FIRESIDE

# THE GARDENER'S

# BASIC BOOK OF
# TREES AND SHRUBS

## STANLEY SCHULER

A FIRESIDE BOOK
PUBLISHED BY SIMON AND SCHUSTER

ISBN 0–671–21481–0 Casebound
ISBN 0–671–22422–0 Paperback
Library of Congress Catalog Card Number 73–7527
Designed by Eve Metz
Manufactured in the United States of America

1   2   3   4   5   6   7   8   9   10

*All photographs by the author unless otherwise noted.*

# CONTENTS

# CRAZY ABOUT TREES

When I was just starting school, my family owned a home with two big Norway maples in the front yard. The one at the north corner of the lot I don't recall very well, but that at the south corner remains clear in mind. My friends and I played under it and in it constantly. It was a grand tree for climbing, once we had shinnied up to the lowest limbs; and the ground around the base was hard and smooth and devoid of vegetation—the perfect place to play mumblety-peg and shoot marbles in cool shade on hot summer afternoons.

I didn't think much about it then, of course, but that maple was my first tree love—in fact, my first plant-of-any-kind love. Since then I have had many more.

There was an old American elm beside the gate of the first house my wife and I bought. We have a black-and-white photograph of it hanging in our bedroom today. It did not have the perfect, symmetrical hour-glass shape that is associated with American elms, but it was beautiful nonetheless. The picture shows it with limbs and twigs laden with snow. But in my mind's eye I can see it pale green in spring and yellow-orange in fall and with our three daughters soaring high on the long rope swing under the dark green canopy of summer.

We had a number of good trees on that property. One was a black locust that looked, against the sky, as if it had been created by an Oriental artist. Another was a charming pink dogwood. But it was the elm

*Our beautiful elm* (Photo by Irving Hartley)

that ever occupied our thoughts. In those days the Dutch elm disease was beginning to run wild in southwestern Connecticut, and we did everything our pocketbook permitted to protect the tree against it. For a long time we succeeded. Then, without warning, the foliage on one high limb withered; and suddenly the whole tree was dead and we had to call in a man to take it down and cart it off to the town dump. The hearts of an entire family went with it.

Within a year we sold the home we had loved and lived in for two decades.

We have had two homes since then and we have planted close to a hundred trees of various sizes, shapes and uses around both of them. But I have never yet enjoyed the experience that so many home owners have had of watching the trees I planted grow tall and wide. That's because we were in our previous house only three years, and have been in our present house less than four. But every time I visit my cousins' plantation just north of Vicksburg, Mississippi, I have some appreciation of this growing-up experience.

Between the old plantation house that belongs to Mary and the new house that Carmichael built there is a large, sloping, grassy area (it isn't really a lawn) populated with five live oaks. My great-grandfather planted them in 1840. Today you could just about hide a Volkswagen behind the trunk of any one of them. The massive limbs stretch far to the sides and almost sweep the ground. Standing under the trees and looking up into the green, rounded crowns, I realize how insignificant I really am. Yet I feel that as long as I remain there I am safe from all dangers. And surely I must be: Just as the oaks themselves have survived ice storms which theoretically should bring their limbs crashing down, my family has survived shelling by Union gunboats, raids by Yankee marauders, floods, tornadoes, boll weevils, pestilence.

There is no reason why the situation should be in any way changed one hundred—even two hundred—years hence.

No, I do not believe I am ascribing to trees an unreal power or charisma. Despite the fact that man has rarely hesitated to chop down trees that did or didn't suit his purposes, the affection of man for trees—and to a lesser extent, for shrubs—is undeniable, and it derives from the qualities of the trees rather than of man.

Trees and shrubs purify the air we breathe by absorbing carbon monoxide and releasing oxygen. They also remove airborne dirt and sand, ash, dust, pollen, offensive odors and pollutants.

Trees provide shade and, along with shrubs, modify the air's temperature and moisture content.

Trees and large shrubs serve as barriers to wind, sound and sight.

Trees and shrubs prevent water and wind from eroding soil and laying waste our land.

Trees and shrubs are homes for birds and squirrels and provide much of the food that keeps these alive.

Some trees and shrubs also yield fruits we savor for their sweet succulence and nourishment.

Trees are playgrounds and hideaways (albeit somewhat precarious) for growing children.

Trees and shrubs fill the air with lovely music as they move in the wind. Some also fill it with rare perfume.

Next to the sky, trees and shrubs are the most beautiful elements of every residential property. They not only have enormous beauty in their own right but they also contribute to overall garden beauty by serving as backgrounds and foils for other garden features. In addition, they cast pretty shadow patterns on the ground; glisten under ice after a sleet storm; and turn into sugar-plum fairies after a snowfall.

Finally, trees—and occasionally large shrubs—have a unique ability to instill in man a sense of silent peace. I can't describe how this happens because it happens in various ways. You can be sitting on a terrace studying the foliage of a tree a hundred feet distant and suddenly you are free of all annoyances, anxieties and distractions. You can be standing under a large tree at night, seeing nothing, and the same thing happens. You can be standing in a cluster of rhododendrons or old boxwoods, and again it happens.

I'm crazy about trees, I admit. I have acquaintances who are equally crazy about certain shrubs. Happily there are millions like us.

My editor was telling me recently about a conversation she had with one of her cousins. He is contentedly married, has seven children, and lives in a tiny house in the deep South. "We ought to move," he said. "But we don't, and it isn't just the money. It's that old magnolia in the back yard. I'd miss it too much if we moved. Some mornings when I see it, I feel like saying, 'Good morning, tree.' It's one of the family."

# ·1·

# SELECTING
# THE RIGHT TREES AND SHRUBS
# FOR YOUR GARDEN

Often when my daughters and their husbands come to visit, the conversation turns to gardens, which is not surprising in a garden-loving family such as ours. All have very different kinds of property, and we have covered a wide variety of subjects, but I guess the thing we talk about most is trees and shrubs. Trees and shrubs are the major elements in any garden, and they can be expensive, so it seems especially important to find the right ones for the right location.

Ashley and Tom wonder what trees they need to give shade, height and texture to their largely open lot; what shrubs will most quickly and effectively hide an ugly foundation wall; and how can they make what they do plant grow better in the dreadful fill the developer poured into their lot.

Randy and Bill are concerned primarily with finding shrubs that will grow in the shade of the old elms and maples that populate their small front yard. Oh, yes, and what would be the best shrubs for screening out one of their neighbors?

Cary and Charlie, new owners of an old property, mull over the advisability of cutting down the hemlocks and firs that black out their windows; and if these are removed, what shrubs should be planted in their place to soften the lines of the aluminum siding thus exposed?

That so much attention should be given trees and shrubs is, of course, understandable. They are the most important plants in any garden, partly because they are the largest and partly because they have the greatest number of roles to play. Unfortunately, they also raise the most questions in the gardener's mind. I don't mean by this that they are unusually difficult to grow, because they are not. If anything, they're the easiest. But just because they are the biggest and most versatile garden plants, they are the most difficult to choose and use.

Hopefully this book will help to make the process easier for you.

## CLIMATE

The selection of trees and shrubs for your garden, my garden and every other garden is dictated by a variety of considerations. Of these, the most crucial is the climate.

There are no perennial* plants that grow in all parts of the world or even in all parts of the United States. For example, the white birch and green ash grow in the north but not in the south. On the other hand, Chinese hibiscus and camellias grow in the south but not in the north. There are also a number of plants that have definite eastern or western preferences, although these are usually less pronounced than north or south preferences.

This probably comes as no surprise, especially if you have traveled around the country to any extent, because you can hardly help noticing that the plants growing in our warmest climates are quite different from those in our coldest. Nevertheless, it is a fact that many people do not realize that all perennial plants have definite climate requirements; consequently they waste considerable money and effort trying to grow things which are foreordained to die.

How can you avoid making the same mistake?

In this book (as in many others) you will find that for all the trees and shrubs described or named I have noted the climate zones in which they grow. These are given in the following ways:

Zones 5–7
Zones 3b–8
Zone 10

* Making growth year after year.

The zone numbers refer to a map prepared by the U.S. Department of Agriculture and reproduced on page 14. On this map, mainland United States and Canada have been divided into ten primary climate zones ranging from No. 1 in the far north to No. 10 in the warmest sections of Florida, Texas and California. Each of these zones is divided, in turn, into two smaller zones—"a" and "b." Minimum temperatures in "a" run about 5 degrees colder than those in "b."

A plant identified as growing in Zones 5-7 grows in all parts, more or less, of Zones 5, 6 and 7. On the other hand, a plant identified as growing in Zones 3b–8 grows only in the southern half of Zone 3 but also grows in all parts of Zones 4, 5, 6, 7 and 8. By contrast, a plant identified as growing only in Zone 10 is strictly a tropical plant.

The way you should use this map is to determine the climate zone you live in. Then you can check the zones listed for each plant described in later chapters to see whether it will grow in your garden. For example, if you live in Zone 6b, you should be able to grow any plant that is identified with the zones in the left-hand column below but you cannot grow those in the right-hand column.

| | |
|---|---|
| 5–7 | 7–10 |
| 3b–8 | 2–6a |
| 2–9 | 9b–10 |
| 4–8 | 8–10 |
| 6b–10 | |
| 2–6 | |

Note that in the preceding sentence I said *you should be able to grow* any plant in the left-hand column; I didn't make the flat statement that you *can* grow it. There are two reasons for this equivocation:

First, because of the great difference between the climate of the far west and that of the east, a plant that thrives in, say, Zones 5, 6 and 7 in the west may not do well in Zones 5, 6 and 7 in the east. This is particularly noticeable in Zone 10. Very few trees and shrubs growing in our colder climates live in southern Florida (Zone 10), yet many of these plants succeed along the northern California coast, which is also in Zone 10.

Second, the entire country contains many microclimates—small areas with climates that differ quite distinctly from the climates of the much

*Palms are an ideal choice for hot, dry climates. Here, Mexican fan palms are seen under the fronds of a date palm. The fronds of the latter are arranged in feather fashion.* (Photo by Arizona Photographic Associates)

*Plant Hardiness Zone Map developed by the Agricultural Research Service of the U.S. Department of Agriculture. On a more detailed version of the map, each zone is divided more or less in half into two sub-zones: "a" and "b." The former is farther north and somewhat colder than the latter.*

larger surrounding areas. These are not shown on the Department of Agriculture's climate-zone map; in fact, I doubt whether anyone in the country has any idea where all of them are. But if you have lived in your present home for any length of time, you have probably noticed whether there is anything peculiar about your immediate climate; and if there is, it is possible that some plants which normally thrive in your climate zone will do badly for you—or vice versa.

When you are making a list of trees and shrubs which you would like to grow in your garden, how then can you be sure that those identified with your climate zone will actually grow for you? One answer is simply to look around your neighborhood. A better answer is to ask a long-time resident who is either an established nurseryman or an experienced gardener.

## LIGHT

Light is an element of climate, but must be given separate consideration when you are choosing trees and shrubs.

Different plants react to light in different ways. Some need just about all the sunlight they can get. Some like sun but also grow in partial shade. Some need partial shade. And some do well in rather deep shade. It follows that the trees and shrubs you buy must be suited to the conditions under which you intend to grow them.

In other words, if your lot is shady, the plants you pick should be capable of growing in shade. On the other hand, if your lot, like so many new suburban lots, is wide open, almost all the plants you buy should be sun-lovers; only those which are planted on the north side of your house should be tolerant of shade.

This is pretty obvious even to some one who has done very little gardening. What isn't so obvious is the fact that the intensity of the light also affects plant selection.

For example, the sun in the south and southwest is much stronger than in other parts of the country; consequently gardeners in these areas

*An Amur maple was chosen for this location, first because it could survive a rigorous climate, and second because it is small enough to be placed close to the house to relieve the blank look of the wall and steep roof.*

must either do without certain sun-loving northern plants, such as lilacs, or they must place them so they will be shaded from about 10 in the morning until 3 in the afternoon.

Another problem is caused by light bouncing off a light-colored wall. This augments the intensity of the light coming straight from the sun. Because of this increase in light, the only plants to place close to the south or west side of the wall should have exceptional resistance to high light intensities; otherwise they will sunburn badly and perhaps die.

## WATER

Three questions must be asked about the moisture requirements of any tree or shrub you consider:

1. Does it need more moisture than nature and you can give it? Actually, trees and shrubs have such large root systems that they can find moisture in the soil when smaller plants are drying up. Nevertheless, there are few species which withstand drought. Most need a more or less constant supply of moisture; and some need a great deal. In either case, if the needed moisture is not supplied by precipitation, you must provide it by a hose whenever the soil around the roots dries out to a depth of about a foot or more. This certainly isn't much work; but it may be an impossible task if your water supply, whether public or private, is inadequate.

2. Does the plant need less moisture than it will get? Among American trees the bald cypress has the rare ability of growing in water. Under similar circumstances, other trees and shrubs would die. In fact, even when no water is visible, trees and shrubs sometimes drown because the soil is so soggy that oxygen cannot penetrate to the roots.

This means that if you have on your lot a low spot that is often filled with standing water or if your soil is poorly drained, you are not going to have much success growing anything except bald cypresses, cattails and other marsh plants.

Even if you don't have a soggy spot in your garden, you may have trouble raising certain trees and shrubs that have very low moisture requirements. The beautiful California shrubs belonging to the ceanothus genus* are an example. Most species use so little water that, if you

---

* A genus is a group of plants with basically similar characteristics. The genus is made up

planted them next to a lawn that you watered once a week, you would kill them within a month or two.

3. How tolerant is the plant of saline soil and water? Salinity is a problem only in dry areas of our 17 western states. There, both the soil and irrigation water contain soluble salts and alkalis which poison many plants if heavy concentrations build up in the soil around the plant roots. True, it is possible to reduce this danger by occasionally dousing the ground with so much water that the salts are carried down out of reach of the roots. Even so, it is a much better idea simply to start out with trees and shrubs that have high tolerance of the salts.

## SOIL

Although beginning gardeners generally believe that the plants they put in must be suited to the soil in their gardens, this actually is not true. Unlike climate, soil can be changed to suit any plant you buy. All problems can be corrected. You can make thin sandy soil fertile; heavy clay soil, light; sour soil, sweet. You can even make saline soil nontoxic (but you can't keep it that way if you irrigate with saline water).

Admittedly, such changes are not always easy or inexpensive to make. That's why you must at least note what kind of soil a tree or shrub prefers, because it doesn't make sense to give yourself extra trouble by putting in a plant which is little if any better than a half dozen other plants that would be perfectly happy in your soil as it is. On the other hand, if your heart is set on a certain plant, don't let its soil preferences keep you from buying it.

## POLLINATION OF PLANTS TO PRODUCE FRUIT

If you ever become interested in botanical study, this is a particularly fascinating subject to delve into. There is no need to go into it deeply here. However, it does have some bearing on your selection of trees and shrubs.

In most species, male and female flowers or flower parts are borne on the same plant, so it is necessary to put in only a single plant to have

of different species; and some species are made up, in turn, of different varieties. When botanical nomenclature is used, the generic name comes first; the specific name second; and the varietal name last.

fruit. Such plants are said to be self-fruitful.

A number of trees and shrubs are self-unfruitful, however. With some, such as hollies, you must plant both a male and a female specimen for pollination and ultimate fruiting to take place. In other words, you must put in two plants even though only one of them, the female, produces berries. With other plants, such as apples, you must plant two different varieties—for example, a Red Delicious and a McIntosh—to have fruit; but in this case, both trees are productive.

Trees and shrubs which are self-unfruitful are pointed out in the descriptive lists of 100 Best Trees and 100 Best Shrubs, and the exact steps you must take to produce fruit are described. In all cases, however, these involve putting in two plants rather than one. Since this may lead either to overcrowding of the garden or to giving up another plant you especially want, you may feel it advisable to do without self-unfruitful species.

## RATE OF PLANT GROWTH

As a gardener, my wife has one great failing: she is impatient to get speedy results. If she wants to screen out the house next door, she wants to do it now. If she wants to fill a gap in the foundation planting, she wants to do it now.

I understand her feeling—just as I understand the millions of home owners who feel the same way. But I must point out that what they are asking is not easy to achieve without some sacrifice. You have three possible courses:

1. You can buy large specimens to start with. This, of course, is costly. For example, a fine 10-foot-high flowering dogwood costs about $60 whereas a 3-foot tree costs only $10. Similarly, a 10-foot Canada hemlock costs $80 whereas a 2-foot tree costs only $5. Obviously, if you are landscaping a barren lot from scratch, you are not going to buy very many large trees and shrubs unless you are wealthy. On the other hand, if you want to shade a terrace within a year or two, the only way you can do it is to plant a sizable tree at the outset.

2. You can buy inexpensive small specimens of trees which grow exceptionally fast. (You can also buy fast-growing shrubs; but since these are so much smaller than trees anyway, their speed of growth is less

*Two paper birches and a Norway spruce—excellent, fast-growing trees. When planted 40 years ago, the spruce was 10 feet tall. It is now 65 feet. The birches, also planted 40 years ago, are almost as tall.*

important.) Unfortunately, however, this approach to the problem is not so good as it might seem. For one thing, a number of our fastest growing trees are poor species which should be avoided. Poplars, for instance, are very rapid growers but the wood is weak and breaks in storms, the roots work their way into drains, and the trees are short-lived. For another thing, most of the fast-growing trees which are worthy of planting in a garden grow to such size that they may dwarf a small house and lot.

3. You can plant small inexpensive specimens of moderately fast-growing trees and encourage them to make faster growth by heavy fertilizing and watering. The extent to which you can stimulate growth by giving trees extra care is indicated by the fact that southern foresters today make pine trees grow 30 percent faster than they naturally do simply by fertilizing the trees every year and by eliminating weeds and shrubs that compete for moisture. Even faster growth is possible in a garden, where you can give each tree maximum attention.

Why do I recommend forcing the growth of moderately fast-growing trees rather than those that grow exceptionally fast? It is not because the fast growers do not respond to the treatment just as well as the moderate growers; on the contrary, they respond even better. My reason is that there is a wider selection of top-notch trees among the moderately fast growers; and many of them turn into small to medium-size plants which are suitable for small properties as well as large.

## SIZE OF TREES IN RELATION
## TO HOUSE AND LOT

Although what I have just said may seem to indicate that small lots should be planted only with small trees, that is not really what I believe.

Many horticulturists and landscape architects *do* make a point of this idea for three reasons. First, small trees fit under electric and telephone wires and do not have to be chopped to bits periodically by the line crews. Second, small trees are a great deal easier to take care of than large trees. Third, when all the major elements of a property—the lot, house and trees—are in scale with one another, the property is more attractive than when the house and lot are dwarfed by the trees.

I concede the first and second points, although it should be noted that as time goes by and more and more wires are installed underground rather than overhead, the first will lose validity. I also agree that there is solid merit in the third point: When the elements of any composition are in scale, the effect *is* more orderly and restful. But I cannot go along

100 percent with this idea, simply because I have seen—as you undoubtedly have, too—a great many small properties with huge trees that look very attractive indeed.

Another point which goes counter to the small-trees-for-small-properties theory is that if you want trees for shade, you cannot depend on small varieties to provide it. You need a rather large tree to shade the roof of a house. You also need a rather large tree with a crown held

*Sawara false cypresses were used to frame the opening to a U-shaped terrace (barely visible at right) because they form neat, feathery, evergreen pyramids that can easily be kept reasonably small by regular pruning.*

high off the ground if you want to walk around and sit on a shaded terrace without a feeling of restriction.

In other words, I doubt the wisdom of making flat statements about the size of trees a home owner should plant if he owns a small property. Trees should be selected for the roles you want them to perform, not simply because they are small.

## WHAT DO YOU WANT YOUR TREES TO DO?

When you select trees (also shrubs, which will be discussed separately) for your garden, you should have clearly in mind what their functions are to be. I have a friend who doesn't follow this rule, but she is a plant collector who has enough acreage so she can put in plants merely for the pleasure of studying them. She is patently an exception. Most gardens today are small and have space for only a few trees—perhaps no more than four or five—and so the trees must be chosen with care.

What roles do you wish them to play?

1. Trees for shade. All trees cast shade, although the way some people talk, you might think that only deciduous trees are shade trees. Trees with high crowns (there are evergreens as well as deciduous trees in this category) cast shade to the side and also on whatever is underneath. Trees with branches all the way to the ground (there are deciduous trees as well as evergreens in this category) cast shade only to the side. (Of course, they also shade the ground underneath; but this doesn't mean very much to the gardener since no one can walk or even sit under such a tree.) Deciduous trees cast shade only in the summer; evergreens, the year round. The trees you plant primarily for shade-making depend on what is to be shaded and when. Here are some of the many possibilities:

For shading the house roof: The best choice, as a rule, is a tall, deciduous tree with a high, wide crown that spreads over the roof only a few feet. (The branches should not extend too far over the roof, because they might break and smash through it in a storm.)

For shading a terrace or patio: If you use the terrace at all hours of the day, plant a tree with branches that will spread over the required area and will grow high enough above the paving so you can walk under them without ducking. Ideally the tree should have somewhat open

*A yellow-wood was selected to shade this terrace because it is shapely, spreading and generally free of problems. Every other year or so it is festooned with wisteria-like flowers.*

foliage so that you can see little patches of sky and so that some sunbeams get through. The tree must not be a litterbug forever dropping leaves, twigs, fruits, etc., that must be swept up; and it should not have flowers or fruits that attract insects.

On the other hand, there might be circumstances under which you should use some other type of tree. To name just one, if a terrace is exposed to the western sun and if you like sunlight on it during the middle of the day, your best choice would be a fairly tall, wide specimen with branches to the ground. This should be planted a fair distance to the west of the terrace.

For shading the house windows: If the windows are close to the ground, small trees will do as well as large. Use a deciduous tree if you want to let in sunlight in the winter but not in the summer. Use an evergreen for year-round shading.

A tree with branches to the ground gives best protection to west windows, but must be planted far enough from the windows so it will not seem oppressive.

For shading a children's play area: A small tree is probably preferable since the low crown gives children a cozier feeling and since they can climb the tree more easily and safely. In colder climates, be sure to use a deciduous tree so the sun can get through and warm and dry the ground in winter.

2. Trees for privacy and screening. If you want privacy throughout the year, you must plant an evergreen. The size and shape of the tree are dictated by the area to be screened and the place from which it can be viewed. For example, you should use a tree with branches to the ground if you are screening a terrace or first-floor bedroom from your next-door neighbor. But if you have a two-story house on a hillside below a neighboring property, use a high-crowned tree to screen your upstairs bedrooms. Evergreen trees are used in the same way to screen out drying yards, dog pens and other unattractive sights on and off your property.

3. Trees for windbreaks and sound barriers. Needled evergreens are your first choice; broadleaf evergreens, the second. But very densely branched deciduous trees such as hawthorns and Russian olives have value.

*Olives are excellent for shade because they cut the sun's glare but let plenty of light through. The trees often have several trunks.*

4. Trees to give elevation to the property. As increasing numbers of one-story houses are built on flat, open lots, this is becoming more important, because if you plant such a property with nothing but small trees and shrubs, the effect is pancake dull. To make the picture interesting, you need a tree or two with strong vertical lines.

Any tall tree will do, but the more slender the specimen, the better. Many small trees, such as the Irish yew and American arborvitae, impart a very strong sense of elevation to a garden simply because they stand out like exclamation points.

5. Trees to direct the eye. One of the aims in landscaping is to exercise some control over what a person viewing the garden sees. There are various reasons for doing this: To direct the eye away from whatever is unsightly; to create a focal point; to alter the impression of what is seen; and so forth.

Trees do all these things well, though obviously no one tree or no one type of tree is suitable for all purposes. For instance, if you want to direct the eye upward out of the garden toward the sky or a distant mountain peak, use a tall, slender, pyramidal tree. To create a focal point or draw attention away from something ugly, use any tree of very distinctive shape or color. To focus attention away from a blank retaining wall separating your garden from an uphill neighbor, plant a high-canopied tree with drooping branches that pull the eye down toward your garden.

6. Trees for beauty. All the trees in the 100 Best Trees descriptive list are beautiful, but they are beautiful for different reasons: for their form, their trunks and branching pattern, their bark, their flowers, their colorful fruits, their foliage texture, their fall color. When you choose a tree strictly for the beauty it will bring to your garden, you make a subjective judgment about the species you consider most beautiful. But you should also consider the situation planned for the tree.

In landscaping parlance, a specimen tree (there are also other kinds of "specimen" plants) is one planted to attract attention to itself because it

*The tall pin oaks in my back lawn and the slender, straight American arborvitaes behind them direct your eyes from the garden toward the sky. Picture taken in early spring reveals the interesting branch pattern of this species of oak.*

is beautiful. But to be an effective specimen, it should be planted in the open where it can develop properly and where it does not have visual competition from other large plants. This means that big trees can be used as specimens only on rather large properties. But there is no reason why small trees such as crab apples and franklinias cannot be treated as specimens on very small properties.

Of course, trees planted for their beauty do not have to be treated as specimens. They are often grouped with other trees and shrubs. One arrangement which is extremely effective is to place a small or medium-size flowering tree in front of a group of dark green conifers. Another excellent idea is to silhouette a tree with a handsome branch structure or with multiple trunks against a wall.

7. Trees for delicious fruit. This is a small group which is usually not considered along with the so-called ornamental trees. But this is a mistake, because many fruit trees are very pretty plants—usually rather small—which will grace any garden. True, they need more attention than other trees if you want lots of top-quality fruit. But that is a small price to pay for the extra pleasure their produce gives.

## WHAT DO YOU WANT YOUR SHRUBS TO DO?

Because shrubs are smaller than trees, the choice between them is less critical. If you make a mistake, it is less obvious and it is also easier and less costly to correct. Nevertheless, when picking shrubs, you should try to make sure that each one is the best choice for the role it is to play.

1. Shrubs for beauty. By and large, shrubs have less interesting or beautiful structures than trees; but there are more that have beautiful flowers. This makes it harder to decide which is the most ornamental because there are fewer criteria by which to judge them.

2. Shrubs to soften the harsh look of walls and to change their lines. These are two jobs that shrubs do better than any other plants except vines.

By no means all walls are unattractive and harsh; but many have a rigid, blank look that should be changed. Just planting any shrub close in front of these makes a great improvement; but you can get the best results with the least number of plants with narrow, vertical shrubs that offer sharp contrast to the long, low, horizontal lines of the wall, or with slender, open shrubs that display a network of upright stems and dancing leaves against the wall.

To change the lines of a wall—which usually involves making a high wall appear lower—simply mass a line of shrubs of more or less the same height along the base of the wall. For this job, many gardeners use evergreen shrubs sheared to a certain height.

3. Shrubs for concealment and screening. This is the principal function of shrubs in foundation borders: to hide the unattractive foundation walls, basement bulkheads, basement windows, electric and gas meters. You may also use shrubs of medium to large size to conceal other sights in the garden, such as clothes lines and boats on trailers.

*Though deciduous, the upright redvein enkianthus is a good shrub to plant at the corner of a house to conceal the downspout. It also serves as a frame for the house.*

As a rule, evergreens are favored. But even in winter, deciduous shrubs with very dense branches are just about as effective and should not be ignored.

4. Shrubs to enclose or define garden spaces. Shrubs used in this way may be planted in hedges or in informal masses generally referred to as shrubbery borders.

On a small lot, shrubbery borders normally are planted along the boundaries to separate the lot from that of the neighbors and to serve as the background for flowers. The shrubs are large or medium size, a mixture of evergreen and deciduous plants that looks attractive and neat with a minimum of pruning and provides a pleasant blend of textures, shapes and colors.

The favorite shrub for hedges is privet, which is deciduous in cold climates, evergreen in warm. But there are many others—both deciduous and evergreen—to consider (see the list on pages 42–43). Those with thorns or spines should be used when you need a hedge to keep out people and animals.

Hedges are pruned more heavily than border plants, but this does not mean that they are always sheared to precise outlines. The height at which a hedge is kept depends on whether you need it—like a pencil line —simply to suggest the separation of one area from another (in this case, the hedge might not be more than 1 foot high) or whether you are trying to control the view into or out of a garden area (in which case, the hedge might be 3 feet high or more).

5. Shrubs serving as backgrounds for other plants. The best ones for this purpose are fairly tall-growing, needled and broadleaf evergreens.

6. Shrubs for holding banks. This is a utilitarian but very important job which is often assigned to rather small shrubs that quickly establish themselves once they are planted and that spread rapidly to cover the banks and keep the soil from eroding.

7. Shrubs for filling in shady places in the garden. This is one of the principal functions of shrubs, because every garden has at least one shady area—at the base of the north wall of the house. And whenever you plant a tree or very large shrub, you create another shady area. In all cases, the shrubs you should plant to fill these areas depend, first of all, on the depth of the shade and second, on whatever else you want the shrubs to do.

*A fine choice for a shady shrubbery border—drooping leucothoe. In the spring it drips with neat clusters of tiny white flowers.*

## COST OF TREES AND SHRUBS

It is inevitable when you are picking out plants for your garden that you will consider their cost. This is not so unfortunate as some dyed-in-the-wool horticultural enthusiasts might suggest.

The cost of trees and shrubs depends on the size of the plant and on how common that particular species or variety is.

Just because a tree or shrub is very common does not mean it is inferior to others which are less common. Trees and shrubs become common because gardeners like them and because nurserymen can propagate them easily and raise them rather quickly to marketable size. Many of the plants named in the best and next-best descriptive lists in this book are very common species, hence rather inexpensive. So there is no reason why you can't find plenty of excellent trees and shrubs that you can afford.

Neither is there any reason why you shouldn't decide on some of the less common, more expensive species. In this case, all you must do to stay within your budget is to buy somewhat smaller specimens and give them extra fertilizer and water so they will grow faster.

## TREES AND SHRUBS FOR SPECIFIC PURPOSES

With the exception of those indicated, the plants named in the following lists are taken only from the descriptive lists of 100 Best Trees and 100 Best Shrubs.

The lists are designed simply to give you a quick idea of what is available if you are looking for a certain *basic* type of tree or shrub (I have not drawn up interesting but relatively exotic lists of, for example, trees with red fall foliage; trees with beautiful bark; fragrant shrubs; etc.). Once you find in these lists the plants that seem to offer the best possibilities for you, turn to the descriptive lists for more complete information about them.

## DECIDUOUS TREES

|  | Climate zones | Height (feet) | Growth speed |
|---|---|---|---|
| Apple | 3–8 | 50 | Moderate |
| Ash, green | 2–7 | 60 | Very fast |
| Beech, American | 3b–8 | 90 | Moderate |
| Beech, European | 5–10 | 90 | Moderate |
| Birch, European | 2–10 | 60 | Fast |
| Birch, white | 2–7 | 90 | Fast |
| Cherry, flowering | 4–10 | 75 | Fast |
| Cherry, sour | 4–7 | 35 | Fast |
| Chestnut, Chinese | 5–8 | 50 | Moderate |
| Corktree, Amur | 3b–10 | 40 | Moderate |
| Crab apple | 2–10 | 50 | Moderate |
| Crape-myrtle | 7b–10 | 25 | Moderate |
| Dogwood, flowering | 5–9 | 40 | Moderate |
| Dogwood, Japanese | 6–10 | 20 | Moderate |
| Elm, Chinese | 6–10 | 60 | Very fast |
| Fig, common | 7–10 | 25 | Fast |
| Franklinia | 6–10 | 30 | Slow |
| Fringetree | 5–9 | 30 | Slow |

| | Climate zones | Height (feet) | Growth speed |
|---|---|---|---|
| Ginkgo | 5–10 | 120 | Moderate |
| Golden-rain-tree | 6–10 | 30 | Moderate |
| Hickory, shagbark | 4–8 | 120 | Moderate |
| Honeylocust, thornless | 5–8 | 130 | Very fast |
| Ironwood | 2–9 | 35 | Slow |
| Jacaranda | 9b–10 | 50 | Fast |
| Japanese pagoda tree | 5–10 | 60 | Moderate |
| Larch, Japanese | 5–9 | 90 | Fast |
| Linden, littleleaf | 3b–10 | 90 | Slow |
| Linden, silver | 5–10 | 90 | Moderate |
| Magnolia, saucer | 6–10 | 25 | Moderate |
| Magnolia, star | 6–8 | 20 | Moderate |
| Maple, Amur | 2–10 | 20 | Slow |
| Maple, Japanese | 6–10 | 20 | Slow |
| Maple, Norway | 3b–10 | 90 | Fast |
| Maple, sugar | 3b–10 | 120 | Moderate |
| Mimosa | 7b–10 | 35 | Fast |
| Mountain ash, European | 3b–8 | 60 | Moderate |
| Oak, bur | 4–10 | 100 | Moderate |
| Oak, pin | 5–10 | 75 | Moderate |
| Oak, valley | 7–10 | 70 | Moderate |
| Oak, white | 5–10 | 90 | Slow |
| Oak, willow | 6–9 | 50 | Moderate |
| Peach | 5–9 | 25 | Fast |
| Pear | 3–9 | 40 | Moderate |
| Pecan | 6–9 | 150 | Fast |
| Persimmon, Japanese | 7b–10 | 40 | Fast |
| Plane-tree, London | 6–10 | 100 | Fast |
| Plum | 3–9 | 25 | Fast |
| Poinciana, royal | 10 | 40 | Very fast |
| Russian-olive | 2–9 | 20 | Moderate |
| Snowbell, Japanese | 6–10 | 30 | Moderate |
| Sorreltree | 6–9 | 75 | Slow |
| Sour-gum | 5–10 | 90 | Slow |
| Stewartia, Japanese | 6–10 | 60 | Slow |
| Sweet-gum | 6–10 | 120 | Moderate |
| Thorn, Washington | 5–10 | 30 | Moderate |
| Tulip tree | 5–10 | 175 | Moderate |
| Willow, golden weeping | 3–10 | 75 | Very fast |
| Yellow-wood | 3b–9 | 50 | Moderate |

## EVERGREEN TREES

|  | Climate zones | Height (feet) | Growth speed |
|---|---|---|---|
| Acacia, silver wattle | 9–10 | 50 | Very fast |
| Arborvitae, American | 6–10 | 60 | Slow |
| Camellia | 7b–10 | 40 | Slow |
| Cedar, Deodar | 7–10 | 100 | Fast |
| Cedar-of-Lebanon | 7–10 | 120 | Slow |
| False cypress, Sawara | 3b–7 | 120 | Moderate |
| Fig, weeping | 10 | 30 | Fast |
| Fir, white | 5–10 | 120 | Moderate |
| Grapefruit | 9b–10 | 30 | Moderate |
| Gum, lemon-scented | 9b–10 | 75 | Very fast |
| Gum, silver-dollar | 6b–10 | 60 | Fast |
| Hemlock, Canada | 3–7 | 90 | Moderate |
| Holly, American | 6–9 | 50 | Slow |
| Holly, English | 6b–10 | 70 | Slow |
| Holly, lusterleaf | 7b–10 | 60 | Slow |
| Ironbark, red | 9–10 | 80 | Fast |
| Madrone, Pacific | 7b–10 | 100 | Moderate |
| Magnolia, southern | 7b–10 | 90 | Slow |
| Mango | 9b–10 | 90 | Moderate |
| Norfolk Island pine | 10 | 90 | Fast |
| Oak, live | 8–10 | 60 | Moderate |
| Olive | 8b–10 | 25 | Slow |
| Orange | 9b–10 | 25 | Moderate |
| Palm, coconut | 9b–10 | 100 | Moderate |
| Palm, date | 10 | 60 | Fast |
| Palm, Mexican fan | 9b–10 | 90 | Very fast |
| Palm, royal | 9b–10 | 80 | Fast |
| Pine, Austrian | 4–7 | 90 | Fast |
| Pine, eastern white | 3–6 | 150 | Fast |
| Pine, longleaf | 8–9 | 120 | Moderate |
| Pine, Scotch | 2–8 | 75 | Fast |
| Pine, western white | 6–8 | 90 | Fast |
| Pittosporum, Queensland | 10 | 30 | Slow |
| Red cedar, eastern | 2–8 | 60 | Moderate |
| Schefflera | 10 | 25 | Fast |
| Sea-grape | 9b–10 | 20 | Moderate |
| Spruce, Norway | 2–7 | 150 | Fast |
| Spruce, Serbian | 5–7 | 90 | Moderate |
| Tea tree, Australian | 9b–10 | 30 | Moderate |
| Umbrella pine | 6–10 | 50 | Slow |
| Yew, Hicks | 3–10 | 20 | Moderate |
| Yew, Irish | 7–10 | 25 | Slow |

## DECIDUOUS SHRUBS

| | Climate zones | Height (feet) | Showy flowers |
|---|---|---|---|
| Azalea, Exbury hybrid | 6b–10 | 10 | Yes |
| Azalea, flame | 6–10 | 15 | Yes |
| Azalea, Ghent hybrid | 5–10 | 10 | Yes |
| Azalea, Mollis hybrid | 6–10 | 5 | Yes |
| Azalea, royal | 5–10 | 15 | Yes |
| Barberry, Japanese | 5–9 | 7 | No |
| Beautybush | 5–10 | 12 | Yes |
| Bluebeard | 6–10 | 2 | Yes |
| Blueberry, highbush | 5–7 | 12 | No |
| Bridal wreath | 5–9 | 6 | Yes |
| Broom, Warminster | 6–10 | 6 | Yes |
| Butterfly bush | 6–10 | 8 | Yes |
| Carolina allspice | 5–10 | 9 | No |
| Cherry, Nanking | 2–10 | 9 | Yes |
| Chokeberry, red | 3–9 | 9 | Yes |
| Cinquefoil, shrubby | 3–10 | 4 | Yes |
| Cotoneaster, rockspray | 5–10 | 3 | No |
| Cotoneaster, spreading | 6–10 | 6 | No |
| Deutzia, slender | 5–9 | 3 | Yes |
| Elaeagnus, autumn | 3b–8 | 12 | No |
| Enkianthus, redvein | 5–10 | 20 | No |
| Euonymus, winged | 3b–8 | 10 | No |
| Forsythia, border | 6–8 | 9 | Yes |
| Fothergilla, Alabama | 6–9 | 6 | Yes |
| Honeysuckle, tatarian | 3b–10 | 9 | Yes |
| Hydrangea, garden | 6–10 | 12 | Yes |
| Hydrangea, oakleaf | 6–10 | 6 | Yes |
| Lilac, common | 3b–8 | 20 | Yes |
| Lilac, littleleaf | 6–8 | 6 | Yes |
| Lilac, Persian | 6–8 | 6 | Yes |
| Mock-orange, Lemoine | 6–9 | 8 | Yes |
| Ninebark, eastern | 2–8 | 9 | Yes |
| Peony, tree | 6–10 | 5 | Yes |
| Privet, Vicary golden | 5–10 | 12 | No |
| Quince, flowering | 5–10 | 8 | Yes |
| Rhododendron, Korean | 5–10 | 6 | Yes |
| Rose, shrub | 4–10 | 8 | Yes |
| Rose of Sharon | 6–10 | 15 | Yes |
| Smokebush | 6–10 | 15 | No |
| Spicebush | 5–8 | 15 | Yes |
| Stephanandra, cutleaf | 6–8 | 7 | No |
| Summersweet | 4–7 | 8 | Yes |
| Tallhedge | 2–8 | 15 | No |
| Tamarisk, Kashgar | 6–9 | 8 | Yes |
| Viburnum, Burkwood | 6–10 | 6 | Yes |
| Viburnum, doublefile | 5–10 | 9 | Yes |

## DECIDUOUS SHRUBS (Continued)

| | Climate zones | Height (feet) | Showy flowers |
|---|---|---|---|
| Viburnum, Korean spice | 5–10 | 5 | Yes |
| Viburnum, Siebold | 5–9 | 10 | Yes |
| Viburnum, tea | 6–10 | 12 | Yes |
| Viburnum, Wright | 6–9 | 9 | Yes |
| Winterberry | 3b–8 | 12 | No |

## EVERGREEN* SHRUBS

| | Climate zones | Height (feet) | Showy flowers |
|---|---|---|---|
| Abelia, glossy | 6–10 | 6 | Yes |
| Andromeda, Japanese | 6–9 | 9 | Yes |
| Andromeda, mountain | 5–9 | 6 | Yes |
| Aucuba, Japanese | 7b–10 | 10 | No |
| Azalea, Indian hybrid | 8b–10 | 6 | Yes |
| Azalea, Kurume | 7–10 | 3 | Yes |
| Azalea, snow | 6b–10 | 6 | Yes |
| Azalea, torch | 6–8 | 10 | Yes |
| Bamboo, yellow-groove | 6b–10 | 25 | No |
| Barberry, wintergreen | 6–9 | 6 | No |
| Box, common | 6–8 | 20 | No |
| Camellia, sasanqua | 7b–10 | 20 | Yes |
| Ceanothus, Point Reyes | 7–10 | 2 | Yes |
| Cotoneaster, willowleaf | 6b–10 | 15 | No |
| Elaeagnus, thorny | 7b–10 | 12 | No |
| Euonymus, evergreen | 8–9 | 15 | No |
| Fatshedera | 7b–10 | 7 | No |
| Fatsia | 7b–10 | 8 | No |
| Firethorn, Laland's scarlet | 6b–10 | 10 | No |
| Fuchsia | 7b–10 | 12 | Yes |
| Hawthorn, yeddo | 7b–10 | 10 | Yes |
| Heavenly bamboo | 8–10 | 8 | Yes |
| Hibiscus, Chinese | 9–10 | 15 | Yes |
| Holly, Chinese | 7b–10 | 10 | No |
| Holly, Japanese | 6–10 | 20 | No |
| Honeysuckle, winter | 6–10 | 6 | Yes |
| Hypericum, Hidcote | 6b–10 | 3 | Yes |
| Juniper, Meyer | 5–10 | 6 | No |
| Juniper, Pfitzer | 5–10 | 10 | No |
| Laurel, mountain | 5–8 | 30 | Yes |

* But a few are deciduous in cold climates

## EVERGREEN* SHRUBS (Continued)

| | Climate zones | Height (feet) | Showy flowers |
|---|---|---|---|
| Lavender | 6–10 | 3 | Yes |
| Leucothoe, drooping | 5–9 | 6 | Yes |
| Mahonia, leatherleaf | 7–10 | 10 | Yes |
| Manzanita, Stanford | 7b–10 | 6 | Yes |
| Myrtle, true | 8–10 | 15 | No |
| Natal plum | 9–10 | 15 | Yes |
| Oleander | 8–10 | 20 | Yes |
| Oregon grape | 6–10 | 6 | Yes |
| Osmanthus, holly | 6b–10 | 18 | No |
| Pine, mugo | 2–9 | 8 | No |
| Pittosporum, Japanese | 8–10 | 15 | Yes |
| Privet, California | 6–10 | 15 | No |
| Privet, Japanese | 7b–10 | 12 | No |
| Rhododendron, Carolina | 6–8 | 6 | Yes |
| Rhododendron, Catawba hybrid | 5–8 | 15 | Yes |
| Sarcococca, dwarf | 7–10 | 3 | No |
| Skimmia, Reeves | 7b–9 | 2 | No |
| Yew, Japanese | 5–10 | 25 | No |
| Yew, spreading English | 6b–10 | 3 | No |
| Yew pine | 8–10 | 10 | No |

* But a few are deciduous in cold climates

## TREES THAT GROW UNUSUALLY FAST

*(Those marked with an asterisk are on the list of Next Best Trees, Chapter 10)*

| | Climate zones | Deciduous or Evergreen | Height (feet) |
|---|---|---|---|
| Acacia, silver wattle | 9–10 | E | 50 |
| Ash, green | 2–7 | D | 60 |
| Cajeput-tree* | 10 | E | 40 |
| Chinaberry* | 7b–10 | D | 50 |
| Cucumber-tree* | 5–10 | D | 90 |
| Dawn-redwood* | 6–10 | D | 100 |
| Elm, American* | 3–9 | D | 120 |
| Elm, Chinese | 6–10 | D or E | 50 |
| Empress-tree* | 6–10 | D | 45 |
| Gum, lemon-scented | 9b–10 | E | 75 |
| Honeylocust, thornless | 5–8 | D | 130 |
| Pine, Monterey* | 8–10 | E | 100 |
| Pine, slash* | 8–10 | E | 100 |

## TREES THAT GROW UNUSUALLY FAST
### (Continued)

| | Climate zones | Deciduous or Evergreen | Height (feet) |
|---|---|---|---|
| Poinciana, royal | 10 | D | 40 |
| Redwood* | 7b–10 | E | 350 |
| Silk oak* | 9b–10 | E | 100 |
| Sycamore* | 5–10 | D | 120 |
| Willow, Babylon weeping* | 6b–10 | D | 30 |
| Willow, golden weeping | 3–10 | D | 75 |
| Willow, Niobe weeping* | 5–10 | D | 40 |
| Willow, Thurlow weeping* | 4–10 | D | 40 |

## SHRUBS FOR SHADY PLACES

| | Climate zones | Deciduous or Evergreen | Height (feet) |
|---|---|---|---|
| Abelia, glossy | 6–10 | E | 6 |
| Andromeda, Japanese | 6–9 | E | 9 |
| Aucuba, Japanese | 7b–10 | E | 10 |
| Azalea, Exbury hybrid | 6b–10 | D | 10 |
| Azalea, flame | 6–10 | D | 15 |
| Azalea, Ghent hybrid | 5–10 | D | 10 |
| Azalea, Indian hybrid | 8b–10 | E | 6 |
| Azalea, Kurume | 7–10 | E | 3 |
| Azalea, Mollis hybrid | 6–10 | D | 5 |
| Azalea, royal | 5–10 | D | 15 |
| Azalea, snow | 6b–10 | E | 6 |
| Azalea, torch | 6–8 | E | 10 |
| Bamboo, yellow-groove | 6b–10 | E | 25 |
| Barberry, Japanese | 5–9 | D | 7 |
| Barberry, wintergreen | 6–9 | E | 6 |
| Beautybush | 5–10 | D | 12 |
| Box, common | 6–8 | E | 20 |
| Bridal wreath | 5–9 | D | 6 |
| Camellia, sasanqua | 7b–10 | E | 20 |
| Carolina allspice | 5–10 | D | 9 |
| Chokeberry, red | 3–9 | D | 9 |
| Deutzia, slender | 5–9 | D | 3 |
| Elaeagnus, thorny | 7b–10 | E | 12 |
| Enkianthus, redvein | 5–10 | D | 20 |
| Euonymus, evergreen | 8–9 | E | 15 |
| Euonymus, winged | 3b–8 | D | 10 |

## SHRUBS FOR SHADY PLACES *(Continued)*

| | Climate zones | Deciduous or Evergreen | Height (feet) |
|---|---|---|---|
| Fatshedera | 7b–10 | E | 7 |
| Fatsia | 7b–10 | E | 8 |
| Firethorn, Laland's scarlet | 6b–10 | E | 10 |
| Forsythia, border | 6–8 | D | 9 |
| Fothergilla, Alabama | 6–9 | D | 6 |
| Fuchsia | 7b–10 | D or E | 12 |
| Hawthorn, yeddo | 7b–10 | E | 10 |
| Heavenly bamboo | 8–10 | E | 8 |
| Hibiscus, Chinese | 9–10 | E | 15 |
| Holly, Japanese | 6–10 | E | 20 |
| Honeysuckle, tatarian | 3b–10 | D | 9 |
| Hydrangea, garden | 6–10 | D | 12 |
| Hydrangea, oakleaf | 6–10 | D | 6 |
| Laurel, mountain | 5–8 | E | 30 |
| Leucothoe, drooping | 5–9 | E | 6 |
| Mahonia, leatherleaf | 7–10 | E | 10 |
| Mock-orange, Lemoine | 6–9 | D | 8 |
| Myrtle, true | 8–10 | E | 15 |
| Natal plum | 9–10 | E | 15 |
| Oregon grape | 6–10 | E | 6 |
| Osmanthus, holly | 6b–10 | E | 18 |
| Peony, tree | 6–10 | D | 5 |
| Pittosporum, Japanese | 8–10 | E | 15 |
| Privet, California | 6–10 | E | 15 |
| Privet, Japanese | 7b–10 | E | 12 |
| Rhododendron, Carolina | 6–8 | E | 6 |
| Rhododendron, Catawba hybrid | 5–8 | E | 15 |
| Rhododendron, Korean | 5–10 | D | 6 |
| Sarcococca, dwarf | 7–10 | E | 3 |
| Skimmia, Reeves | 7b–9 | E | 2 |
| Stephanandra, cutleaf | 6–8 | D | 7 |
| Summersweet | 4–7 | D | 8 |
| Tamarisk, Kashgar | 6–9 | D | 8 |
| Viburnum, Burkwood | 6–10 | D | 6 |
| Viburnum, doublefile | 5–10 | D | 9 |
| Viburnum, Korean spice | 5–10 | D | 5 |
| Viburnum, Siebold | 5–9 | D | 10 |
| Viburnum, tea | 6–10 | D | 12 |
| Viburnum, Wright | 6–9 | D | 9 |
| Yew, Japanese | 5–10 | E | 25 |
| Yew, spreading English | 6b–10 | E | 3 |
| Yew pine | 8–10 | E | 10 |

## HEDGE PLANTS

| | Minimum trimmed height (feet) | Space between plants (feet) | Deciduous or Evergreen | Climate zones |
|---|---|---|---|---|
| Abelia, glossy | 5 | 3 | D | 6–10 |
| Arborvitae, American | 8 | 2 | E | 6–10 |
| Barberry, box | 1½ | 1 | D | 5–9 |
| Barberry, crimson pygmy | 1 | 1 | D | 5–9 |
| Barberry, Japanese | 3 | 2 | D | 5–9 |
| Barberry, wintergreen | 3 | 1½ | E | 6–9 |
| Beech, European | 15 | 5 | D | 5–10 |
| Box, common | 3 | 2 | E | 6–8 |
| Box, edging | 1½ | 1 | E | 6–8 |
| Bridal wreath | 6 | 2 | D | 5–9 |
| Cherry, Nanking | 6 | 4 | D | 2–10 |
| Cinquefoil, shrubby | 1 | 1½ | D | 3–10 |
| Cotoneaster, spreading | 3 | 2 | D | 6–10 |
| Deutzia, slender | 1½ | 1½ | D | 5–9 |
| Elaeagnus, thorny | 4 | 3 | E | 7b–10 |
| Elm, Chinese | 8 | 3 | D | 6–10 |
| Euonymus, compact winged | 4 | 2 | D | 3b–8 |
| Euonymus, evergreen | 4 | 3 | E | 8–9 |
| False cypress, Sawara | 10 | 4 | E | 3b–7 |
| Firethorn, Laland's scarlet | 4 | 3 | E | 6b–10 |
| Hawthorn, yeddo | 4 | 3 | E | 7b–10 |
| Hemlock, Canada | 8 | 3 | E | 3–7 |
| Hibiscus, Chinese | 6 | 3 | E | 9–10 |
| Holly, American | 4 | 3 | E | 6–9 |
| Holly, Burford | 5 | 2 | E | 7b–10 |
| Holly, convex Japanese | 2 | 2 | E | 6–10 |
| Honeysuckle, tatarian | 6 | 3 | D | 3b–10 |
| Honeysuckle, winter | 3 | 3 | E | 6–10 |
| Hypericum, Hidcote | 1½ | 1½ | E | 6b–10 |
| Myrtle, true | 6 | 4 | E | 8–10 |
| Natal plum | 3 | 2½ | E | 9–10 |
| Ninebark, eastern (nanus) | 1½ | 1 | D | 2–8 |
| Osmanthus, holly | 6 | 2 | E | 6b–10 |
| Pine, mugo | 2 | 2 | E | 2–9 |
| Pittosporum, Japanese | 4 | 2 | E | 8–10 |
| Privet, California | 3 | 1 | E | 6–10 |
| Privet, Japanese | 4 | 1½ | E | 7b–10 |
| Privet, Vicary golden | 1 | 1 | D | 5–10 |
| Quince, flowering | 4 | 2 | D | 5–10 |
| Rose, shrub | 3 | 2 | D | 4–10 |
| Russian-olive | 10 | 5 | D | 2–9 |
| Sarcococca, dwarf | 1½ | 1 | E | 7–10 |
| Skimmia, Reeves | 1½ | 1 | E | 7b–9 |

## HEDGE PLANTS (Continued)

| | Minimum trimmed height (feet) | Space between plants (feet) | Deciduous or Evergreen | Climate zones |
|---|---|---|---|---|
| Stephanandra, cutleaf (crispa) | 3 | 2 | D | 6–8 |
| Tallhedge | 10 | 3 | D | 2–8 |
| Tea tree, Australian | 10 | 4 | E | 9b–10 |
| Yew, Hicks | 6 | 2½ | E | 3–10 |
| Yew, Japanese | 3 | 2 | E | 5–10 |
| Yew pine | 4 | 2½ | E | 8–10 |

# ·2·

# ACQUIRING
# THE MOST DESIRABLE
# TREES AND SHRUBS

There are several ways to acquire trees and shrubs for the garden, and I have found that almost all can be good. To be sure, I usually get best results from plants which have been grown by knowledgeable nurserymen. But occasions frequently arise when it seems like a good idea to use the somewhat less reliable acquisition methods.

## BUYING TREES AND SHRUBS

In recent years a notable change has occurred in the outlets through which trees, shrubs and other plants are sold: A great many variety chains, supermarkets and discount houses have gone into the business; and a number of independent so-called garden centers have sprung up in shopping centers and along heavily traveled suburban thoroughfares. All these outlets have made it much easier for gardeners to shop for trees and shrubs; and they have helped materially to hold down the cost of the plants. But apart from these two advantages I am not at all certain that gardeners are well served.

To begin with, the people working in these outlets don't know much about gardening, and, since many of them commute to work, they generally know even less about local gardening conditions and the best plants for the area in which they work. So if you are looking for sound information, you are usually out of luck.

In the second place, the selection of trees and shrubs offered by these outlets is limited to the commonest species and varieties.

Finally, while the available trees and shrubs have been propagated and grown in big wholesale nurseries by competent people, they are often not of No. 1 quality. Even worse, they may have been raised in a warm climate and may be unable to make the transition to a cold climate.

In short, my enthusiasm for these new low-cost plant outlets is restrained. They would be acceptable if they were frequented by experienced gardeners, who could cope better with the plants they buy, than with those beginning gardeners who actually shop there.

(A source of plants I definitely advise against is the door-to-door salesman who drives up with a truck loaded with "outstanding bargains.")

I buy trees and shrubs from two types of outlet. When I want fruit trees and when I am not in a hurry for ornamental plants to make an immediate show, I buy from nurseries that sell by mail. Some of these firms advertise their plants at such outrageously low prices that I refuse to patronize them on the theory that what I receive is bound to be small and wispy and will require a lot of hard work. Others, such as Wayside Gardens and Stark Brothers, have been known and respected by experienced gardeners for several generations.

These leading mail-order nurseries are not cheap. The trees and shrubs they sell are small. All are bare-root plants which are shipped during dormancy. Usually they arrive when you are not quite expecting them and may not be ready to plant them. These are the disadvantages of buying by mail.

The principal advantage of the top mail-order nurseries is that they offer a very wide selection of plants. Often they have varieties that are difficult to find anywhere else. To stay in business, they are continually propagating and seeking out new and improved varieties. And the plants they ship are strong and of excellent quality.

The other plant sources I rely on are established local nurseries. I go to these when I need large, well-filled-out specimens of ornamental trees and shrubs and large or small evergreens (which should always be sold with a ball of earth around the roots).

Local nurseries range in size from many small businesses that carry a rather limited assortment of trees, shrubs and vines to a few big businesses offering a wide selection. Since the plants are larger than those sold by mail, they are proportionally more expensive. Unlike the mail-order firm's plants, which are guaranteed no matter what, the local nursery's plants may be guaranteed only if you let the nurseryman plant them for you (this adds to the price).

In the past, local nurseries raised everything they sold, so the plants were well acclimated to the area when they were finally delivered to gardeners. Today the nurseries still raise much of their stock; but they also buy from wholesalers. If you are given a choice, take the home-grown material.

Aside from the fact that the local nurseries are the only source of trees and shrubs that are too large or heavy to be sold by mail, they have one main attraction to gardeners: If they have been in business for any length of time, they know the area in which you live; they are pretty sure which plants will thrive and which will not; and they can offer sound advice when you need it.

I once asked the nurseryman who supplied most of the trees and shrubs for my previous home what he thought about my putting in an Oregon grape. "I can get it for you," he answered, "but I don't advise it. It does all right in the area where you used to live down near the water; but out here we're high and a lot colder, and it just doesn't come through."

Information of that sort makes the local nurseryman very valuable to the gardener.

As I indicated earlier, trees and shrubs bought from mail-order nurseries come with bare roots (because they cost less to ship). Those from local nurseries come with roots encased in a ball of earth.

Since bare-root plants must be planted when they are dormant, they are shipped to you in the spring before they leaf out. Some species may also be shipped in the fall after losing their leaves. On their arrival, you will find that the bare roots are wrapped in fibrous material, plastic sheeting and heavy brown paper. If the fibrous material and roots are damp—as they should be—you can safely wait a day or two before planting as long as you keep the wrappings tight and set the plant in a cool, shady place. If the roots happen to be dry on arrival, they should be soaked in a bucket of cold water for a couple of hours. You should then set the plant out in its permanent location or heel it in.

Heeling-in is a process used to keep trees and shrubs which you cannot plant for several days in good condition. Simply dig a rough trench in a shady spot; remove the wrappings from the plants, and lay the roots in the trench so the plants are on a 45° slant. Then cover the roots with soil and dampen thoroughly.

Plants from local nurseries are sold with the root balls either wrapped in burlap or enclosed in large metal, plastic or fiber cans. The former, known as "balled & burlapped" or "B & B" plants, are generally bigger than canned plants; but there is no other real difference between them. Canned plants can be planted at any time during the growing season— from early spring through the summer and until mid-fall. Balled & burlapped plants which were dug up from wherever they were growing in the nursery and wrapped in burlap while they were dormant—before they put out new spring growth—can also be planted at any time during the growing season. However, if you buy a tree or shrub while it is still growing in a nursery, it can be dug up and transplanted to your garden only in early spring before it makes growth, or in the fall after growth has stopped.

One thing you can do when you buy a tree or shrub from a local nursery that you cannot do when you buy by mail is to inspect the plant to make sure it is a good specimen in good condition. Here are things to look for:

The ball of earth, whether in burlap or a can, is firm and damp. The burlap is stretched tight around the ball. The plant trunk or stems do not wobble in the soil.

There are no large scars on the trunk; no large broken branches.

If the plant is in leaf, the color is bright and fresh-looking. Yellowing of foliage indicates something is wrong.

The plant is a desirable shape. If it is a needled evergreen, it has dense foliage and the branches are closely spaced up and down the trunk.

## BUYING SEEDLING TREES

Seedling trees are of no interest to anyone who is trying to get good-sized trees on his property in a short time. They are usually planted

*A seedling Douglas fir less than a foot high is putting out growth within a fortnight after planting in early spring.*

only by people who are reforesting land or who want to raise Christmas trees for sale. But it is conceivable that if you are landscaping a better-than-average-size lot by easy stages, you might put some seedlings in as a future source of cheap plant material.

Seedling trees (there are also seedling shrubs, but I have never heard of any for sale) are young plants less than a foot tall and without branches. They usually are nothing more than a shoot with roots. Most of those for sale are needled evergreens; only a few are deciduous species.

The principal sources of seedling trees are the state forestry departments, which raise the plants by the hundreds of thousands every year. If you are a resident of a state, you can buy seedlings from the state forest at one or two cents apiece provided you meet certain conditions. For instance, you must agree to set out a minimum number of trees (usually several hundred); you may have to plant a minimum number of acres; and you may be required to own a certain number of acres. In addition, you must agree, as a rule, not to use the trees for landscaping purposes—only for reforestation, timber or Christmas trees.

But there are other sources of seedling trees that do not impose any such restrictions. These are mail-order firms such as Rayner Brothers in Maryland and Western Maine Nurseries in Maine, which sell seedlings for any purpose of your choosing in lots of ten and up. The cost: in the neighborhood of 15 to 25 cents per tree, depending on the species and the quantity you purchase.

## COLLECTING PLANTS FROM OTHER GARDENS AND THE WILD

This is the least reliable way of acquiring trees and shrubs because those that spring up and grow without assistance do not have the compact root systems of those raised in a nursery. The result is that when you dig them up, it is difficult to get all the roots, and thus the plants' chances of surviving the move into your garden are lessened. On the other hand, this method is a cheap source of plants—sometimes very sizable plants—and if you don't succeed in pulling through a plant that no one wants, or which is growing in the wrong place, you waste nothing except effort.

Of course, the first thing you should remember about collecting trees and shrubs is that they probably belong to somebody; so you should secure permission to dig them up before you lay hands to shovel.

The next thing to note is that the plants must be dug and planted while they are dormant. Early spring is the best time in most areas and for most plants. Mid- to late fall is the only other choice.

If you are not in a rush to move a plant, you should root-prune it the first spring and move it the second spring. This forces it to develop a strong, compact root system which makes it easier to move. Root-pruning is done with a sharp spade which is thrust straight down into the ground all the way around the plant in a circle. The diameter of the circle should be close to 15 inches for any plant with a trunk or stems under 1 inch thick. Increase the diameter 12 inches for each additional inch of trunk thickness or fraction thereof. To reach as many of the roots as possible, drive the blade of the spade all the way down. Give the plant a few weeks to recover from this operation; then fertilize it and keep it watered through the summer and fall.

In the second spring, cut around the circle once more. Then dig a trench around it; work a spade in under the root ball; and lift the plant out of the ground. The soil should be damp so it sticks together. If you can wrap a piece of burlap or other strong material around the root ball, this will help to hold it together during the move.

A more-hazardous-to-the-plant method of transplanting that may be attempted with any deciduous tree or shrub, but only with evergreens less than 18 inches tall, is simply to dig around the plant with a spade and carefully pry out the roots with whatever soil sticks to them. Don't worry if you cut some of the roots—even some of the big ones; just try not to mutilate too many. When the plant is out of the ground, trim off the ragged root ends with pruning shears. The new planting hole should be big enough so the roots can be spread out more or less naturally.

The actual method of planting trees and shrubs from the wild is identical to that for nursery plants. One additional step must, however, be taken with both bare-root plants and those with root balls: to compensate for the inevitable loss of roots when you dig up the plants, prune back the tops by removing some of the branches entirely or reducing the length of all of them about 25 to 30 percent. This can be done at any time before, during or after moving the plants.

# ·3·

# PROPAGATING
# YOUR OWN TREES AND SHRUBS

When I was growing up, my mother embarrassed me because she always carried a very sharp knife in her pocketbook, and whenever she spied a plant she admired, she would stop, open the knife, and cut off a sprig without asking anyone's permission. Then she would take the piece home and put it in damp sand or peat moss until it developed roots and was ready to be moved into the garden.

Once I became a gardener, I discovered that what Mother did, a lot of other gardeners do also. In fact, in the gardener's world, swiping cuttings for propagating purposes doesn't really rate as a crime as long as it isn't overdone. However, it is much nicer to ask the owner of the plant you covet if you may take a cutting from it. Gardeners being gardeners, the chances are you will be told, "Why, of course. I'm so glad you like the plant."

But I am getting ahead of myself.

No home owner who wants to populate an open yard with trees and shrubs is going to propagate many of his own plants, because it takes several years to produce plants of any size. But if you are simply trying to fill in various empty spots in the garden and are not in any great hurry about it, propagating trees and shrubs—but especially shrubs—is a good idea. It saves a lot of money. It's fun. And it is sometimes the only way you can acquire a species or variety that strikes your fancy.

Basically, there are two ways of propagating plants: from seed and from various parts of growing plants. The former method is called sexual reproduction; the latter, asexual or vegetative reproduction. Some plants are best handled the first way, some the second; and some can be handled both ways. The one thing to be borne in mind about *all* plants is that if they are hybrids, they will not come true if you grow them from seed. Instead of having, say, the pink flowers of the plant from which you took the seeds, the new plants may have the white flowers of one of the two plants which were crossed to produce the hybrid. The only way you can make an exact reproduction of a hybrid plant—assure that it will come true—is to propagate it vegetatively.

## RAISING TREES AND SHRUBS FROM SEED

This is not so easy as raising flowers and vegetables from seed; and I therefore recommend it for only a few trees and shrubs. For these, you simply collect the seeds when the fruits containing them ripen (this is usually indicated by a color change in the fruits, and the fruits may start to fall from the plant). It is then generally advisable but not always necessary to remove the pulp covering the seed. Finally, you sow the seed in an outdoor seedbed.

In due course—usually the following spring—the seedlings push up out of the ground. In the subsequent months, you should fertilize them lightly and water them regularly while they are making active growth. Screen them partially from the sun until they are about 4 inches high. You can move the little plants to their permanent location or a larger nursery bed any time in early spring after they have established good roots.

## PROPAGATING TREES AND SHRUBS BY SUCKERS

Suckers are the new plants that come up from an established plant's roots. Lilacs, fatsias and sour-gums are examples of trees and shrubs that sucker rather prolifically.

To propagate such plants, just dig down around a sucker and cut it

[LEFT] *Suckers springing up around the base of a common lilac are not only unsightly in themselves but even more unsightly because they trap leaves. But they are useful for propagating new plants.* [RIGHT] *Two weeks after a sucker was removed from the lilac, it put out leaves and started growing vigorously.*

off with a section of the root attached. Cut back the top of the sucker to compensate for the loss of the whole root that formerly nourished it. Then plant the sucker in humusy soil at the same depth it originally grew. Keep it watered until it starts to make growth, and feed it lightly at that time.

## PROPAGATING TREES AND SHRUBS BY LAYERING

A number of plants develop roots wherever low-growing or pendulous branches touch the ground. This is natural layering—a process you can easily duplicate.

On the plant you elect to layer, pick out a vigorous, rather young branch that is growing low to the ground, and with a sharp knife make a slight diagonal cut partway through the bottom of the branch 12 to 18 inches from the tip. Stick a toothpick or other sliver of wood into the cut to keep it open. Scoop out the soil under the cut to a depth of 2 to 3 inches; press the cut into this, and pile soil on top of the branch. To hold it down, weight it at the cut with a rock or clamp it down with a U-shaped piece of heavy wire.

When roots form at the cut (this usually takes about a year), sever

*How to propagate a plant by layering. Roots will form at the cut after the branch is buried in the ground and weighted down.*

the branch below the cut and plant the rooted section upright in good soil. Water and fertilize to stimulate growth.

## PROPAGATING TREES AND SHRUBS BY AIR-LAYERING

This method is used less often than conventional layering, but it works well. All you have to do is buy a simple air-layering kit from a garden-supply store and follow directions.

Select a stem that developed in the previous year and make a small notch in it with a knife. Dust the cut with the hormone powder in the layering kit; then wrap it in sphagnum moss which has been soaked in water and squeezed dry. Cover the moss completely with plastic film, and seal the side and end laps with plastic tape.

Open the wrappings now and then to check whether roots are developing. When a nice little bundle finally forms, cut the stem below it; and move the new plant into good garden soil to grow. Water and fertilize as you do other new plants.

## PROPAGATING TREES AND SHRUBS BY GREENWOOD STEM CUTTINGS

A greenwood stem cutting is a short piece cut from the tip of a young stem which is making vigorous growth. As a rule, the best time for taking such cuttings is in spring or summer; but with some tropical plants it is possible to take cuttings whenever the plants are in an active growth period.

Cut through the stem ¼ to ½ inch below the sixth or seventh leaf from the tip. Make the cut on a slant. Then remove all but the four top leaves.

The mixture in which you root the cuttings (called the propagating or rooting medium) should consist of two parts by volume of finely shredded peat moss and one part of clean builder's sand. Wet this with water just enough so that, when you squeeze it, it gives off only a few drops.

If you are propagating only one or two or three plants at a time, pour a 4-inch layer of the dampened rooting medium into the bottom of a large, deep, clean plastic freezer bag. Firm it well. Dip the base of each cutting 1 inch deep into a hormone rooting powder available from a garden-supply store. Then with a pencil poke a hole 1 inch deep in the

*The best way to propagate a few greenwood stem cuttings is to place them in plastic freezer bags, which are then sealed to hold in moisture.*

*To make a quantity of greenwood stem cuttings, put them in a flat filled with rooting medium; then cover it tightly with plastic film. Instead of a sheet of film, a large plastic bag is used here.*

rooting medium; insert the bottom of the cutting; and firm the medium around it.

After inserting all your cuttings in the rooting medium, dampen the leaves very slightly with water, and close and seal the bag to hold in humidity. The bag should not touch the cuttings. Put it in a spot where there is plenty of light but no sun.

In the succeeding weeks, keep an eye on the cuttings and if you see any signs that they or the rooting medium are drying out, open the bag and dampen the medium promptly. Also keep an eye out for mildew or other fungus in the bag; and if you see any, spray the cuttings with a fungicide such as captan.

After about four weeks, start checking the cuttings for root formation (it does no harm to pry them carefully out of the rooting medium and then to replace them). When roots are ½ inch or longer, transplant the cuttings outdoors into a good mixture of well-drained loam, sand and humus. Even sun-loving species should be shaded lightly from the sun until they revive from the shock of transplanting. Water regularly and fertilize lightly until you are ready to move the plants into their permanent locations.

If you are propagating a lot of stem cuttings, follow the same procedure; but instead of starting them in plastic bags, place them in a wooden flat filled with rooting medium. To maintain humidity around them, build a "tunnel" of several U-shaped wires over each flat; and stretch polyethylene film over these and down around all four sides of the flat. Tack the plastic to the bottom of the flat.

## PROPAGATING TREES AND SHRUBS BY HALF-HARDWOOD STEM CUTTINGS

A half-hardwood cutting is one taken from the end of a stem which has lost some of the soft suppleness of a greenwood cutting. Otherwise, the propagating procedure is the same.

## PROPAGATING DECIDUOUS TREES AND SHRUBS BY HARDWOOD STEM CUTTINGS

A hardwood cutting is taken from that part of a pencil-size stem which has been growing six months or longer. The cuttings are made in the fall. You can make several from a single stem. Each piece should be 6 to 10 inches long. At the bottom, the cutting is cut off at right angles to the stem ½ inch below a leaf joint. At the top, cut ½ inch above a leaf joint and slant the cut so you can tell top from bottom.

*Hardwood cuttings are made from pencil-size branches. The cuts at the top are made on a slant; those at the bottom straight across.*

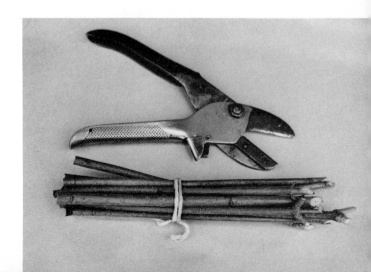

Bundle about a dozen of the cuttings together with the tops pointing in the same direction, and tie them with a string. Dig an outdoor trench about 18 inches deep, put in 3 inches of sand and lay the bundle on this. Then fill the trench completely with sand and cover it with a thick layer of leaves or hay.

When spring comes, separate the cuttings and arrange them in a row, bottoms down, in a trench filled with two parts peat moss and one part sand. (Work fast; don't let the cuttings dry out.) Only the two top buds should protrude above the surface of the rooting medium. Water well, and keep the medium damp all summer (it is very porous and will dry out rapidly).

The cuttings should be rooted come fall. Move them into a bed of soil mixed with humus and keep them watered until winter. Don't apply fertilizer until the next spring.

## PROPAGATING BROADLEAF EVERGREEN TREES AND SHRUBS BY HARDWOOD STEM CUTTINGS

Take the cuttings from stem ends that have been growing for about six months. Make the cuttings in early fall and follow the procedure for propagating plants by greenwood stem cuttings. If you live in a climate where the temperature does not go below freezing, leave the cuttings outside in their plastic bags or in a plastic-covered flat. In colder areas, bring them indoors into a bright but not sunny room with a low temperature.

The cuttings usually will not be well rooted until spring, when they should be planted in good, humusy soil outdoors. Fertilize them a few weeks after transplanting. Keep them watered at all times.

NOTE: In the descriptive lists of best trees and shrubs, propagating procedures are recommended only for those species which are relatively easy to work with.

# ·4·

## SUCCESSFUL PLANTING

Because of their size, most of us think of trees and shrubs as being rather self-sufficient; so, once they are growing well, we tend not to pay them a great deal of attention. This is not very smart—but habit is hard to break.

However, because we do treat these important plants in such a cavalier manner, it is essential to give them the best possible start in the garden. In short, the planting operation must not be rushed or skimped in any way. The more carefully you carry it through, the better the plants will grow.

### TIMING

The best time to plant trees and shrubs is in the early spring. Fall planting, however, is possible with many species; and in warm climates it is quite common. If you are thinking about setting out a certain tree or shrub in the fall, a good nurseryman will automatically advise you against it if there is any risk involved.

Bare-root deciduous plants must be planted in the spring before they get their leaves, or in the fall after their leaves drop. Small bare-root evergreens are also planted in the spring, or in the fall between September 1 and a month before the ground freezes.

Plants which have been dug and put in burlap or cans before they leaf out in the spring can be planted from that time until mid-fall. But if you buy a plant that is growing in the ground in a nursery, you must plant it on the same schedule as a bare-root plant—in early spring or late fall.

## SOIL

One thing I strongly believe all gardeners should do is to have their soil tested before they do any kind of planting. This is a very easy task and it will probably cost you less than $2 as all state agricultural extension services (listed on pages 309–310) offer soil tests as a basic service to gardeners and farmers.

The first step is to dig up samples of soil from about six to ten different locations around your property. For soil testing for trees and shrubs, the samples should be taken from the top 12 inches of soil (if we were talking about lawns or vegetables, the samples would be taken from half this depth). Mix the samples together thoroughly when they are fairly dry. Then put about a cupful in a plastic freezer bag or any other small container. Return the rest of the soil to the garden.

Send the bag of soil to your extension service with a request that they test it for you. Your letter should include the following information: (1) The size of the area you intend to plant. (2) The plants you intend to grow. You don't have to be specific; just say "deciduous and evergreen trees and shrubs" or whatever the facts are. (3) The plants that are growing in the area at the moment. There is no more need to be specific about these than about the plants you intend to grow. (4) What if anything you have done to improve the soil. (5) What the soil drainage is like.

Within a few days, you should receive a form describing the condition of your soil and suggesting ways to make it better.

Regardless of the report's recommendations, one thing you should definitely do to your soil is to mix in humus to make it lighter, more moisture-retentive and more nourishing. Humus is decayed organic matter. Leaves, grass clippings and hay which are piled in a heap to decay make excellent humus when they break down to a dry, crumbly consistency. But most gardeners use peat moss simply because it is available at reasonable cost in ready-to-use form at supermarkets and garden-supply stores. As a very rough rule of thumb, add one part peat moss (or other kind of humus) to two parts soil in every planting hole you prepare. This amount can be decreased in rich soils; increased in very poor soils. In the case of the latter, you should also add an equal quantity of loam.*

If your soil is acid,† as it is in many parts of the country, you can sweeten it by mixing in ground limestone. Use about one kitchen cupful in a small planting hole; two in a large hole.

If your soil is neutral or alkaline and you want to make it acid to suit such acid-loving plants as azaleas and camellias, the peat moss you add for humus should do the trick; or you can use well-rotted oak leaves or pine needles. Another way to make soil acid is to mix powdered sulfur into the top inch of soil after a plant has become established. Use ¼ cup per plant in sandy soil; ½ cup in heavier soil. Add this a little at a time over a period of several weeks so you run no risk of injuring the plant roots.

Changing the water-holding capacity of soil is often more difficult than improving its ability to nourish plants. For instance, if your soil is so sandy or gravelly that moisture goes through it as if it were a sieve, you must fill it with large quantities of clay and peat moss. Lacking clay, use a heavy loam with the peat moss. Peat moss alone is unsatisfactory because it doesn't give the soil sufficient body.

To make a heavy, slow-draining soil drain a bit faster, add sand and crushed rock along with peat moss.

Dense clay soil is hardest of all to cope with. Where I used to live, the ground soaked up and held so much water in winter and spring that several trees and shrubs I planted died for lack of oxygen. In a situation like this, dig each planting hole 6 inches deeper than normal and fill this space with coarse crushed rock; then mix a large quantity of fine crushed rock and peat moss into the soil around the plant roots. This should correct matters; but you can't be sure it has until the plants have been in for about a year. During wet weather, if they show any

* A rich soil made up of approximately equal amounts of silt, sand and clay. A handful of dry loam holds together reasonably well when squeezed.

† The acidity or alkalinity of soils is indicated by their pH. Soil with a pH of 7 is said to be neutral. If the pH is much below 7, the soil is acid. If the pH is much above 7, the soil is alkaline.

signs of illness such as sudden yellowing or dropping of leaves, you should immediately run a 4-inch drainage pipe from the bottom of each planting hole to some distant outlet point.

## DIGGING THE PLANTING HOLE

The first step in planting any tree or shrub is to measure the depth and width of the root system. If the plant is in burlap, measure the ball at its greatest width and height. If in a can, measure the can at its widest point and measure the depth of the soil in the can. If the plant is bare-root, raise it off the ground and measure the roots as they dangle. (The top of the root system should be considered to be the same as the soil line on the trunk.)

The hole you dig should be half again deeper than the root system and twice as wide at both top *and bottom*. For economy of labor, make the hole with vertical sides. But it does no harm if the sides slant, as long as the hole is wide enough at the bottom.

If you are planting in an area where the soil taken from the hole will mix with and perhaps damage the ground on which it is piled (as in a lawn area), cover the ground with a tarpaulin, burlap or large sheets of corrugated board and pile the soil on this.

Place the sods and other vegetation you dig out in one pile; the good topsoil in another pile; and the subsoil in a third pile. Roots, rocks and building rubble should be put in a fourth pile for later removal to the dump.

If you run into ledge rock or a very large boulder before you reach the desired depth, you must either devise some method of getting it out or desert the hole and move to another location. If you hit hardpan (extremely dense clay) or caliche (rock-hard calcium salts, found in the southwest), you must dig down into them with a pickax to a depth at least 6 inches greater than the required planting depth in order to improve drainage.

When the hole is completed, toss the sods upside down in the bottom to rot and enrich the soil. Then fill in above them with topsoil and finally with subsoil. As you throw the soil in, add peat moss and mix it in well.

Fill the hole a little more than one-third of its depth; then jump in and tramp the soil down firmly. Add or take out soil as necessary to bring the hole to the exact depth of the root system. To measure accurately, lay a board across the top of the hole and measure down from this with a rule.

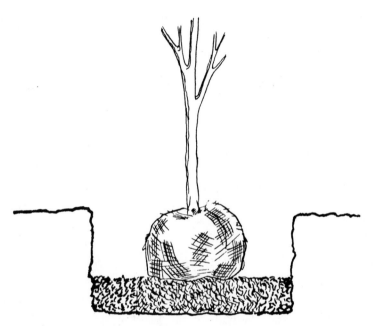

*The planting hole for a tree or shrub should be twice as wide as the root ball and half again as deep.*

## PLANTING TREES AND SHRUBS

First take a look at the plant from all sides, and decide how it should be placed for best effect.

If the plant is balled and burlapped, leave the wrappings as they are. But if the plant is in a can, this must now be removed by cutting it from top to bottom on opposite sides. Use a knife on material that is easily cut, but avoid slicing deeply into the root ball. Metal cans must be opened with tin snips. This is a mean task; get the nurseryman to do it for you before you leave the nursery.

Trees and shrubs with soil balls must be handled very carefully when you lift them into their planting holes or whenever else you move them, because if the balls are not solid, they are likely to crack away and damage the roots. Since this is especially likely to happen if you lift plants by their trunks, old-time nurserymen make it a rule always to lift them by the root balls. But this, alas, is heavy, hard work. For that reason, I feel the rule should be enforced only when you are handling a canned plant, because once it is out of the can, the only way to hold the soil ball together is with your hands. On the other hand, the soil ball of a balled and burlapped plant cannot fall apart, although it can crumble if it is dry; therefore, as long as it is damp and hard, it is fairly safe to lift the plant by the trunk. Bare-root plants, of course, are always lifted by the trunks.

If a plant has a root ball too heavy for one person to lift, call in a strong, healthy helper and place the plant on a piece of stout canvas. Drag the plant on this to the planting hole. Then grasp the canvas on opposite sides and lower it with the plant into the hole. Pull the canvas out by tilting the plant slightly to one side, bunching the canvas up under it, and then tilting the plant to the opposite side to free the canvas.

If the plant has bare roots, center it in the hole and spread the roots out more-or-less naturally. Balled and burlapped and canned plants need only be centered. Make sure the plant is standing upright (you may need someone to hold it). Then start filling in around the roots with topsoil which has been mixed with peat moss. When you run out of topsoil, switch to the subsoil—which must also be mixed with peat moss. Whatever the soil, firm it frequently with your foot to eliminate air pockets. Work it into the roots of bare-root plants with a stick.

When you have filled in around the bottom two-thirds of the root system, fill the top third of the hole with water and let it soak in out of sight. Then untie or carefully cut the burlap loose from a balled and burlapped plant; pull it away from the top of the soil ball, and spread it out to the sides of the hole. It need not be removed completely because it will disintegrate and disappear within several months.

Fill in the hole the rest of the way with your soil-and-peat-moss mixture. Make sure it is firm. The soil level should be no higher than the original soil line on the trunk.

*A young bare-root Chinese chestnut has been cut back at the top to compensate for loss of roots during the transplanting operation. The watering saucer is filled with a mulch of wood chips.*

Now build a ridge, or dike, of soil all the way around the edges of the hole to form a watering saucer. This should be about 3 inches high for small plants; 6 inches for very large plants. Fill the saucer with water; and if there is no rain, fill it twice a week (three times a week in an arid climate) for the next three weeks. From then on it is highly advisable to keep the saucer filled with an organic mulch* of peat moss, chopped bark, hay, etc., to hold in moisture and keep down weeds.

The final steps in planting trees and shrubs involve protecting the

* A mulch is the equivalent of a blanket. It may be made of organic or inorganic materials.

trunks against sunscald and staking to hold the plants upright.

Sunscald is an ailment that causes the bark on tree trunks to split so that other disease organisms can enter. Any tree can be affected; but precautions to prevent scalding must be taken only in the case of deciduous trees and evergreens with exposed trunks when they are planted in the fall or planted in the spring in our warmest climates. Just wrap the trunks from the ground up to the first branches with strips of burlap or heavy kraft paper; or paint the trunks with whitewash. The covering should be maintained for about six months.

Staking is essential for all trees and for any shrub that is considerably taller than wide and planted in a spot where it may be blown over by wind or knocked down by traffic.

*Until its roots take hold, this newly planted pine will be held upright by three guy wires running to stakes in the ground. The wires are run through short lengths of hose to protect the trunk.*

To protect a shrub or a tree under about 5 feet high, drive a stake deep into the soil beside it. The stake should be at least 1½ inches diameter. Leave a space of 2 to 3 inches between it and the trunk or main stem of the plant, and tie the two together loosely but securely.

In extremely vulnerable locations, use two stakes rather than one, and center the trunk between them.

Larger trees should be anchored in an upright position by three strong guy wires looped around heavy wood stakes or iron pipes driven into the ground around the tree. The wires should be looped around the tree trunk 3 to 6 feet above the ground (the taller the tree, the higher the wires). The angle of the wires to the trunk should be about 45°. To keep the wires from cutting into the trunk, run them through short lengths of hose at the upper end.

Stakes should be kept in place for at least a year—even longer if a tree does not appear to be thriving. Stakes for dwarf fruit trees should be maintained permanently.

## PLANTING LIVE CHRISTMAS TREES

The process is like that just described. Just make sure you keep the tree well watered and in a fairly cool room over the holiday, and move it outdoors as soon as possible—before New Year's Day. In cold climates, dig the planting hole before the frost gets into the ground; and keep the soil you remove from freezing so you can easily replace it after Christmas. To do this, cover it with a thick blanket of leaves. If you neglect to dig a hole before the ground freezes, you can thaw the soil by building a fire on top of it or by dousing it with boiling water.

## PLANTING SEEDLING TREES

If you want to plant seedling trees like large trees, there is no reason why you shouldn't. Undoubtedly the trees will respond to such attention by growing faster and bushier than they normally do when planted in sod in a field. But the main idea in growing seedlings is to raise lots of trees at minimum cost, and so they are planted rapidly with minimum preparation directly in sod. Note, however, that only evergreens can be handled this way. Deciduous seedlings must be planted in ground that is plowed, as for a vegetable garden, and kept cultivated for at least three years thereafter.

When planting seedling evergreens, carry them in a bucket of cold water. They must never dry out. To make a planting hole, simply drive a sharp spade straight down into the soil and push the handle away from you to open a narrow slit. Without bothering to spread the roots, drop them straight into the slit. Then pull out the spade and step on the slit to close it and to firm the soil around the roots.

If the weather is dry, give each tree a little water to get it going; and if the weather continues dry, water several times again, if possible. However, seedlings are often planted in remote fields where watering of any kind is unfeasible; and in that case, all you can do is hope that they will pull through without moisture at planting time.

# ·5·

# WATERING AND FERTILIZING

The two pin oaks in my rear lawn have grown to 70 feet in, as near as I can figure, 40 years. That's fast growth even for pin oaks. But there's an obvious reason for it: Much of the fertilizer and water that have been applied to the lawn has actually been taken up and utilized by the trees.

Somehow I doubt that the couple who developed the garden deliberately intended this result. And I must admit that when I feed and water the lawn, my only concern is the grass. So what has happened has been providential as well as accidental.

This really is not the way anyone should take care of trees and shrubs. As the most important plants in the garden, they theoretically deserve most attention. The fact that they don't get this yet continue to thrive attests to their innate vigor and serves as a reasonable excuse for not giving them as much nourishment in proportion to size as you give smaller plants.

## WATERING

More trees and shrubs die for lack of moisture than for lack of fertilizer. During periods of drought you can see them drop almost like flies. This may not be preventable in forests and along highways, where the plants are beyond reach of a hydrant, but it is unpardonable in a garden that is served by an adequate water supply.

Unfortunately, however, the watering of plants is a very inexact science. The only certain way to tell when a tree or shrub needs to be watered is to wait until the leaves begin to wilt and drop. But if you put the plant to this test very often, you will weaken it to such an extent that it will eventually die.

Another good way to tell when a plant needs water is to install in the ground a pair of tensiometers, which automatically measure the amount of moisture in the soil at different depths. Even expert gardeners generally ignore these valuable devices, however; and perhaps they are right in doing so, because while the indicated moisture level may be critically low for one species of plant, it may be quite acceptable to another.

In other words, if you were to ask, "How often should I water my trees and shrubs?" I could not give a precise and acceptable answer. Each gardener must come up with his own answer. This you acquire through experience. You also have the following basic facts to guide you:

1. As pointed out in Chapter 1, some plants have more natural resistance to drought than others. Resistance is most notable in species that are native to arid regions.

2. Young plants need a more constant supply of moisture than old. For example, the California Agricultural Extension Service recommends that during the dry season in that state, orange trees purchased at one year of age should be watered every seven to ten days during their first year in the garden; every 14 days during the next two years; and every two to six weeks, depending on the soil and climate, during their remaining lifetime.

3. Small plants need proportionally more moisture than large because they have less extensive root systems and cannot reach out so far for moisture.

4. The more closely plants are spaced, the more moisture they all need. This is because there is so much competition among them for the available moisture.

5. Plants' need for water grows as the soil surrounding the upper parts of their root systems dries out. As a general rule, small and me-

dium-size shrubs need to be watered when the upper 12 inches of soil have become completely dry. Trees and large shrubs need to be watered when the upper 18 inches of soil are dry. Short of installing tensiometers, the best way to tell the condition of the soil is to dig a hole or to drive a soil probe into the ground, pull it out and examine the sample brought up.

6. In colder climates, where frozen ground keeps the precipitation from reaching the roots of trees and shrubs, you should make sure that all evergreens get lots of water in the autumn after growth has stopped and before the ground freezes. The reason is that, even in winter, evergreens transpire* to a certain extent; and if they don't have an ample supply of moisture to draw on, they may die of drought.

## HOW TO WATER TREES AND SHRUBS

There are two things you should note before getting into the mechanics of watering.

First, during dry spells, instead of sprinkling trees and shrubs lightly every few days, you should wait until the soil dries to the critical depth mentioned above. You should then pour on enough water to saturate this entire space from top to bottom. The exact amount of water to apply depends on the nature of your soil. Generally speaking, to wet dry soil to a depth of 1 foot, you should apply ¾ to 1 inch of water if the soil is sandy; 1½ to 2 inches if the soil is loam; and 2½ to 3 inches if the soil is clay.

Second, remember that in addition to penetrating deep into the ground, the roots of trees and shrubs spread to all sides as far as the branch tips and sometimes even farther. Every square foot within this entire area must receive the same amount of water—not just the small area around the base of the plant.

To apply so much water over such a large area without losing some of it through runoff is not always easy. Sprinkling is usually the best answer under trees with high crowns. But under low-growing plants you should use either a soaker hose or a watering saucer.

Whether made of porous canvas or perforated plastic, soaker hoses do an excellent job, even on sloping ground, because they emit water so

* Give off moisture through the pores of the leaves.

slowly that almost all of it is soaked into the soil and there is little runoff. But it takes a long time to water a plant—especially a tree—to the necessary depth.

On flat ground, a watering saucer (see Chapter 4) is better than a hose because it is faster. And you can more easily gauge how much water you give the plant during each application. The diameter of the saucer should equal the diameter of the plant's canopy.*

## HOW TO CONSERVE MOISTURE

The suggestion was made in Chapter 4 that after you plant a tree or shrub and keep it watered for several weeks, you should fill the watering saucer with an organic mulch. Ideally, except for trees and shrubs which are for appearance's sake closely encircled with grass or a ground-cover, all of them—regardless of age—should be mulched.

Organic mulches do a number of valuable things:

—retard the loss of moisture from the soil through evaporation;

—smother weeds, which are not only unsightly but also compete with the tree or shrub for moisture;

—add vital nutrients to the soil as they disintegrate;

—keep plant roots cooler in summer and warmer in winter;

—retard runoff of water and thus minimize or prevent erosion.

There are many organic mulching materials, but some are too unattractive to go into prominent parts of the garden. These include hay and straw, leaves, ground corncobs, peanut shells and sawdust. Chopped branches from the chippers of the utility line crews are also unattractive when fresh, but become less so after aging.

The most attractive mulching materials are chopped tree bark and buckwheat hulls—both do everything a mulch is expected to do. But the bark has the advantage of being fairly coarse and heavy; consequently it does not blow or wash away as readily as the hulls.

Cocoa beans are another good-looking material, but unless they are mixed with sawdust, they develop a slimy mold. And they should never be used around azaleas and rhododendrons because they contain more potash than is good for these plants.

Peat moss is also a fairly attractive mulch, but it has the peculiar

* The crown of a plant; the spreading section covered with leaves.

characteristic of losing absorbency when it dries out. Then, instead of letting water seep into the soil, it causes some of it to run off.

Whichever mulching material you use, it should be spread over the entire root system of each tree or shrub if this does not detract from the beauty of the garden or interfere with its use. The thickness of the layer can range from 2 to about 5 inches. In a shrubbery border, use a 2-inch thickness directly under each shrub; about 5 inches in the sunny openings between shrubs.

## FERTILIZING TREES AND SHRUBS

The best fertilizer for trees and shrubs is a balanced formula containing the three major plant nutrients: nitrogen, phosphorus and potassium. The law requires that the formula for each mixture be printed on the bag in the form of three numbers separated by hyphens. The first number stands for the percentage of available nitrogen in the fertilizer; the second, for the percentage of available phosphorus; and the third, for the percentage of available potassium, or potash.

A good fertilizer for most trees and shrubs is one containing a little more nitrogen than phosphorus and potassium—for example, 10-6-4, 12-6-4 or 16-8-8. But for broadleaf evergreens and fruit trees, 10-10-10 or 8-8-8 are slightly better formulas. In areas with peculiar soil deficiencies, magnesium, manganese, copper or other elements may be added to balanced fertilizers.

Bone meal and cottonseed meal are two other fertilizers that are popular, particularly with older gardeners. The former may be applied to all kinds of trees and shrubs. The latter is recommended especially for azaleas, rhododendrons and other plants growing in acid soils.

## WHEN AND HOW MUCH TO FERTILIZE

Until very recently the fertilizing of trees and shrubs was even less a science than watering. Then Dr. Robert J. Schramm, Jr., of the University of Connecticut, made the discovery that he could greatly increase growth by fertilizing trees and shrubs in spring, summer, fall and winter. This was in direct violation of conventional belief, which held that, in all except our warmest climates, trees and shrubs should be fertilized only in spring and early summer, because if they were fertilized later, this would force them to put out new growth which would be killed by winter cold. Through experiment, however, Schramm found that winter-killing can be avoided. The secret is to make an annual soil test and then to apply a balanced fertilizer that compensates for any lack of nutrients in the soil and gives each plant a perfect diet.

The importance of this discovery to gardeners and nurserymen, both of whom want to grow strong plants in the shortest possible time, cannot be minimized. But I am sorry to report that it is a discovery you cannot take advantage of at this writing if you live outside Connecticut. No other state agricultural extension service is as yet set up to make the necessary soil tests and recommend a year-round feeding program. So until that day comes, you must stick with old fertilizing methods.

Actually there is nothing wrong with these. They simply are not scientific and precise. For instance, the only thing I am reasonably positive about is this: To make the fastest possible growth, plants need fertilizer most when they are young. This does not mean, of course, that fertilizer alone can produce fast growth. The soil in which the plant is set is far more important. If that is properly prepared according to directions in Chapter 4, plants will grow well without further assistance. But fertilizer added to good soil *does* yield astonishing results.

The first feeding should be given three or four weeks after a new tree or shrub is planted in the spring (fall-planted specimens should not be fed until the following spring). The delay of several weeks after planting gives the roots a chance to start functioning well enough to absorb the fertilizer. For a small shrub or a tree whip,* scratch about two handfuls of fertilizer into the soil and water it in. For larger plants use about a cupful of fertilizer.

Feed the young plants early every spring for the next four to six years. Increase the dosage about one-half cupful per year for shrubs; one cupful for trees.

Whether you should continue to feed the plants after this depends on whether they have made satisfactory growth. If you feel they still need pushing, keep on feeding on a slowly increasing scale. (If you want maximum production from fruit trees, these should always be fed

---

* A whip is a young shoot without branches. Most of the fruit trees sold are one-year-old whips.

every year on a schedule recommended by your state agricultural extension service. Some particularly spectacular flowering shrubs, such as azaleas, rhododendrons, camellias, Chinese hibiscus and tree peonies, are also usually fed every year.) On the other hand, if you are happy with the appearance and condition of the plants at this point, annual feeding can be stopped.

Established trees and shrubs growing in a shrubbery border or a foundation planting under an organic mulch usually get all the nourishment they need from the mulch. But if you do not use a mulch, fertilize the plants every second or third year. Use two to three cupfuls for shrubs; five to ten for trees. Just scratch it lightly into the soil and water it in well.

Established trees and shrubs which are surrounded at their base by a groundcover or other small plants can be handled in the same way. You should, however, increase the fertilizer applications about 50 percent in order to satisfy the needs of all the plants.

Established trees and shrubs whose root systems are partially covered by paving should usually be fertilized at least every other year to compensate for the fact that some of the roots receive little nourishment. Use the amounts recommended for plants in shrubbery borders; but in order to avoid possible burning of the small root area receiving the food, apply half the amount in early spring and the second half in mid-spring.

Established trees and shrubs growing in a lawn area usually get all the nourishment they need from the fertilizer broadcast over the lawn; but because of them, the grass may not get as much nourishment as *it* needs. If this seems to be the case, make one application of lawn fertilizer in early spring and a second in mid-spring. Each should equal about two-thirds of the amount specified for a normal single application. (Although lawn fertilizer normally has a higher nitrogen content than the formulas recommended for trees and shrubs alone, no harm will come to the large plants because of this. However, if you apply a combination fertilizer and weed-killer to your lawn, make very certain that the weed-killer is safe to use under trees and shrubs.)

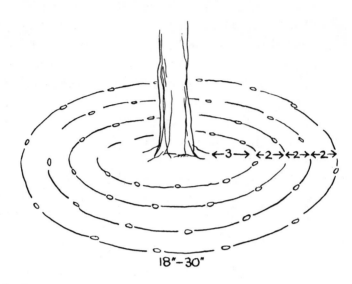

*To feed a large tree, poke deep holes in the ground at 18- to 30-inch intervals in circles 2 feet apart. Divide the fertilizer as evenly as possible among these. The last ring of holes should be 2 feet out beyond the tips of the branches.*

## FERTILIZING TREES AND SHRUBS WHICH MAY BE EXPOSED TO A FATAL DISEASE

This is purely a preventive measure—similar to taking vitamins to ward off colds and flu. I am not at all sure that there is any conclusive evidence that it works. Nevertheless, when you know a favorite plant may be stricken, you are usually ready to try almost anything to protect it.

I am most familiar with the frantic efforts that owners of American elms in the east have made to save these beautiful trees from the Dutch elm disease by fertilizing and spraying them every spring. In most cases, the trees have died anyway. But every once in a while the results have been encouraging.

The treatment for threatened shrubs calls for an annual early spring feeding. Use two to three cupfuls of fertilizer for small and medium-size shrubs; four to six cupfuls for progressively larger shrubs. Work it into the soil over the entire root zone and water in well.

To make sure fertilizer reaches tree roots lying far below the soil surface, it should be placed in 18-to-24-inch-deep holes made with a crow-bar or power-driven earth auger. The holes are made in concentric circles around the tree. The innermost circle is 3 feet from the trunk; the outermost, 2 feet out beyond the ends of the branches. The circles in between are 2 feet apart. Within each circle, the holes are spaced 18 to 30 inches apart.

Give each tree 3 to 5 pounds of fertilizer per inch of trunk diameter at breast height (for example, a tree with a 12-inch trunk should be given 36 to 60 pounds of fertilizer). Use the lower figure for very vigorous trees, the higher figure for less vigorous trees. Divide the total amount equally between all the holes. Spoon the fertilizer in carefully so you don't burn any grass around the holes. Then fill the holes to the top with soil and peat moss.

## FERTILIZING TREES AND SHRUBS THAT HAVE BEEN DEFOLIATED, DISEASED OR INJURED

Plants that lose their leaves in the spring and early summer—most often because of an insect attack—should be fertilized immediately in the way just described. But if the loss comes in the late summer, withhold treatment until early the following spring.

Plants that are badly injured in a storm or by an errant automobile should be handled similarly.

But if individual branches on a tree or shrub suddenly turn yellow and then die, you should get expert opinion on what is causing the trouble before applying fertilizer. In some cases feeding may be helpful; in others it may have no effect; and in still others it may actually be harmful. (Pears, for example, are subject to a serious disease called fire blight which is stimulated into action by too much fertilizer.)

# ·6·

## PRUNING AND TRAINING

Many years ago, when my wife was showing an old friend—an expert gardener—around our garden, she happened to point out a mountain laurel that was growing up in front of a dining-room window. "Stan hasn't figured out what to do about its growing so large," she remarked.

Our friend minced no words in her answer: "Doesn't he know what pruning shears are for?"

I am wiser today. But many gardeners are not. Some refrain so assiduously from using pruning tools that you might think they were completely unaware that tools existed. Others use pruning tools with a vengence to whack innocent pretty trees and shrubs into dreadful unnatural shapes.

Pruning has several functions:

To keep plants from outgrowing their locations.

To help maintain the health of plants by removing diseased, dead and excess branches. This also serves to keep the plants from littering the ground underneath with broken branches.

To reshape plants which have been battered by storms.

To make plants more shapely and attractive.

And to promote production of fruit.

Obviously, pruning is a rather vital function if you want good-looking, healthy trees and shrubs.

This fine white oak was at one time so filled with dead and dying wood that its chances of survival seemed bleak. But a tree service cleaned out all of this —plus a lot of unnecessary live wood—in half a day; and the tree is today growing vigorously. It also looks much better.

## HEAVY PRUNING, TREE SURGERY AND TREE REMOVAL

Most pruning work on most residential properties is simple enough and safe enough for the home owner to do himself. But if you have any big trees that need attention, a reputable professional tree service should be employed for almost all work except the cutting of branches fairly close to the ground. Such a service is expensive; however, it may not only save your life but also save a tree you would otherwise lose.

Jobs to leave to a tree service include all high-off-the-ground pruning of limbs; removing trees that are so big or so situated that they must be taken down piece by piece from the top; cleaning out and filling large cavities in trunks and limbs; bracing weak trunks and heavy branches with steel rods or cables.

## PRUNING TOOLS FOR HOME USE

The first and only pruning tool you will need until your trees and shrubs are large is a pair of pruning shears. The so-called snapcut type has a single sharp cutting blade that presses against a flat, anvil-like surface. The other type of shears has two overlapping cutting blades. Professionals generally prefer the latter because they cut more cleanly; but this is true only if you buy the most expensive models—cheap models

*Lopping shears will cut through branches about 1½ inches thick.*

*The pole pruner cuts through the smaller part of a branch when the rope is pulled. The pole saw, which cuts on the pull stroke, is for removing larger branches.*

cut very badly. By contrast, snapcut shears almost always do a good job.

Other pruning tools you may find you need are described as follows:

Lopping shears are like small pruning shears but have long handles and larger throats so you can cut through much bigger branches.

Pruning saws have coarse teeth for fast cutting of all kinds of wood. (You can use a carpenter's saw, but the going is painfully slow.) Saws with straight blades cut, like a carpenter's saw, on the push stroke. Those with slender, curved blades cut on the pull stroke. The latter are used primarily on extension poles for cutting branches above the head.

Pole pruners are designed for high-up removal of branches less than about 1 inch in diameter. The pruning head slips over the branch; the cutting knife is then pulled through the branch by means of a rope or long handle.

Power-driven chain saws are used for effortless cutting of very large branches and tree trunks. But they are worth buying only if you have a sizable woodland. For occasional use, rent a saw.

Hedge shears or electric hedge clippers are necessary only if you have a hedge or keep individual shrubs and small trees trimmed to definite shapes.

Three rules for using all pruning tools are: (1) Keep them sharp. (2) Paint them a bright color so you can find them if you put them down or drop them. (3) Sterilize the cutting edge with denatured alcohol after pruning a sick plant. In fact, if you are pruning a tree that has a disease such as fire blight, you should disinfect the cutting blade after every cut so you do not transmit the disease from one branch to another.

After cuts more than 1 inch in diameter are made in deciduous plants and broadleaf evergreens, the cuts should be dressed with tree paint to keep out disease organisms. The paint can be applied by brush or aerosol spray can. If a wound oozes sap, wait until this dries before painting. Conifers need not be protected with paint because they cover over the wounds by themselves with resin.

## WHEN TO PRUNE TREES AND SHRUBS

Cut out broken, diseased and dead branches; one of any two branches that rub against each other; suckers from the roots and water sprouts* on trunks and branches at any time of the year. The sooner you get rid of such things, the better.

But when you are pruning to improve the appearance of a tree or shrub or to control its size, the best time to do the job is in the spring. Except for fruit trees, plants that bloom in the spring are usually pruned right after the flowers fade. All other plants—those that bloom in summer or fall, those without important flowers, and fruit trees—are pruned in very early spring.

## HOW TO PRUNE MOST TREES AND SHRUBS

When removing an entire branch from a trunk or from a larger branch, make the cut as close as possible to the trunk and parallel with it. If using shears, try either to cut from the bottom up or with the cutting

---

* Slender, unbranched shoots resembling suckers, which grow more or less straight up from the trunk and larger branches.

*This is why one of two branches that rub together should be cut out. If the top branch does not break where it has been worn thin, it will eventually die for lack of nourishment. The lower branch, in this case, is not badly harmed.*

*How to remove a large tree limb. Make the first cut part way into the bottom; then cut all the way down through from the top a little farther out on the limb. Remove the stub that is left.*

blade edge parallel to the trunk in order to keep the bark on the trunk from tearing as the branch falls. When a heavy limb is to be removed by saw, cut about one-third up through the bottom of the limb 10 inches from the trunk. Then cut all the way down through the limb 12 inches from the trunk. Finally cut off the stub that is left close to the trunk. This procedure also prevents damage to the trunk bark and wood when the limb falls.

When shortening a branch, cut it off just above a bud or side branch which is pointed in the direction you want the branch to go. The cut

*When cutting back a branch, cut it just in front of a side branch or bud that is growing in the desired direction. These are snapcut shears.*

*How to cut a branch above a side branch. The first has too much stub. The second is cut too close. The third is just right.*

should be angled at about 60° to the branch and pointed in the direction of the bud or side branch.

When shearing a plant or a hedge (this is also a shortening process) it is unnecessary to cut every branch just above a bud or side branch, because any unsightly stubs which are left will soon be hidden by the dense growth that develops. However, you should take pains never to cut below the last green growth on a needled evergreen branch, because branches without needles soon die.

To shape a shrub that has numerous stems, cut some of the older stems all the way back to the ground. Pruning the stems at the top gives the plant an ugly flat-topped look and also encourages the stems to put out vigorous new growth just below the cut ends.

*This heavenly bamboo was butchered by having its top cut off, but such is its innate beauty that it is attractive anyway. The proper way to prune shrubs like this is to cut out the stems at the base when they grow too large.*

*To slow the growth of a white pine and make it thicker, pinch out the center candles in each cluster. This forces the side candles to make stronger growth than they would normally.*

When shortening branches that have grown too far out to the sides and top of a tree or shrub, cut them off inside the plant (behind the ends of nearby branches). This conceals the stubs.

To make evergreens dense, cut off the growing tips at the ends of the branches. If you undertake this operation as soon as the tips start growing in the spring, you can pinch them off with your fingers.

## HOW TO KEEP TREES AND SHRUBS SMALL

If you don't want plants to reach their full size, you should prune them every year after they have become established and start making strong growth. Should you fail to do this, the plants will get away from you and you will suddenly discover that you can reduce their size only by rather severe surgery, which may detract from their appearance.

The best way to control the growth of all species of trees and shrubs is to prune the roots in early spring. The work is done with a sharp spade. Drive this straight down into the ground to its full depth in a circle all the way around the plant. If you encounter large roots which are hard to cut without mangling, use shears.

The first year that you root-prune a plant, measure the thickness of the trunk just above ground level. If it is less than 1 inch across, make the circle 15 inches in diameter. For each additional inch of trunk thickness, increase the diameter of the circle 12 inches. (If you're working on a multistemmed plant, you will just have to guess what the diameter of the stems would be if they were bundled together into a single stem.) Once the roots have been pruned to a certain diameter, you can continue pruning them year after year to the same diameter. Or if you want to let the plant make further upward growth, you can gradually increase the diameter of the circle.

As an alternative to root-pruning, you can control the growth of many plants simply by removing the growing tips of the branches when they start elongating in the spring. This, however, is a much more time-consuming undertaking.

## HOW TO REDUCE THE SIZE OF TREES AND SHRUBS THAT HAVE GROWN TOO BIG

Many shrubs that put up a cluster of stems, such as rhododendrons, azaleas, mountain laurels, andromeda and lilacs, can be rejuvenated when they get too tall and leggy by cutting them down to within a few inches of the ground. If this is done early in the spring, the plants will make substantial new growth before the following autumn. All the

*On a rhododendron, the large buds are flower buds; the small buds (fore-ground, left), leaf buds. Both have small axillary buds at their base (but here visible only around the leaf bud). To make a plant bush out and bear more flowers, nip off the leaf buds but be careful not to hurt the axillary buds. The flower buds should also be removed, but only after they bloom, of course.*

stems can be shortened at the same time; but in order not to leave a big gap in the garden, it is usually best to do the job a few stems at a time over a period of about three years.

Although some single-stemmed trees and shrubs will also put up new growth when cut to the ground, plants of this type are more commonly reduced in size by cutting back the top and sides. How ruthless you are

*This soft-foliaged western white pine could undoubtedly have been prevented from developing this odd structure if the lowest limbs had been cut out when they first appeared.*

depends on how desperate you are for results. The fact that a large tree will live even after a storm takes off two-thirds of its crown indicates that trees and shrubs have a remarkable capacity for survival. Nevertheless, it is generally a better idea to cut plants back gradually in order to avoid too much shock to their systems.

In doing this kind of major pruning, if you have to remove entire branches, note the angle at which they grow from the trunk. The wider the angle, the stronger the crotch; the narrower the angle, the more likely the branch will split away from the trunk if it is heavily laden with snow, ice or fruit. In other words, if there is any choice between the branches to be removed, save those with the widest crotches.

## HOW TO PRUNE DECIDUOUS FRUIT TREES

A fruit tree requires considerably more pruning than an ornamental because you must keep the center of the crown fairly open to let in sunlight and thus promote better fruit production. Pruning starts as soon as young trees (which are almost always bare-root specimens) are planted, and continues every year thereafter.

With all except peaches, nectarines and apricots, early pruning is designed to develop a central trunk, referred to as the leader, with four or five large "scaffold" branches growing in different directions and spaced at least 6 inches apart up and down. The lowest branch should be about 30 inches from the ground.* Smaller branches—also well spaced —are allowed to grow from the scaffolds.

Once the fruit tree reaches 16 to 18 feet in height, it should not be allowed to grow any taller. This makes all care and harvesting of fruit much easier.

Peaches, nectarines and apricots are trained by the so-called "open-center method," which gives them a vase shape. At planting, the trunk

* The height of a branch on a tree trunk never changes even though the tree itself may grow much taller. In other words, a new branch appearing on a trunk at a height of 30 inches is still 30 inches above the ground after 25, 50 or 100 years.

*To make this apple tree more manageable and more productive, I cut it back about a third over a period of 3 years. Several of the branches removed were 3 to 4 inches in diameter. As shown here, the tree is now about 15 feet high and open at the center to let in light.*

is cut back to about 2 feet high. Three or four branches rising from the stub are developed as scaffolds from which smaller branches are allowed to grow. The maximum height of a tree should not exceed 8 to 10 feet.

After the basic structure of all fruit trees has been developed, annual late winter or early spring pruning consists mainly of removing dead and broken branches, water sprouts, branches that crisscross and any other branches that make the crown too dense.

## HOW TO TRAIN AND PRUNE HEDGES

Whether you shear a hedge to a formal shape or allow it to grow more-or-less naturally into an informal shape, training should start soon after the plants are in and growing strongly. Waiting until the hedge reaches the desired height before you prune makes shaping very difficult.

A cardinal rule in training all hedges is to keep the sides either vertical or slanting outward toward the bottom. Thus the sun can reach the branches at all levels. If the top is allowed to get wider than the bottom, the branches at the bottom will eventually be shaded out.

A second cardinal rule—which I find most people ignore to their ultimate sorrow—is to keep a hedge narrow enough so you can easily cut the top without climbing into the hedge. This is especially important in the case of tall hedges that must be trimmed from a ladder.

Maximum width of a hedge no higher than your armpits is 6 feet. Maximum width of taller hedges that must be cut from a ladder is 5 feet, if the ground on both sides is flat and firm. But if the ground is flat and firm on only one side, so that you can cut the hedge from that side only, the maximum width should not be more than 3 feet. (If the ground slopes away from a hedge on both sides, making it impossible to set a ladder safely, you should not let the hedge go over 4 feet in height.)

Except for broadleaf evergreens, which are usually trimmed before growth starts in the spring, most hedges are trimmed soon after growth starts. One trimming a year is enough for many evergreens; but some deciduous hedges need to be trimmed once or twice during the late spring and summer to keep them under control.

To keep the tops of hedges smooth and level from one end to the other, always trim them to a string stretched taut between stakes.

My house was unoccupied for several years before I bought it, and no one had pruned the false cypress hedge around the swimming pool. Consequently, to clear the deck around the pool, I was forced in some places to cut the hedge back below the last green growth. This left the dead, dark holes that show here. These will never fill in.

*Interesting shapes on a handsome terrace: espaliered crab apples at left; rounded boxwoods at center. All have been shaped by pruning.*
(Photo by United Press International)

## HOW TO ESPALIER TREES AND SHRUBS

An espalier is a tree, shrub or vine trained to an ornamental, flat, two-dimensional shape. Because the branches grow out on directly opposite sides of the trunk, the plant has no thickness. It is like a fence.

Espaliers are most often grown in front of walls in order to relieve the flat, blank look of the walls and also to silhouette the plants. But they are sometimes grown in the open, where they serve the purpose of dividing one part of the garden from another.

Trees and shrubs that make especially good espaliers are identified in the 100 Best descriptive lists beginning on pages 119 and 220. If these plants are to be grown in the open, you must first set posts firmly in the ground and stretch stout galvanized wires tightly between them. Space the wires 1 foot apart. To train an espalier in front of a wall, the proper procedure is to erect a similar wire trellis 6 inches out from the wall.

This allows air to circulate on all sides of the plant and also permits you to clean and paint the wall. Many people, however, fasten the espalier directly to the wall.

The actual technique of espaliering is quite simple. Decide first on the shape you want the plant to have. Then, starting when the plant is small, select young, supple branches which are growing more or less in the direction in which you want to lead them, and tie them firmly in place at 8-to-12-inch intervals. Cut out all other branches; and rub out* twigs and buds that you don't want on the espaliered branches. When the plant has attained the desired size, limit further growth by nipping off new growth points that develop.

The basic shaping and pruning of an espalier is done in early spring while the plant is dormant. But you must remove unwanted new growth as it develops during the spring and summer.

* This is the easiest way to remove small, succulent growths arising from stems and branches. You simply rub them off with your thumb.

# ·7·

# CONTROLLING PESTS

Many insects and diseases, and a few animals and birds, attack trees and shrubs. I do not minimize the damage they can do. American chestnuts have been wiped out by the chestnut blight. American elms are in the process of being wiped out by the Dutch elm disease. White pines by the hundreds of thousands are being deformed by the white pine weevil.

Yet I don't think there is any reason for the average gardener to become unduly alarmed. I have I don't know how many trees and shrubs in considerable variety on my property, yet I have had little trouble with pests. From experience, I know what problems *may* arise, and if I elect to do something to prevent them—I don't always—little work is entailed.

For instance, I know that my two beautiful pin oaks may be defoliated every year by inchworms, so I have them sprayed annually by a professional; and at the same time I have the sycamores sprayed because their leaves are attacked almost every year by a fungus disease.

I know that the Japanese andromedas are browned by the lacebugs which feed on the undersides of the leaves, so I myself spray the plants the last week in May.

I know that the lilacs may be covered by unsightly but not serious mildew in late summer; and if I am sufficiently annoyed when it appears, I get out my sprayer again.

I know that a spruce has lost its leader to weevils every year; but this has been happening for so long—even before I bought the place—that it matters no more. The tree will never develop properly no matter what I do to protect it.

Finally, I know that if I want good crops of apples, cherries, peaches and pears, I must spray the trees about every ten days throughout the growing season. This, I admit, is something of a chore, but it's a price I —and everyone else who wants to grow delicious fruit—must pay for it. No trees or shrubs require more attention than these—but that is only if you want fruit.

*Spraying a plum tree. If fruit and ornamental trees are kept under about 18 feet in height, you can cover them efficiently with a small pressure sprayer.*

Despite my rather casual attitude, I have lost just one plant—a large Douglas fir. One autumn it looked strong and healthy. Suddenly, early the next spring, it began to shed its needles, and it was dead. I could find no explanation. The tree man who took it down had none either.

The thing we all forget is that trees and shrubs, like men, are mortal. A few have been around for several thousand years, but none lives forever. Some, in fact, have rather short lives.

*To spray large trees, however, you must hire a tree service. The large hose here is fed by a tank truck almost 100 feet away.*

Another thing that writers of garden books forget (I have been guilty, too) is that there is nothing to be gained by describing *all* the insects and diseases that attack trees, because the only trees that gardeners can properly spray themselves are under about 15 feet tall. To take care of larger trees, you have to hire a tree service with a huge spray outfit. So of what practical value is it to you to know what is eating the top out of a tree? The only thing you need to know is that something's wrong and that you'd better call in expert help.

Of course, in some cases, you may be too late and the plant will die despite all ministrations. But this generally isn't true. You can console yourself with the thought that many trees and shrubs are doomed to die even before they show any signs of sickness. On the other side of the coin, many, many more trees and shrubs survive ailments you might think would kill them. This is especially true of those which are attacked by insects. For example, in the east, thousands of oaks are stripped of foliage every spring by inchworms; but as a rule, the only oaks that die are those defoliated two or three years in a row during periods of drought.

Trees and shrubs can survive most attacks by insects and disease if you keep them in healthy condition by watering, mulching, feeding and pruning. This is the best way to protect them. Preventive spraying, as for lacebugs on my andromedas, is called for only when you have reason to believe that your plants are likely to be attacked by certain pests. And control spraying (or some other form of treatment) is required when an attack does occur.

## SPRAYING EQUIPMENT

There are several ways to cope with garden insects and diseases, but spraying is by far the most common as far as trees and shrubs are concerned. Unless you want to spend a lot of money, you have a choice of two types of sprayer: a compressed-air sprayer and a hose sprayer.

Theoretically, a hose sprayer should be the more useful for tree and shrub work. It is advertised as being able to deliver a stream for 30 feet or more; therefore you should be able to spray medium-size trees. But, unfortunately, at this distance, the stream is more of a jet than a spray; and it isn't easy to hit every leaf and branch with a jet. Furthermore, in order to use the sprayer, you must drag a watering hose around after you wherever you go; and that isn't always easy either.

I prefer a compressed-air sprayer of about 2-gallon capacity. A man can carry one easily even when full. And even though this sprayer, too, works better close up to a plant than at a distance, it delivers a coarse but drenching spray for about 15 to 18 feet. When I first started raising fruit, I bought a much bigger orchard sprayer in order to reach the tops of large trees; but when something went wrong with it, I switched to my small garden sprayer and found it did just as good a job and was much less arduous to handle.

One thing you must be sure to do when using any kind of sprayer is to rinse it out thoroughly after every use in order to clean out possibly corrosive chemicals and particles that may clog the nozzle. Repeated careful washings of the sprayer with household ammonia are called for after you have used it for applying weed-killers.

## WHEN TO SPRAY

Preventive spraying is done just before the pest you are worried about becomes active. Control spraying is done just as soon as you notice the pest. Applications should be made right after a rain, and when there is relatively little breeze. (Breeze, however, is not a serious problem if you are treating a small plant at close range.)

## SPRAY CHEMICALS

The list of insecticides and fungicides is long. Some chemicals—the so-called "broad spectrum" type—are effective against numerous pests. Others are effective against only a few pests. Although you may need the latter on occasion, it's silly to buy them until needed. If you buy Sevin and malathion for use against insects, plus captan, ferbam or zineb for use against diseases, you are ready for most problems you will encounter.

## COMMON INSECT PESTS

This is an abbreviated list, for as I said earlier, it is of no avail to know what a pest is if you must hire an expert to cope with it. Furthermore, if you run into an unusual pest on a small plant that you yourself can spray, it takes only a couple of days to send it to your state agricultural extension service for identification and information about the latest methods of controlling it.

Insects that attack edible fruits are also omitted because if you follow the regular spray program recommended by your state agricultural extension service, you won't have any trouble from them and, indeed, may never even see them.

*Aphids* Tiny insects that collect in white, green, grayish, or reddish masses on many trees and shrubs throughout the country, suck the plant juices, and eventually cause distortion of leaves and flowers and general plant malaise. They are also troublesome because they transmit plant diseases. Spray with malathion or lindane. Destroy large anthills, because ants hoard aphids in their hills; but be kind to all ladybugs, because they feed on aphids.

*Bagworms* One-inch caterpillars with small silky bags covered with fragments of the conifers, sycamores, maples, lindens and citrus trees they feed on. They are found in the eastern half of the country, mainly in the south. Spray with Sevin in the spring. Pick off and burn the bags.

*Borers* These are various kinds of caterpillars and grubs that attack many trees and shrubs throughout the country. They bore holes in the branches and trunks, weaken the plants, and permit the entrance of disease organisms. You can kill the pests with a wire probe or by injecting carbon bisulfide in the holes. Work paradichlorobenzene crystals into the soil all around trees in the fall.

*Carpenter worms* Two-and-a-half-inch white caterpillars with brown heads bore into oaks, elms and other deciduous trees. Control like borers.

*Elm spanworms*   Spanworms are larvae of the snow-white linden moth. The long, thin caterpillars that hatch from barrellike eggs in mid-spring have the habit of congregating at midday and weaving the upper parts of their bodies to and fro. Found in the northeast in company with gypsy moths, they defoliate oaks, hickories and ashes primarily. Spraying for gypsy moths controls spanworms, but a newly discovered parasitic wasp does an even better job without any urging from you.

*Fall webworms*   Common, 1-inch-long, hairy caterpillars with a dark stripe on the back, yellow stripes on the sides. They make silken tents at the ends of branches of deciduous fruit and other trees, and eat the leaves. You may encounter them in mid-spring, late summer or fall. Cut off and burn the tents. Spray with Sevin.

*Gypsy moths*   Extremely serious pests that are rapidly spreading out of New England into Pennsylvania and the upper south. They have also leapfrogged to a small area in Florida. The hairy caterpillars are the real villains. When full grown they are about 2 inches long, brownish, with three light stripes on the back. They raise and lower themselves by long threads; and with solid footing, they loop themselves along. They are commonly called inchworms, cankerworms or measuring worms. They start feeding on the leaves of trees soon after these develop in the spring. Favorite targets are oaks; then white and gray birches, willows, lindens, apples and Colorado spruces; and from these they move to other spruces, hemlocks and pines. They are best controlled by spraying soon after leaves develop with Sevin or bacillus thuringiensis (B.t.). A second application about three weeks later is advisable during the worst infestations. You should also apply creosote to the brown egg masses found on trunks and garden walls in early spring. Banding tree trunks with Tanglefoot does away with climbing caterpillars.

*Japanese beetles*   Handsome metallic-green beetles with coppery wings found east of the Mississippi. They chew holes in the foliage of various small trees and shrubs during the summer. Kill the grubs before they emerge by dusting the lawn with chlordane. To kill the beetles, spray with Sevin. It's also easy to pick beetles off small plants into a bucket of kerosene.

*Lace bugs*    Several different little bugs with large lacy wings. They are found almost everywhere, feeding on the undersides of leaves on most deciduous trees, andromedas, azaleas, rhododendrons and ceanothus. Leaves look mottled; later turn pale brown. Spray several times in the spring with malathion.

*Leaf miners*    Tiny larvae of several insects found almost everywhere. They are almost impossible to see because they burrow inside leaves; but you can tell they are present because the leaves become spotted with translucent blotches. Birches and hollies are favorite targets. Spray with Sevin or malathion as new foliage develops.

*Leaf rollers*    Little caterpillars which roll leaves around themselves and then have a happy time eating. They attack most deciduous trees everywhere. Spray in spring with malathion.

*Red spider mites*    Widespread, microscopic sucking insects that feed on the needles of hemlocks and other evergreens. The needles turn brown and fall. Spray with a miticide such as Kelthane as soon as you suspect trouble.

*Sawflies*    Sawflies look like wasps with transparent wings. Their variously colored caterpillars chew in the spring on the foliage of larches and most other conifers and some deciduous trees. Control with malathion.

*Scale insects*    Several different pests which are a nuisance everywhere. These are tiny insects with a hard, scaly covering that congregate in masses on the trunks and limbs of many trees and shrubs. By sucking the plant juices, they reduce plant strength, cause loss of foliage and sometimes death. Spray with malathion or Sevin, preferably when you see the scales moving around. Repeat treatments will probably be necessary.

*Tent caterpillars*  Caterpillars that build silken tents in the crotches of many fruit and shade trees, then emerge and feed voraciously on the leaves. They are common almost everywhere. Destroy egg clusters in the winter. Remove tents by hand and burn them (but never burn the nests in the trees). Or spray tents and caterpillars with malathion.

*White pine weevils*  One-quarter-inch, reddish-brown beetles with white spots, which chew on the new leaders and branch ends of eastern white pines and sometimes other conifers. If they kill the leaders, the trees then develop several leaders, which turn into multiple trunks. No satisfactory way to control the pest has been found despite years of work by the U.S. Forest Service. But you have a chance of protecting individual trees if you spray malathion on the new, developing growths on pines under 15 feet tall.

## COMMON DISEASES OF TREES AND SHRUBS

*Anthracnose*  A widespread fungous disease which causes gray, brown, black or white spots, often with whitish centers, on leaves and sometimes twigs of numerous trees and shrubs. The leaves and twigs die. Control by spraying with zineb several times at ten-day intervals after the leaves start to develop.

*Canker*  Another widespread disease which causes large sores on trunks of maples and oaks. Let an expert take care of these.

*Cedar-apple rust*  This disease shows up in red cedars and junipers in the spring in the form of red, gelatinous galls (swellings or growths). When the galls open, the spores are transmitted to nearby apples, hawthorns, quinces, pears and mountain ashes, where they cause distortion and death of the foliage. Control by spraying cedars with ferbam in the spring.

*Chlorosis*  This disease occurs when, for one reason or another, a tree or shrub is unable to absorb sufficient iron from the soil. The leaves then turn yellow between the veins, which remain green; and they may fall. You can correct the problem, however, by applying iron chelates to the soil.

*Dieback*   This disease causes twigs and branches of oaks, maples and other trees to die back from the end. There is no good control. Just cut off the dead growths several inches farther down and burn them.

*Dutch elm disease*   American elms are the only plants affected. Leaves suddenly yellow and die on individual branches or sometimes on the entire tree. Then the tree dies. The disease is thought to be transmitted by beetles and also through the roots of trees growing close together. Once a tree is infected, you can't save it. But sometimes the disease can be warded off by heavy fertilizing of trees and spraying to kill the beetles in the spring. It is because the disease is so deadly that planting of this gorgeous tree can no longer be recommended.

*Fire blight*   A disease common to pears, apples, quinces, cotoneasters, firethorns and other deciduous plants, fire blight causes leaves to blacken and die; then the twigs blacken, become wizened-looking and die. Spray plants several times while they are in bloom with Bordeaux mixture. Cut out blighted twigs immediately. Make the cuts 6 inches below the affected area and sterilize your shears between cuts. Do all other pruning in late winter. Fertilize plants sparingly: overfeeding stimulates the disease.

*Leaf spot*   A very common disease, rarely fatal, but causing unsightly dark-edged spots with distinct centers on leaves of many plants. Spray several times with zineb or ferbam when you first notice trouble.

## OTHER PESTS

*Deer*   Deer do very extensive damage in the garden by chewing many shrubs—both evergreen and deciduous—to the ground; by nibbling on the tips of fruit tree branches; and by rubbing the bark off tree trunks with their antlers. In a few states shooting out of season is permitted. You can also erect an 8-foot wire-mesh fence or an electric fence. But probably the most practical way to protect plants is to apply a nasty-tasting repellent such as Arasan 75 or Improved Z.I.P. to shrubs and the tips of tree branches within 8 feet of the ground. Follow the manufacturer's directions carefully.

*Dogs*    Man's best friend is his shrubs' worst enemy, and I have yet to find a good way of coping with him. My best advice is to give him a swat every time you catch him in the act, or douse him with a pail of water. You can also surround his favorite shrubs with wire mesh, but that doesn't add to the beauty of the plants.

*Mice*    Mice are most troublesome in orchards and tree plantations, where they establish huge colonies; but they may eat the bark on the trunk and roots of almost any tree. If they completely girdle a trunk, the tree dies. To thwart them, keep grass around the trees cut low so they cannot establish nests in the vicinity; keep organic mulches pulled about 6 inches away from the trunks. Use traps, but not poison baits which pets and children can get at. In extreme situations, surround tree trunks with wire mesh. This should be sunk 4 inches into the ground and extend to 20 inches aboveground.

*Rabbits*    These also eat the bark from the trunks of trees, especially young trees; but they do less damage than mice. Use taste repellents to keep them off, or encircle trunks with wire mesh. This must extend to about 18 inches above the normal snow level.

*Slugs and snails*    These night workers do most damage in flower and vegetable gardens, but may also chew sizable holes in the young foliage of rhododendrons and other shrubs. You will see the holes the morning after. To control the pests, scatter metaldehyde baits among the shrubs and cover them loosely with boards to provide the damp, dark hiding places the miscreants like.

*Woodchucks*    Woodchucks occasionally feed on tree bark but can be held at bay with taste repellents or wire-mesh guards around trunks.

*Woodpeckers*    Every once in a while a woodpecker takes it into its head to drill holes up and down old tree trunks looking for insects. The result is not only unsightly but also allows disease organisms to enter the trees. Shooting is the best way to prevent further trouble; but you might well take a tip from a friend of mine who saved his home from destruction by mounting a papier-mâché owl on the chimney cap. Why not try one in your tree?

# ·8·

## SOME USEFUL
## FACTS ABOUT TREES AND SHRUBS

You may never need to know any more about growing trees and shrubs than you have read in the preceding seven chapters, but I wouldn't bet on it. On occasion you must give them special attention.

### WINTER PROTECTION

If you take pains to select plants suited to your climate, it should not be necessary to protect them against winter weather. I feel very strongly that gardens in winter should not be unsightly; for that reason I dislike the use of plants which must be wrapped in swaddling clothes for four or five or six months of the year. Nevertheless, since I cannot prevent you from buying species that may be doubtfully hardy in your climate, I am forced by my desire to make this a useful book to tell you what should be done in the event that you ignore my advice.

To protect evergreens against cold winds and/or drying sun, surround them on their exposed sides with burlap or snow fencing. The former is more often used, but it is a nuisance because you must erect a sturdy frame to which the stretched burlap is stapled. To keep the burlap from sagging and flapping in the wind, it must be attached at both top and bottom to heavy wires or boards stretched between the uprights of the frame.

Snow fencing is much easier to handle, and even though the spaces between the slats are about 2 inches wide, the fencing does as good a job of screening as burlap.

Another form of winter protection is required by fragile evergreens and dense deciduous species planted in foundation borders under the eaves of steep roofs. The only sure way to keep these from being crushed under heavy, wet snow and falling icicles is to erect little roofs of plywood over them. However, these are so hideous that I recommend two less than perfect alternatives: To stop snow from coming off the roof in avalanches, install steel snow stops in multiple rows from one end of the roof to the other. And to prevent the formation of icicles as snow melts and runs down the roof, install electric heating cables along the eaves' edges and in the gutters and downspouts.

In heavy snow country it may also be necessary to protect certain evergreens which are growing out in the open. In my experience, arborvitaes need attention most because they become badly bent under snow and often break; but large vase-shaped yews are also vulnerable. For the latter and also for multistemmed arborvitaes, the best protection is afforded by wrapping a stout twine around them in a spiral from the bottom to the top. This should be just tight enough to pull the branches in a bit so they cannot spread. Small columnar, single-stemmed arborvitaes can be tied at several places near the top to stout stakes.

Actually, the best way to take care of evergreens and deciduous trees and shrubs with weak wood when you have a blizzard or a very wet snowfall is to go out with a broom or long bamboo pole and knock off the snow. Do this during the storm and also after it stops. But don't belabor the plants lest you break the branches yourself. Work from the bottom up and just push the limbs enough to dislodge the snow. Besides arborvitaes, plants that especially need help are southern broadleaf evergreens such as boxwood and the southern magnolia. And don't overlook deciduous plants if you happen to have a snowfall before the leaves drop in the autumn or after they appear in the spring.

Two other things you should certainly do if you live in snow country are to place tall stakes beside small plants that might be knocked down by skiers, sledders and snowmobilers, and to plant small shrubs several feet away from either side of your driveway so they will not be crushed under the snow pushed aside by plows.

## PROTECTING TREES AND SHRUBS
## FROM STRANGULATION

At my former home, I had a couple of acres of woods which had been taken over by bittersweet. When I finally cut through the tangle, I was amazed to see how many large trees had deep spiral grooves in the trunks where the vines had climbed up around them. A number of the trees were dead.

Not all vines are tree killers; but watch 'out for those that climb by twining—bittersweet, poison ivy, honeysuckle, etc. If you find these growing up into trees and shrubs, pull them down promptly. If they won't come down, cut them off at the base; then, about a year later, when the dead stems have become brittle, they can usually be removed without any trouble. The live roots should be removed, too. If you can't grub them out, let them put up a new stem for about a foot; then bend this over and dip it in a jar filled with a solution of Ammate.

On occasion trees may also strangle themselves by developing "girdling" roots. These are roots that curl tightly around the trunk, usually just above ground level. The presence of below-ground girdling roots is indicated if you notice a tree trunk which grows straight down into the ground instead of flaring slightly outward. However the roots are growing, just cut them off before they can do any harm.

## RAISING THE GROUND LEVEL
## AROUND A TREE

With very few exceptions, trees die when you pile more soil over their roots than they have been accustomed to or if you mound soil up against the trunks. So when it is necessary to raise the grade around a sizable tree you cherish, extensive steps must be taken to protect it.

Cover the entire root system (from the trunk to the outermost tips of the branches) with a 6-to-12-inch layer of coarse crushed rock; and over this spread about 2 inches of fine rock to keep soil out of the coarse layer.

Around the trunk, build a well about 3 feet across and up to the level of the new grade. You can construct the walls of concrete blocks,

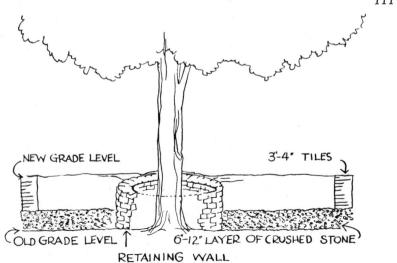

NEW GRADE LEVEL    3"-4" TILES

OLD GRADE LEVEL ↑    6"-12" LAYER OF CRUSHED STONE

RETAINING WALL

*How to raise the grade level around a tree. The vertical tiles are necessary only if you are raising the grade more than about 2 feet or if the soil is extremely dense.*

bricks or stones. In order to allow water which enters the well to drain off rapidly, do not use mortar. To keep out children, animals and debris, cover the well with a steel grating or fill it to the top with very coarse crushed rock.

It is now safe to fill in around the tree with soil. Thanks to the well and the layer of rock, air and moisture can reach the tree roots, and the tree will live. However, if you raise the grade a great deal—say 2 feet or more—one final step is in order: Place a ring of 3-to-4-inch-diameter vertical drainpipes or tiles around the tree under the tips of the branches. Space these 3 to 4 feet apart and cover the tops with wire mesh so they will not become clogged with grass clippings and other debris and also to keep people from stepping into them. Their purpose is further to assure that adequate air and moisture reach the roots.

## LOWERING THE GROUND LEVEL AROUND A TREE

The main job in this case is to retain as much soil around the roots as you can. If necessary, however, you can safely reduce the diameter of the root system 50 percent.

Make a circle around the tree halfway between the trunk and the outermost tips of the branches and dig a trench down to the new grade level. Cut off the roots in the trench. Then build up in the trench a retaining wall of concrete, brick masonry or stone masonry. The wall should be about 3 inches higher than the old soil level so that water, instead of running off, sinks down to the roots.

The soil outside the retaining wall can then be removed down to the new grade level.

This project should be undertaken as early in the spring as possible so the tree will have plenty of time to recapture its strength before frost. To assist it, give it about 5 pounds of balanced fertilizer per inch of trunk diameter at breast height. Feed the tree through crowbar holes driven into the ground inside the retaining wall (see Chapter 5). Apply half the fertilizer at the time the wall is built and the remaining half six to eight weeks later.

## PAVING AROUND TREES AND SHRUBS

When solid paving—for example, concrete, blacktop or bricks laid in mortar—covers the roots of a plant, oxygen and moisture are cut off and the plant dies. There are, however, two ways to prevent this outcome.

If you put in solid paving, do not cover more than half of the plant's root system, and leave an open space 1 to 2 feet wide between the paving and the trunk.

A better alternative is to lay paving blocks, such as bricks or flagstones, loose (without mortar) on a bed of sand. Since water and air will pass through the joints between the blocks, it is safe to pave over the entire root system.

## PROTECTING TREES AND SHRUBS
## FROM SALT DAMAGE

On a recent springtime trip down the Merritt Parkway in Connecticut I was horrified to notice how many of the shrubs and trees in the median and close to the sides of the road had dead lower limbs. The villain was obvious: Salt spread to keep the road open in winter had been splashed up on the trees by the thousands of passing cars.

Similar damage occurs every year in every state that uses road salt— and it isn't confined to major highways. You can see it along suburban streets and country lanes. I once had a neighbor who lost a whole row of lovely hemlocks to salt.

The only sure way to keep your own trees and shrubs safe is to plant them at least 6 feet back from the road—even more if there is high-speed traffic on the road.

If for one reason or other you do not do this, you should at least make sure to slope the ground away from the plants so the salt water will not have time to penetrate to the roots. Build a plywood screen in front of evergreens. And don't wait for the highway or street department to clear storm drains so the salt melt water will run off rapidly; get out your shovel and open them yourself.

Extraordinary high tides which occasionally flood waterfront properties are much less damaging to trees and shrubs than road salt. In fact, although I know a good many people who have been flooded repeatedly—sometimes two or three times in a year—I have never known them to lose large plants. Nevertheless, if you feel particularly solicitous about a tree or shrub, there is no reason why you shouldn't race out with a hose when the ocean recedes and soak the soil around the plant with fresh water to wash out the salt. This can do no harm and just might do much good.

## PROTECTING TREES AND SHRUBS FROM POLLUTED AIR

There is much growing evidence that air pollution injures many plants and has, indeed, killed many sturdy trees. The most dramatic evidence of this comes from a mountain area 100 miles east of Los Angeles where more than a million majestic ponderosa pines are dead or dying from southern California smog.

Unfortunately, short of cleaning up the atmosphere, there is nothing to be done to prevent this. But if you live in an area with a bad pollution problem, you can at least select plants which seem to have unusual resistance to smog. Deciduous specimens are the best; but even among the evergreens, there are certain species identified in the 100 Best Trees list on page 119 which are better than average.

One other step you should take, especially with your evergreens, is to hose them off frequently with water. This removes the visible grime and allows the leaves to function more normally.

*When bark on a tree is wounded, trim it out in an ellipse or diamond so that water will drain out.*

## REPAIRING BARK WOUNDS

If the bark is torn from a tree trunk or large stem on a shrub, carefully trim around the wounded area with a sharp knife or hammer and chisel. Shape the opening like an ellipse or a diamond pointed at top and bottom; and try not to cut through the cambium layer just beneath the bark. Then coat with tree paint.

## REPAIRING SMALL CAVITIES IN TREES

Let a professional take care of cavities more than about 3 inches across or 2 inches deep. For smaller cavities, cut out any decayed areas with a knife and sharp chisel, and smooth the wood in the cavity. Slant the bottom of the cavity toward the front so that water which enters will pour out, but don't enlarge the hole any more than necessary. Then disinfect the wood with alcohol; and when this evaporates, apply tree paint. If you can find the cavity filler used by tree surgeons in a garden-supply store, it is advisable then to fill the wound with this.

## REPAIRING BROKEN BRANCHES AND STEMS

If a small branch or stem is partially split by a storm or accident, it is often possible to repair the damage if you act immediately. Close the break and make sure the edges are smoothly aligned. Then drive several brass screws or bolts through the break. Finally, tie the branch to a stake or another branch with strips of cloth to reinforce the break while it knits.

## REPAIRING A DAMAGED LEADER

When the top of the trunk—the leader—of a conifer is broken or killed by insects, the branches just below the break begin to grow upward instead of outward and eventually the tree has several leaders and its natural pyramidal symmetry is destroyed. I happen to think that this sometimes results in a more interesting, picturesque tree; but that is my opinion. If it isn't yours, you can easily maintain the symmetry of the tree by the following actions:

Trim the broken leader off just above the topmost branches. Select the branch that you think will make the best replacement leader (this may be the longest branch or the one that grows out of the trunk at the most acute upward angle). Tie a stick to the top of the trunk with strips of cloth. The end of the stick should project above the tree. Then gently bend the selected branch upright and tie it to the end of the stick. In

*How to make a conifer develop a new leader in a hurry.*

the succeeding months, as the branch becomes accustomed to its new position, you can pull it closer to the stick.

This hastens the development of a vigorous new leader and discourages the other top branches from trying to become leaders too. However, if one of these branches does start growing upward, it should be removed.

## RIGHTING TREES AND SHRUBS THAT BLOW DOWN

If the roots have not been too badly mangled and if the plant isn't too large, you should waste no time in trying to save it. First trim the broken ends of the roots and cover all that are exposed with damp burlap, straw—anything that will keep them from drying out.

Open the hole in the ground as necessary to accommodate the roots. Then pull the plant upright and secure it in position with guy wires (see page 66). On large trees, use a couple of sets of guy wires, one above the other. Keep the plant well watered for several weeks, and fertilize it if the blow-down occurred before July 15. (Except in warm climates, an application of fertilizer after this date might force the plant to make new growth which would later be killed by frost.)

## FELLING TREES

As I said earlier, leave the felling of large trees or trees which are in difficult situations—near a house or electric wires, for example—to a professional. But you can take down small trees and even quite large trees if there is plenty of open space around them.

Study carefully the direction in which the tree should be felled. (If it grows on a slant, don't try to fell it in the opposite direction unless you put a rope around it.) Then with an ax and/or saw cut a V-shape notch almost half through the trunk on the side in the direction of the fall. To save a little work, you can make this close to the ground; then you won't have to cut off a stump after the tree is down. Generally, however, it's easier to make the notch a foot or so above the ground.

Then saw through the trunk from the opposite side a couple of inches above the apex of the V. When the tree begins to creak and then bend, stand as far away as you can while sawing, and make sure the tree is not bending in your direction (despite the notch, a tree will sometimes do this because of the way it has been growing).

To reduce the risk of having a tree come down on you as you cut, it is a splendid idea to attach a long guide rope to it. You should also use a rope if you have to bring down a tree into a narrow opening between other plants. Tie the rope before you start cutting the tree—as high up in the crown as you can safely climb. The free end should be handled by someone strong who stands in front of the tree and pulls it down.

Once a tree is on the ground, cut it from the stump. Then saw the stump off flush with the ground (though in informal settings, tree stumps make excellent seats to perch on when you wish to take a rest from your gardening labors).

## REMOVING STUMPS

The fastest—and also the most costly—way to get rid of large stumps is to have a tree service cut them down below ground level with a chipping machine. The alternative is to treat the stump with a stump-killing chemical available from garden-supply stores.

Drill a couple of 1-inch holes down through the top of the stump to a depth of about 10 inches. Also drill a couple of slanting holes through the sides of the stump to meet—if possible—the vertical holes. Cram the holes about three-quarters full of the chemical and wet it with water. Then fill the holes to the top with chemical and cover the stump with a piece of plastic.

Let the chemical work for two months. Then remove the plastic, saturate the stump with kerosene, and set it on fire. It will not make much of a blaze but should slowly burn away.

## KILLING STUMPS

If you simply want to keep a stump from sprouting, saturate it with 4 pounds of Ammate dissolved in 1 gallon of water. For a stump less than 6 inches across, make a few ax cuts in the surface and slowly pour on the chemical until no more can be absorbed.

For larger stumps, make a series of deep, slanting, overlapping ax cuts in the sides of the stump. Be sure you go through the bark. Then pour on the Ammate solution, and fill each ax cut with a heaping table-spoonful of Ammate crystals.

# ·9·

# THE 100 BEST TREES

ACACIA, SILVER WATTLE. *Acacia decurrens dealbata*. Zones 9–10. Broad-leaf evergreen with compound* leaves containing numerous small, silver-gray leaflets, giving the tree a feathery look. Grows very rapidly to form a spreading, 50-foot tree but lives only about 25 years. Covered in late winter with round clusters of small fragrant yellow flowers. The profuse pollen these shed sticks to the tops of cars, house windows, etc.

Plant in a sunny spot in any good soil. Cut off the lower branches of young plants to encourage them to develop as trees rather than as shrubs. Keep staked for several years. Prune annually after flowering to keep the center of the tree open.

Many other good species and varieties of acacia are available.

APPLE. *Malus pumila*. Zones 3–8. Deciduous. Standard trees make moderate growth to as much as 50 feet; but if you grow them for fruit, they should be held at 15 to 18 feet. The smallest dwarf apples reach no more than 6 feet; semidwarfs go to about 15 feet. All trees bear white spring flowers, followed by luscious red, yellow or green fruits from mid-summer to late fall, depending on variety.

To raise apples for fruit, you must put in at least two compatible varieties that bloom at the same time. For example, plant Red Delicious

* A compound leaf is one having several blades on one leafstalk.

with Cortland; Rhode Island Greening with McIntosh; Rome Beauty with York Imperial; Lodi with Yellow Transparent. Plant the trees in the full sun in better-than-average, well-drained soil. Prune early every spring to keep the trees open, and fertilize them at the same time. To control the many insects and diseases that attack apples, you must also spray them at roughly 10-day intervals from early spring until harvest.

If you're not interested in fruit, but want to grow apples simply as ornamental shade trees—which they are—such frequent spraying is unnecessary. You should, however, keep excess small branches cut out; otherwise the trees get cluttered-looking. To prevent fruit formation, plant only one variety; or, if your neighbor has an apple tree, spray your tree with a chemical that keeps fruit from setting. Naphthalene-acetic acid is an example.

Apple trees also make excellent espaliers either with or without fruit.

ARBORVITAE, AMERICAN. *Thuja occidentalis.* Zones 6–10, but hardy as far north as Zone 2 if you don't object to the brown color of the foliage in winter. Evergreen. Tiny leaves growing tight together are arranged in flat, fanlike sprays. Small, erect cones. Tree forms a narrow column; makes moderately slow growth to 60 feet.

Arborvitae is a favorite for framing doorways but really looks its best when used as a tall accent plant spearing up against the sky. It survives in fairly deep shade, but grows much taller and denser in full sun or light shade. Plant in average, well-drained soil. Watch out for red spider mites and bagworms.

ASH, GREEN. *Fraxinus pennsylvanica lanceolata.* Zones 2–7. Deciduous. Grows very rapidly to 60 feet. Dense, rounded crown. Compound leaves up to 12 inches long have 7 to 9 elliptical leaflets which turn yellow in the fall.

There are better trees than this, but if you want quick shade for your house or garden, you must consider it. Plant in full sun in average soil.

*In the next ten years this green ash will develop a much wider, rounded crown.*

*Given ample space, as here, the mighty American beech grows tall and wide
—a magnificent sight.*

BEECH, AMERICAN. *Fagus grandifolia.* Zones 3b–9. Deciduous. Grows
at moderate speed to a height of 90 feet and almost the same width.
Massive trunk and branches covered with beautiful smooth, light-gray

bark. Serrated elliptical leaves with pronounced veins turn bronze in the fall and remain on the tree for a long time.

Although the American beech grows in partial shade when young, it should be planted in the middle of a large, sunny lawn and treated as a specimen which children will delight in climbing. It is a magnificent sight in all seasons. It can also be used to shade a terrace provided you cut out very low-growing branches which may develop.

Plant in average soil. Requires little attention once established.

BEECH, EUROPEAN. *Fagus sylvatica.* Zones 5–10. Similar in all respects to the American beech but with branches often sweeping the ground. Several varieties are weeping trees with branches almost as pendulous as those on willows. But while these form huge, attractive mounds in summer, they look odd and even ghoulish in winter when they are bare. The conventional upright tree is therefore recommended.

European beech foliage is also variable. The leaves of the species are dark green and elliptical. But the variety known as the Purple Beech has lustrous purple leaves; the Copper Beech, copper-colored leaves; and several varieties have deeply cut fernlike leaves.

All in all, this is an extremely ornamental tree; but it needs a great deal of space to grow, and also to allow you to view it in its entirety. Requires sun and average, well-drained soil.

BIRCH, EUROPEAN. *Betula pendula.* Zones 2–10. Deciduous. Grows quickly to 60 feet. Forms a rather narrow crown, but some varieties are fairly wide. Somewhat pendulous branches have a pronounced weeping habit in several varieties. Lovely white bark. Nicely chiseled leaves turn yellow in the fall.

This is an outstanding tree for small gardens as well as large. Despite its considerable height, it seems reasonably small. This is because of its overall grace and delicacy. As a shade tree it is of little value, but it brings great beauty to any corner of the garden the whole year around. The true European birch is especially desirable because it is not so densely covered with leaves as the varieties, and the slender, white trunk is therefore clearly visible.

Plant in the sun in average soil. Borers and leaf miners sometimes cause serious problems but can be controlled by spraying.

*The European beech at the corner of the wall has oval purple leaves. The European beech behind it has weeping limbs and finely cut, fernlike green leaves.*

BIRCH, WHITE. Also called Paper Birch and Canoe Birch. *Betula papyrifera.* Zones 2–7. Deciduous. Fast growth to 90 feet. Upright, somewhat pyramidal habit. Glistening white bark with few black marks peels off in papery sheets. Bright-green, heart-shaped leaves with numerous little teeth around the edges turn yellow in the fall.

The white birch is less graceful than the European birch but even more beautiful. This is mainly because of its bark; but its sturdily handsome stature and its leaves that flutter in the breeze cannot be discounted. For maximum effect, it should be silhouetted against the sky or an evergreen background. Under no circumstances plant the tree where the big, white trunk will be hidden. Needs sun and average soil.

If you decide to plant a white birch, make certain that the tree you buy is indeed a white birch and not a gray birch. The latter also has white bark, and for that reason is often mistaken for a white birch. It also has gained some popularity because it often has several trunks and thus forms an attractive clump. But it is an ordinary-looking tree with numerous dark spots on the bark. And it is a poor tree because it may be bent over by heavy snow; when that happens, it usually stays bent for life.

CAMELLIA. *Camellia japonica.* Zones 7b–10. Broadleaf evergreen. Normally grown as a shrub, but if given plenty of time may reach 40 feet. About as wide as high when fully developed. Lovely double, semi-double and single flowers sometimes more than 5 inches across appear from autumn into late winter. Colors range from white through pink to red. There are also variegated forms. The leaves are glossy, elliptical and toothed, up to 4 inches long.

The camellia is everyone's favorite. The only trouble you'll have in buying plants is to decide which of the hundreds of splendid varieties you like best. Plant in full sun or partial shade. The soil should be well drained, rich in humus and slightly acid. Keep plants mulched and watered. Fertilize and prune after flowering. Most serious problem is flower blight, characterized by sudden browning and then death of the blossoms. This can be controlled by good sanitation* and by spraying

---

* In the garden, good sanitation calls for removal of dead and diseased leaves and branches, elimination of weeds and control of insects.

*On the true European birch, the main branches grow upright; the branchlets are pendulous. The effect is lacy and delightful.*

the soil around the plants with Terrachlor.

You can propagate your own camellias by half-hard stem cuttings taken from plants in April or May.

A common camellia making a gay display of flowers in early March. The sasanqua camellia is very similar but blooms earlier and is somewhat more open in habit.

*A parklike setting in a North Carolina residential property. The slender, symmetrical conifer is a deodar cedar. The trees with very long needles are longleaf pines. A flowering dogwood is in the foreground.*

CEDAR, DEODAR. *Cedrus deodara.* Zones 7–10. Evergreen. Fast growth to 100 feet. Forms a wide pyramid with nodding leader. Pendulous branches covered with rather short, stiff needles in upright bunches. Beehivelike cones grow upright to a length of 4 inches.

The Deodar Cedar is one of our most graceful needled evergreens. Unchecked, it is too large for the average property, but it can be kept to manageable size by annual pruning in late spring. Plant in full sun in average soil.

CEDAR-OF-LEBANON. *Cedrus libani.* Zones 7–10. Variety *stenocoma* also grows in Zone 6. Evergreen. Slow growth to 120 feet. Very similar to the foregoing but has stiffly horizontal branches.

This historic species starts life as a slender pyramid requiring little space, but with age it spreads wide and becomes very picturesque. Though well known, it is rather hard to come by. Grow in sun and average soil.

*The hardy variety of the cedar-of-Lebanon thrives as far north as Boston.*

*An old weeping Higan cherry is a billowing mass of pink when the breeze blows.*

CHERRY, FLOWERING. *Prunus* species. Zones 4–10. Deciduous. Fast growth to as much as 75 feet, but most varieties only a third of this size. Variable in shape from stiffly upright to weeping. Covered in spring with lovely white or pink single or double flowers. Asiatic species bloom very early, before leaves appear. On American and European species, leaves and flowers appear together. Some species with glistening, rich reddish bark. All require full sun for best bloom, but only average soil. Prune after flowering. Rather short-lived.

Flowering cherries are famed for their springtime show, but they are not particularly notable at other times. The exceptions are those with handsome bark, which shows up beautifully on the winter landscape. The Japanese, Sargent and Higan cherries are outstanding species. The double-flowered Kwanzan cherry, a Japanese variety, is probably the most spectacular in bloom, but the weeping Higan cherry is a more graceful tree.

CHERRY, SOUR. *Prunus cerasus.* Zones 4–7. Deciduous. Fast-growing, to 35 feet, but should be kept lower. Dwarf varieties are available but produce too little fruit to bother with. White flowers in mid-spring are followed by sour red fruits in early summer.

As an ornamental tree, the sour cherry is pleasant but not spectacular and should not be given a front-row position in favor of a number of prettier trees; but this doesn't mean you should hide it either. Plant in full sun in good soil containing considerable humus. Fertilize and prune in late winter, and spray regularly until just before harvest.

I recommend sour over sweet cherries because (1) they are self-fruitful; (2) not so large; (3) require a little less care; and (4) the birds do not go after the fruit so greedily—meaning that you have a better chance of getting it for yourself.

*Profuse flowers on a sour-cherry tree foretell a bumper crop of fruit about two months hence.*

*In its twelfth year, this rounded, spreading Chinese chestnut produced a bushel of nuts.* (Photo by the Connecticut Agricultural Experiment Station, New Haven)

CHESTNUT, CHINESE. *Castanea mollisima.* Zones 5–8. Deciduous. Grows slowly when young, but then rapidly to 50 feet and even greater spread. Coarsely toothed elliptical leaves turn yellow-brown in the fall; when young they are covered with dense hairs. Dark-brown edible nuts are borne in spiny burs, which open in the fall to let the nuts drop to the ground.

The Chinese chestnut is a good-looking rounded tree with branches sweeping close to the ground. Plant it in full sun in good soil in an open area where it has plenty of room to spread. You must plant two trees to have nuts. They will start to bear within about five years and will give larger and larger crops as they age.

You can grow your own trees by storing nuts over the winter in barely damp peat moss in the fresh-food section of the refrigerator and planting them outdoors in the spring. Cover with 2 inches of soil and protect from squirrels with wire mesh.

CORKTREE, AMUR. *Phellodendron amurense.* Zones 3b–10. Deciduous. Very wide-spreading tree making moderate growth to 40 feet. Trunk and massive limbs covered with deeply fissured bark resembling cork. Unimportant whitish flowers in panicles in the spring followed by clusters of small black berries in the fall. Compound leaves with up to 13 oval leaflets.

The corktree is most impressive in winter when its mighty outstretched limbs are fully revealed. In the summer its chief value is for providing light shade on a terrace. Needs sun and average soil. If you know anybody who has a corktree, all you have to do to get one for yourself is to dig up one of the seedlings which come up everywhere.

CRAB APPLE. *Malus* species. Zones 2–10. Deciduous. Moderate growth to 50 feet, but most species much smaller. Profuse flowers in spring range from white to pink to various shades of red. Flowers are single, semidouble or double; usually fragrant. Red or yellow fruits in summer range from 2 inches down to small berries. A few are used for jelly; a few others hang on the tree through the winter. Applelike leaves are generally green but in a few cases reddish. Only a few species have colorful fall foliage.

Crab apples are variable in habit but are generally shapely. They are of value primarily for their flowers and fruits. Plant in the sun in aver-

*Deeply fissured bark gives the Amur corktree its name.*

age soil. Among the best trees for ornament are the Arnold, Dorothea, Hopa, Katherine, Radiant, Red Jade, Sargent, Tea, Redbud and Japanese crabs. For fruit, use Dolgo, Hyslop, Jacques or Young America. All these varieties are self-fruitful.

CRAPE-MYRTLE. *Lagerstroemia indica.* Zones 7b–10. Deciduous. Moderate growth to 25 feet in height and about equal width. Delightful light-brown flaking bark on angular trunks. Dense privetlike foliage turns yellow in the fall. Crinkled or crepey 1½-inch flowers from pink to red appear in terminal clusters in midsummer.

The crape-myrtle can be grown as a shrub but is best as a tree with a cluster of trunks forming a base. It is attractive the year round, but especially so in summer and winter. Plant in the sun in average soil. New plants are easily and quickly propagated by greenwood stem cuttings. Aphids and mildew are sometimes problems.

*Crape-myrtles are small and very ornamental the year round. The bark on the sturdy but slender trunks is two-colored.*

DOGWOOD, FLOWERING. *Cornus florida.* Zones 5–9. Deciduous tree making moderate growth to 40 feet. Outreaching branches with oval leaves turning deep red in the fall. Large four-petaled flowers in mid-spring are white or pink. Bright-red berries in the fall attract birds.

The flowering dogwood is one of the outstanding small trees for gardens; and it is also outstanding among trees of all sizes. It is beautiful in every season, close up or from afar. Plant it as a specimen or against an evergreen backdrop or house wall. Grows in sun or partial shade in average soil. Requires minimum attention, but keep an eye out for borers. Small trees that spring up from the seeds are easily transplanted. You can also raise your own plants simply by sowing the berries about ½ inch deep in the fall.

In recent years many named varieties have been offered for sale. These differ chiefly in the color of the flowers. Whites range from pure white to cream; pinks from pale pink to red.

DOGWOOD, JAPANESE. Also called Korean dogwood. *Cornus kousa.* Zones 6–10. Moderate growth to 20 feet. Outstretched branches with dense foliage turning bright red in the fall. White late-spring flowers like four-pointed stars. Large red fruits in the fall resemble strawberries.

The Japanese dogwood is not well known but is commonly available. It is fully as outstanding and useful as the flowering dogwood and sufficiently different so you should not hesitate to plant both species. The flowers appear about three weeks later than those of the flowering dogwood. On many plants they are so profuse that the leaves are almost hidden.

Plant in sun or light shade in average soil.

ELM, CHINESE. *Ulmus parvifolia.* Zones 6–10. Deciduous. Very fast growth to 60 feet. Bark flakes off irregularly to expose lighter underbark. Leathery, oval, evenly toothed leaves to 2½ inches long turn reddish in the fall. Small clusters of flowers in late summer or fall (an important point to note because the Siberian elm, which is sometimes sold as a Chinese elm although it is not as good a tree, flowers in the spring).

The Chinese elm is a very decorative rounded tree, and its exceptionally fast growth should be a boon to families starting off in treeless developments. Use it for screening out your neighbors or the sun; and

*The Japanese dogwood has the same four-petaled flowers as the flowering dogwood, but the former are star-shaped, always white, and appear in late June.*

by all means locate it where you can see the attractive bark.

One variety of the Chinese elm is known as the evergreen elm and is identified either as *Ulmus parvifolia sempervirens* or *U. p. pendens*. It is especially popular in southern California, where it retains its leaves until the new ones appear in the spring; but it is also hardy, though deciduous, in colder climates. The tree is very wide-spreading and develops weeping branches that may touch the ground.

Plant both the true Chinese elm and its evergreen variety in the sun in average soil. Staking is necessary for several years—especially in the case of the evergreen variety—until the trunk is stout enough to support the weight of the crown.

*The Chinese elm is much less formal and shapely than the great American elm, but is resistant to the Dutch elm disease, which attacks the latter.*

FALSE CYPRESS, SAWARA. *Chamaecyparis pisifera.* Zones 3b–7. Exergreen with tiny needles arranged in fernlike sprays similar to the arborvitae. Pyramidal tree makes moderately fast growth to 120 feet. Trunk with shredding, reddish-brown bark.

The Sawara false cypress is a handsome, rather feathery-looking tree which can be held to moderate size by selective pruning in late winter or early spring. It also makes a splendid dense, tall hedge or windbreak. Does best in sun but tolerates partial shade. Plant in average, well-drained soil.

An excellent variety is the Moss False Cypress (*C. pisifera squarrosa*). This is considerably smaller and has much softer foliage with a bluish tinge.

FIG, COMMON. *Ficus carica.* Zones 7–10. Deciduous. Fast grower reaching 25 feet. Large leaves with three to five lobes. In warmest climates the plant develops into a tree with a big, gnarled, gray-barked trunk. In colder areas, where it may be killed back by frost, the plant becomes a multistemmed shrub. Sweet seedy brown, green or purple fruits are produced in summer. Some varieties have two crops.

An old fig tree is picturesquely handsome; and even those plants which develop as shrubs have ornamental value when clothed with leaves. Nevertheless the common fig is grown mainly for its fruit.

Plant in full sun. A good location is about 4 feet out from the south wall of a house. Soil must be well drained and enriched with humus. Fertilize twice in the spring. Maintain a mulch and water regularly in the summer.

The best varieties for colder areas are Brown Turkey and Magnolia, because they will produce fruit the same year they are hit by frost. For warmer areas try Celeste, Green Ischia, Kadota or Hunt. The favorite variety in California is Mission. All varieties are self-fruitful.

FIG, WEEPING. *Ficus benjamina.* Zone 10. Broadleaf evergreen. Fast growth to 30 feet. Pendulous branches densely covered with lustrous, leathery, elliptical leaves. Small red, inedible fruits in the summer.

In Zone 10, the ornamental fig and rubber trees (they belong to the same genus) are very popular despite the fact that many of them are such huge vigorous plants that they envelop small gardens. But the

*The common fig has handsome leaves and delicious fruit.* (Photo by the Florida Agricultural Extension Service)

weeping fig is just as attractive as its big brothers and requires much less space. Plant it near the terrace or in a courtyard. It also makes a good espalier. Grows in sun or shade in average soil.

Fir, white. *Abies concolor.* Zones 5–10. Needled evergreen. Grows moderately fast to form a dense narrow pyramid up to 120 feet high. Bluish-green needles often 2 inches long or more. Cones 5 inches long resemble a large thumb.

A western native, the white fir is a fine specimen tree for the larger property. Its unusually long (for a fir tree) needles give it a rather soft appearance, and their color contrasts nicely with other evergreens. The

*The distinctive white fir is clothed with blue-green needles.*

tree is more tolerant of drought and city conditions than many conifers. Plant it in average soil in a sunny location.

FRANKLINIA. *Franklinia alatamaha.* Sometimes identified as *Gordonia alatamaha.* Zones 6–10. Deciduous. Slow grower to 30 feet. More or less pyramidal habit. Bright-green oblong leaves turn scarlet in autumn. White single 3-inch flowers with yellow centers in late summer and fall.

The franklinia is an uncommon and uncommonly pretty tree. Its lovely flowers appear at a time when very few other trees and shrubs are blooming, and they last a long time. Frequently there are flowers after the leaves have turned red. Nature offers few more brilliant displays.

The tree grows in partial shade—and needs it in warm climates—but does best in full sun. Average soil.

*The charming white and yellow flowers of the franklinia appear in the late summer and sometimes continue blooming after the foliage has turned brilliant red.*

*In July the fringetree, a relative of the lilac, puts out huge, feathery white flower panicles of gentle fragrance.*

FRINGETREE. *Chionanthus virginicus.* Zones 5–9. Deciduous. Slow growth to 30 feet. Crown narrow, with numerous branches, and oval leaves dark green above, paler beneath. Foliage is bright yellow in the fall. Fragrant white flowers with fringelike petals are borne in loose, drooping clusters in late spring. Clusters of small blue-black fruits in the fall.

The fringetree seems to take forever and a day to leaf out in the spring, but once it does, you will concur with the general opinion that it is an exceptionally beautiful small tree. It does especially well in the east and south, where it is native.

Plant in a sunny location in average soil. Watch out for scale insects.

*This fairly young ginkgo is just starting to leaf out. Behind it is a well-shaped American holly just about to shed its dark-green winter leaves for a new coat of bright-green spring leaves.*

GINKGO. *Ginkgo biloba.* Zones 5–10. Deciduous. Moderate growth to 120 feet. Unusual leaves resemble a lady's fan with a notch at the top;

they turn a pretty yellow in the fall. Yellowish-to-greenish 1-inch fruits on female trees have a foul odor.

The ginkgo is one of the oldest trees on earth and it is also one of the most satisfactory because it demands almost no attention, has no pest problems and thrives in the worst city atmosphere. It is a big, wide, irregular tree with branches thrusting up and out from the trunk in all directions. It is picturesque in all seasons. Use it as a specimen in a sunny, open location with average soil.

Be sure to buy male plants only.

GOLDEN-RAIN-TREE. *Koelreuteria paniculata.* Zones 6–10. Deciduous. Moderate growth to 30 feet. Large compound leaves with up to 15 coarsely toothed, long oval leaflets. Small yellow flowers in upright pyramidal clusters up to 18 inches long in early summer. Conspicuous papery yellow-brown seedpods in the fall.

The flat-topped golden-rain-tree puts on a brilliant show when in bloom, and although it is not overly distinctive in other seasons, this is sufficient reason to include it in your garden. It is not particular about soil but should have full sun. Needs regular pruning while young to shape it properly. Its major drawback is its rather weak wood.

GRAPEFRUIT. *Citrus paradisi.* Zones 9b–10. Broadleaf evergreen. Moderate growth to 30 feet in height, and equal width. Large, lustrous, oval leaves with a small leaflet at the base. Waxy white flowers. Big yellow fruits in the winter.

All citrus trees are beautiful dark-green, rounded plants; and except for the fact that it is a little larger than most species, the grapefruit is not outstanding. But next to the orange, it produces the most important fruit.

Marsh, Royal, Ruby and Triumph are good varieties. All are self-fruitful. Though you can grow trees from seeds, you will get more fruit if you buy grafted plants. Plant in full sun in a frost-free location (on the south side of the house or a hedge, for example). The soil must be well drained and enriched with humus; keep it covered with an organic mulch. Water trees regularly, especially when young, if you live in a dry region. Follow fertilizing and spray schedules recommended by your state agricultural extension service.

*The golden-rain tree is small and rounded, and in early summer it is bright with yellow flowers.*

*A lemon-scented gum towers above a California hillside house. The base of the trunk is a full story below the house.*

GUM, LEMON-SCENTED. *Eucalyptus citriodora.* Zones 9b–10. Broadleaf evergreen. Grows very rapidly to 75 feet. Slender trunk and limbs covered with whitish to pinkish bark. Long, narrow, yellow-green leaves have a lemony fragrance.

This is one of the most graceful eucalyptus trees; it enhances the beauty of the garden no matter where it is located. The slender trunk is bare halfway up; the foliage crown is irregular and open.

Grow from seed harvested from a neighbor's tree and sown in a flat. Plant in sun in average soil. Stake young trees, and thin out the branches and cut back the trunk to promote trunk growth. Once established, the tree does not require much water. It is pest-free.

GUM, SILVER-DOLLAR. *Eucalyptus polyanthemos.* Zones 6b–10. Broadleaf evergreen. Fast growth to 60 feet. One or more trunks. Young leaves are round to oval and greenish-gray; mature leaves are lance-shaped. Bark mottled.

This is another outstanding eucalyptus—slender, erect and graceful, with very pretty foliage. Needs sun and average soil. Avoid damp locations. Little pruning is required. Propagate from seeds.

HEMLOCK, CANADA. *Tsuga canadensis.* Zones 3–7. Needled evergreen. Moderately fast growth to 90 feet. Informally pyramidal. Short, flat, blunt needles in two layers on opposite sides of the twigs; bright green on top, bluish-green beneath. Numerous cones less than ¾ inch long.

You'll have to look hard to find a lovelier, more adaptable conifer than the Canada hemlock. Its slender branches stretch far to the side and many droop gracefully. The general effect is feathery.

Hemlocks do not take kindly to city smog. They grow in partial shade but do best in the sun. In fact, they must receive sun from all sides if you don't want the upper limbs to shade out and eventually kill the lower limbs (as happens in the forest). Soil needs to be of only average quality but should be well drained; and it's a smart idea to mix in lots of humus. The appearance of a tree is not seriously affected if it puts up a second trunk, but generally a single-stem tree is better. Red spider mites and gypsy moths are occasional pests.

Hemlocks make beautiful dense hedges over 6 feet tall. These can be sheared to smooth sides and top, but are much prettier when feathery.

*Some people might maintain that these Canada hemlocks are all out of scale with the house; but they make a very pleasant setting for the house anyway.*

*One look tells why the shagbark hickory got its name.*

HICKORY, SHAGBARK. *Carya ovata.* Zones 4–8. Deciduous. Moderate growth to 120 feet. Light-gray bark peeling off in long, thick, shaggy strips. Large compound leaves with 5 to 7 rather big elliptical leaflets turning yellow-brown in the fall. Sweet white nuts in smooth green or brown husks that split open in four segments.

The shagbark hickory is a not-too-wide, upright tree with a picturesquely craggy look. It's good for shading a house because the crown develops high off the ground. Among the better nut-producing varieties are Davis, Fox, Weschke and Wilcox. Plant in sun in average soil.

*Female holly flower at left; male flower at right.*

HOLLY, AMERICAN. *Ilex opaca.* Zones 6–9. Broadleaf evergreen. Grows slowly to form a pyramid 50 feet tall. Neatly elliptical leaves to 4 inches long with sharp spines around the edges; dull green above, dull yellow-green beneath. Bright red berries on female plants develop in the fall and persist well into the winter.

This is a topnotch tree for every garden. It can be allowed to grow to full size if you have space; or it can be kept small by pruning. Plant in a sunny spot that is not exposed to cold winter winds. Soil needs to be of only average quality but should be well drained and very slightly acid. Prune early in the spring before growth starts. Leaf miners may be troublesome on this and all other hollies.

The main problem with most hollies is that you need both male and female plants if you want berries. You must, therefore, acquire plants from some one who can tell the difference between the sexes. This is possible to do only when the plants are in flower. The best guide is the shape of the flowers, as shown in the sketch. As a rule, male plants have many more flowers than female plants and the flowers appear in clusters of three to seven arising from a single stem. Female flowers are borne singly, each on its own stem.

HOLLY, ENGLISH. *Ilex aquifolium.* Zones 6b–10. Broadleaf evergreen growing slowly to 70 feet. Pyramidal. Leaves less regularly shaped than the above; glossy dark-green on top, paler beneath. The spines on the edges are large and triangular. Bright-red berries in big clusters on female plants.

The English holly is generally considered to be the best of the genus, but unfortunately it is rather finicky about climate. It does best in the Pacific Northwest but can be grown in other regions near a large body of water. Grow like American holly. You need both male and female specimens to have berries. Numerous varieties are available.

*A well-filled-out, 8-foot English holly. Although the Connecticut property where it grows is named Hollycroft, the climate is too rugged to permit the tree to attain the height of northwestern specimens.*

*The lusterleaf holly has unusually large leaves. The small red berries grow in tight clusters.*

HOLLY, LUSTERLEAF. *Ilex latifolia.* Zones 7b–10. Broadleaf evergreen. Slow growth to 60 feet. Rounded plant. Dark, shiny leaves as long as 8 inches, with finely toothed edges. Large red berries in the fall are produced in tight clusters suggestive of ears of corn.

This is another handsome, dense holly—not well known but worthy of wider use because of its distinctive features. Grows in light shade as well as sun. Average, well-drained soil. You must plant both male and female specimens to have fruit.

HONEYLOCUST, THORNLESS. *Gleditsia triacanthos inermis.* Zones 5–8. Deciduous. Makes very fast growth to 130 feet. Compound leaves with numerous small leaflets that dance in the slightest breeze.

Several named forms of the thornless honeylocust are on the market. Some have narrow crowns, but I prefer those with spreading crowns because, despite their often large size, they have a delicate grace. Even more important, they are outstanding shade trees because they shield a large area but are open enough to let through considerable light. Moraine is an especially good variety.

Honeylocusts are generally free of troubles and do well under city conditions. Plant them in average soil in full sun.

*Thornless honeylocusts shade a walk at the base of the wall. The small, mounded plants are Korean box, a very hardy variety of littleleaf box.*

IRONBARK, RED. *Eucalyptus sideroxylon.* Zones 9–10. Broadleaf evergreen. Grows rapidly to 80 feet but is often much lower. Slender, blue-green leaves turn bronze in winter. Bark almost black. Hanging clusters of fluffy pink to red flowers from fall to spring.

The red ironbark is a variable tree and you should choose specimens carefully for what you want them to do. They may be slender or wide; open or dense; short or tall; upright or weeping. But in any case, you'll like what you get.

Plant in average soil in the sun. Once established, the tree requires little attention, is generally free of pests.

IRONWOOD. Also called American Hornbeam and Blue Beech. *Carpinus caroliniana.* Zones 2–9. Deciduous. Slow growth to 35 feet. Trunk or trunks twisted, angular and muscular-looking; covered with blue-gray bark. Zigzag branches. Pointed, oval, sharply toothed leaves turn brilliant orange-red or deep crimson in the fall. Small ribbed nuts are borne in leafy clusters in the fall.

The ironwood is an attractive, interesting tree which should be planted where you can get a good look at the unusual trunk—near the terrace, for example. It is especially valuable because it thrives in fairly deep shade (it grows wild in forests) and in damp soil of average quality.

*The ironwood develops a muscular trunk covered with attractive gray bark, here spotted with lichens. The tree grows naturally in forests.*

*The jacaranda (here sandwiched between the roofs) has feathery foliage that contrasts sharply with the broad leaves of a sea-grape in immediate foreground.*

JACARANDA. *Jacaranda acutifolia.* Zones 9b–10. Deciduous. Fast growth to 50 feet. Compound leaves with many small leaflets arranged in featherlike or fernlike fashion. Tubular violet-blue flowers in numerous 8-inch clusters in spring and summer.

This irregular, open tree with one or more trunks is a top favorite of gardeners in our warmest climates because of its lovely flowers. But even without flowers, it would win a high rating because of its charming foliage that dances in the wind.

Plant in the sun in average soil and keep it staked until established. Tree needs regular watering, but don't overdo it. Protect from hard winds—the branches are rather brittle.

A fairly young Japanese larch shortly after leafing out in the spring. The bright-green needles grow in tufts.

JAPANESE PAGODA TREE. *Sophora japonica.* Zones 5–10. Deciduous. Grows at moderate speed to 20 feet and then slowly to 60 feet. Dense, very wide, round crown covered in late summer with showy, upright, pyramidal clusters of white flowers. These are followed by yellowish beanlike pods containing seeds. Compound leaves with small, dark-green leaflets have a feathery effect.

The Japanese pagoda tree is an excellent specimen tree for the lawn area but its limbs grow a little too close to the ground for sitting under it comfortably. Furthermore, if allowed to grow over a terrace, the fallen seedpods might stain the paving.

Plant in sun in average soil. Withstands city smog and is free of pests.

LARCH, JAPANESE. *Larix leptolepis.* Zones 5–9. Deciduous conifer. Makes fast growth to form a slender, 90-foot pyramid. Small bright-green needles in dense clusters appear in the spring, then turn yellow in the autumn and finally drop. Small ornamental cones are purplish-red at the start, then turn brown.

This is a charming, lacy, almost gossamer tree, unlike anything else in the garden. Plant it in a sunny spot far enough from the house or terrace so you can take it all in at a glance. It is particularly pretty seen against the sky, but is also effective mixed in with darker evergreens. Needs only average soil. Watch out for larch casebearers—miners that bore into the needles and spoil the looks of the tree for the rest of the summer. These can be controlled by spraying several times with malathion as the needles are developing.

LINDEN, LITTLELEAF. *Tilia cordata.* Zones 3b–10. Deciduous. Slow growth to 90 feet. Dense heart-shaped leaves, dark green above, paler beneath. Inconspicuous, whitish, very fragrant flowers in early summer.

The littleleaf linden develops into a rounded, symmetrical pyramid that makes a fine lawn specimen. But it is too large for most suburban properties, and if that is true in your case, you should select one of its much smaller varieties, such as Rancho or Greenspire. All are excellent trees for metropolitan areas.

Plant in the sun in average soil. In the northeast all lindens are subject to attack in the spring by gypsy moths.

LINDEN, SILVER. *Tilia tomentosa.* Zones 5–10. Deciduous. Moderate growth to 90 feet, and about half that width. Leaves like rounded hearts are green on top, white and hairy beneath. Small yellowish flowers in early summer are very fragrant.

This is one of the very best of the many handsome lindens, especially when the wind blows and exposes the bottoms of the leaves. The tree is broadly pyramidal with erect branches. It looks almost as if it had been carefully trimmed to shape.

Plant in sun in average soil. Has good resistance to drought once it is growing strongly.

MADRONE, PACIFIC. *Arbutus menziesii.* Zones 7b–10. Broadleaf evergreen. Moderate growth to as much as 100 feet, but often a great deal less. Rounded crown. Leathery, egg-shaped leaves are dark green and shiny on top, gray-green beneath. Red-brown bark peeling off to expose light-red underbark. White lily-of-the-valleylike flowers in clusters in the spring. Clusters of bright red-orange berries in fall and winter.

These many fine features make the Pacific madrone an excellent choice provided (1) you put it in average soil in a sunny spot where the litter it is forever dropping will be more-or-less invisible (in a shrubbery border, for example); (2) you start with a tree under 2 feet tall (larger ones are very difficult to transplant); and (3) you do not overwater it.

MAGNOLIA, SAUCER. *Magnolia soulangeana.* Zones 6–10. Deciduous. Moderate growth to 25 feet in height and equal width. One or several rather twisting trunks with good gray bark. Coarse leaves to 8 inches long but pleasantly green. Cup-shaped flowers up to 10 inches across in spring before the leaves unfold are white or pink to purple. Oddly twisted pods open in the fall to display bright red seeds.

The saucer magnolia is a popular small tree and understandably so because it makes a gay show when the forsythia starts to bloom in the spring. Often planted in the lawn, it is actually much better in a border because when the flower petals fall, they make an awful mess. But this is the tree's only serious fault.

Plant in a sunny location in average soil. Prune after bloom. There are several good varieties to choose from.

*When the wind blows, the silver linden shows the whitish undersides of its heart-shaped leaves.*

*The saucer magnolia blooms before the leaves open. Note the Douglas fir at left: After its top was blown out in a storm, a branch started growing upward to take the place of the lost leader.*

MAGNOLIA, SOUTHERN. *Magnolia grandiflora.* Zones 7b–10. Broadleaf evergreen. Dense, pyramidal tree making slow growth to 90 feet. Glossy, leathery leaves to 8 inches long. Spectacular, very fragrant flowers to as much as a foot across in late spring and early summer. Seedpods display bright-red seeds in the fall.

The southern magnolia is a magnificent tree in all seasons. It tolerates considerable shade (it grows happily in southern forests) but it fills out and makes its best display when in the sun in an open area. It is a gorgeous tree to plant in a lawn either near the house, so you can enjoy the flowers to the utmost, or at a distance, so you can appreciate the form of the tree. It also makes a spectacular espalier.

The tree should be under 4 feet tall when planted. Plant in good soil in which you have incorporated a lot of humus. Keep well watered. During heavy, wet snowfalls, gently knock the snow from the branches every hour or so.

*Close-up of a flower on the magnolia opposite.*

*The star magnolia has double white flowers with up to 15 petals. It is the first magnolia to bloom.*

MAGNOLIA, STAR. *Magnolia stellata.* Zones 6–8. Deciduous. Moderate growth to 20 feet in height and equal width. Small, oblong, dark-green leaves turn bronze or yellow in the autumn. Twisting, irregular branches with pretty gray bark. Very fragrant white flowers with many petals in early spring. Seedpods with red seeds in the fall.

This is the hardiest magnolia and one of the most attractive. Grow it in a shrubbery border in the lawn or next to the house or terrace. Plant it in a sunny spot; but if you live in Zone 6a, it is advisable to place it on the north side of the house, adjacent to a high wall or a high hedge so it will not bloom before the last frost. Give it average, well-drained soil containing plenty of humus. Prune after flowering.

*The southern magnolia is a dense pyramid of glossy, dark-green leaves spotted with beautiful, fragrant white flowers. (Photo by Warwick Anderson)*

MANGO. *Mangifera indica.* Zones 9b–10. Broadleaf evergreen. Makes moderately fast growth to 90 feet. Handsome lance-shaped leaves to 15 inches may start out purplish or reddish, then turn dark green. Panicles of pink winter flowers followed in late spring and summer by delectable greenish, yellow or red fruits much like nectarines.

The mango is an exceptionally beautiful roundheaded tree, which grows tall when placed close to other trees, or spreads wide when given ample room in the sun. Even without fruit it would be a standout feature of any garden.

But if you want fruit—and of course you do—plant a grafted tree in a sunny location protected from the wind. The soil can be of average quality but should be well drained and enriched with humus. Apply fertilizer on a schedule recommended by your state agricultural extension service. Weekly spraying with captan or copper fungicide from the time the flowers open until fruits are of good size is essential to control of anthracnose.

Mangoes are self-fruitful. Haden is the most popular variety but other good ones include Poe, Joe Welch, Kent, Momi K and Pirie.

MAPLE, AMUR. *Acer ginnala.* Zones 2–10. Deciduous. Grows slowly to 20 feet. Leaves with three lobes,* the center one very long, are dark green above, lighter below; turn scarlet in the fall. Fragrant, small, yellowish flowers. Winged seeds are bright red.

This small rounded maple has very dense foliage which makes a pretty background for the red winged seeds when they ripen in the summer. If you wish, you can train the tree as a multitrunked shrub and use it as a screen; but it is much more attractive with a single trunk.

Plant in sun in average soil.

MAPLE, JAPANESE. *Acer palmatum.* Zones 6–10. Deciduous. Grows slowly to 20 feet. Deeply cut, finely chiseled leaves with 5 to 9 lobes. Depending on the variety, the leaves may be red throughout the seasons or start out red in the spring, then turn green, and then turn red again in the fall. Most varieties have a spreading, often irregular branch pat-

---

* The lobes of a leaf are the points, though these may be rounded. The sinuses are the indentations between the lobes.

*The two large, rounded trees at the foot of this Hawaiian lawn are mangoes. The luster of their beautiful leaves is visible from afar.*

*The spiderleaf Japanese maple forms a low, wide mound. The tree to the left above it is a larger variety of Japanese maple.*

tern; but some are weeping plants forming large rounded mounds.

The Japanese maple is a superlative tree which is beautiful every month of the year. Plant it in a prominent place far enough away from other trees and shrubs so you can enjoy it to the utmost. There are many excellent varieties differing in the color and shape of their leaves and in their habit. *Atropurpureum, sanguineum,* and Burgundy Lace are several of the best. The Threadleaf and Spiderleaf varieties are outstanding for their delicate, fernlike leaves.

The Japanese maples can be grown in sun or partial shade but are usually most brilliantly red in the sun. The soil should be well drained and rich in humus for best growth, though the trees do quite well in average soil.

MAPLE, NORWAY. *Acer platanoides.* Zones 3b–10. Deciduous. Fast growth to 90 feet and considerable width. Extremely dense foliage. Leaves large and bright green, turn bright yellow in the fall. Small fragrant yellowish flowers in the spring.

The Norway maple is too big for small properties mainly because it casts such dense shade over such a wide area that there would be little chance to grow anything else. But there are much smaller varieties which have gained wide acceptance. *Columnare,* for instance, forms a rather narrow column while *globosum* is something like a blunt-ended football that fits neatly under electric wires.

Whatever the variety, this is an excellent tree because of its fast growth, fine foliage and attractive shape. Plant in full sun in average soil. It requires almost no attention except for occasional pruning to thin out some of the branches. Since the seeds are produced in great profusion and sprout with abandon, it is easy to acquire as many new trees as you want.

MAPLE, SUGAR. *Acer saccharum.* Zones 3b–10. Deciduous. Moderately fast growth to 120 feet. Rounded crown. Medium-gray bark. Coarsely toothed five-lobed leaves turn fiery red in the fall.

There are few trees that make such a brilliant show in the fall. This is enough reason to plant a sugar maple, yet it is not the only one. Whether in leaf or bare, the tree has a distinctive handsome shape. In youth a thicket of small and medium-size branches spear up from the

At this stage in the spring the Norway maple is a mass of fragrant yellow-green flowers. Two weeks later it will have such heavy, rich green foliage that the sun cannot get through to the ground underneath.

*This handsome sugar maple is about 30 years old. The dense, rounded plant at the left is a Hicks yew that was allowed to develop naturally, with little if any pruning.*

trunk at acute angles; with the passage of time, some of the branches die and fall and the tree becomes more open, rounded and spreading. As a shade tree to sit under it is excellent, because the branches are high above the ground and the foliage is sufficiently open to allow a few sunbeams to get through. (Smaller plants which would be killed by the dense shade of the Norway maple do quite well under the sugar maple.) Finally, if you want to tap the tree in late winter, you can make your own maple syrup.

Plant sugar maples in average soil in an open, sunny location. Except for removal of dead wood, they ask nothing from the gardener.

MIMOSA. Also called Silktree. *Albizia julibrissin.* Zones 7b–10, but variety *rosea* will grow as far north as Zone 6b. Deciduous. Fast growth to 35 feet and even greater width. Flat-topped and spreading. Multiple trunks. Compound leaves with innumerable tiny leaflets look like fern fronds. Covered with bright-pink flowers for several months in the spring and fall.

The mimosa is one of the top favorites among gardeners in warm climates. It is lovely in flower and out. Not many trees have such delicate foliage and branch structure. It is at its best when planted on a hillside so that you can look up into it or down on it; but if you don't have a hillside, plant it anyway. Its main fault is that it is a dirty tree, dropping bits and pieces throughout the year and should therefore not be planted to shade a terrace—which is a shame, because it is an excellent shade tree.

Because the true mimosa is attacked by a serious wilt disease, plant only varieties that are resistant to the disease—Charlotte, Tryon or *rosea.* Plant in the sun in average, well-drained soil. It also does well in poor, sandy soil. Stake young trees and protect them against winter cold in more northern areas. Rub out buds that develop low on the trunks.

MOUNTAIN-ASH, EUROPEAN. Also called Rowan tree. *Sorbus aucuparia.* Zones 3b–8. Deciduous. Moderately fast growth to 60 feet. Small white flowers in flat clusters in late spring are followed in the fall by large clusters of brilliant red berries. Compound leaves with 9 to 15 leaflets are reddish in the fall.

Not many plants have more showy fruit. The tree grows slim and

*Even in youth the mimosa is wide-spreading and has ever-so-delicate foliage.*

*The European mountain ash has feathery foliage, white flowers and spectacular red berries. In 3 years this tree shot up from about 12 to 18 feet.*

erect when young, but becomes wider and more open with age. It can be planted in partial shade but does much better and makes a more colorful display in the sun. The soil can be of average quality but should be well drained and sweetened with lime. Spraying the trunk in April with Sevin helps to control the borers that may attack the tree and eventually kill it. Spraying may also be necessary to control scale insects.

NORFOLK ISLAND PINE. *Araucaria excelsa.* Zone 10. Needled evergreen. Makes moderate growth to form a 100-foot pyramid. Sharp-pointed, curving, needlelike leaves become flat triangles when mature. Large, heavy cones.

You have probably seen this unusual tree in pots and admired it. You will admire it even more outdoors in tropical climates. It grows straight and tall, with wide spaces between the tiers of branches. Plant in the sun in average soil.

OAK, BUR. Also called Mossycup oak. *Quercus macrocarpa.* Zones 4–10. Deciduous. Moderate growth to 100 feet. Straight branches slanting upward. Corky ridges on the sides of young branches. Somewhat hairy leaves divided almost in two by deep, rounded sinuses on opposite sides of the midrib; turn reddish-brown in the fall. Acorns almost enclosed by mossy cups.

The bur oak grows particularly well in the Mississippi River Valley, and is probably at its best in southern Illinois and Indiana. It looks rugged and is rugged. Plant in the sun. Average soil is adequate; however, for fastest possible growth, it should be well enriched with humus.

*The bur oak has big, straight, upward-slanting limbs.*

OAK, LIVE. *Quercus virginiana.* Zones 8–10. Broadleaf evergreen. Moderate growth to 60 feet in height; spreads two or three times as wide. Massive, horizontal limbs. Broadly elliptical leaves persist until new leaves have developed, then fall. Small, elliptical acorns.

This is the great oak of the deep south—one of the most awesomely handsome trees alive. At full size it will shade an entire average-size suburban lot. Happily the shade is not so dense that you cannot grow camellias and many other good shrubs under it.

The live oak must have sun and prefers a rich, humusy soil, although it does well in poorer soil. When it gets old and large, the outreaching lower limbs may have to be guy-wired to the upper limbs to keep them from breaking under occasional ice storms and strong winds.

OAK, PIN. *Quercus palustris.* Zones 5–10. Deciduous. Makes moderately fast growth to form a rather slender beehive 75 feet high. Leaves with 5 to 7 toothed and bristle-tipped lobes and wide, deep sinuses turn reddish-brown in the fall. Half-inch acorns.

The pin oak, compared to other oaks, which grow to great size, is slender, almost delicate and neat. Its bottom branches are drooping; middle branches, horizontal; and top branches, almost vertical. It is an outstanding tree for almost every garden, regardless of size. Use it in a lawn or to shade the house or terrace. In the latter case, however, it will probably be necessary to cut out the lower branches because they sometimes touch the ground.

Plant pin oaks in a sunny spot in well-drained soil containing enough humus to retain moisture and encourage vigorous tree growth.

OAK, VALLEY. Also called California white oak. *Quercus lobata.* Zones 7–10. Deciduous. Moderate to fast growth to 70 feet and equivalent width. Four-inch leaves with rounded lobes and sinuses; dark green above, pale beneath. Huge trunk and limbs with dark-gray, checkered bark.

This is California's equivalent of the white oak. It is a gorgeous tree for shading a large garden or huge terrace. Grow in the sun. Given a

*An ivy-festooned live oak in the garden of one of Natchez' famous antebellum homes.*

better-than-average, humusy, well-drained soil, it will grow as much as 3 feet a year. If you have an old oak, water it thoroughly in dry weather but only out around the branch ends—not close to the trunk. Also fertilize the tree through crowbar holes made under the branch ends in early spring. This treatment helps to ward off attacks by a common root fungus.

OAK, WHITE. *Quercus alba.* Zones 5–10. Deciduous. Fairly slow growth to 90 feet. Enormous limbs. Leaves with 7 to 9 rather narrow lobes with rounded ends, the sinuses usually extending more than halfway to the midrib, turn rich purple-red in the fall. Sweet, small, beehive-shaped acorns loved by squirrels.

Whenever anyone makes reference to the Mighty Oak, this is the tree he's talking about. In an informally rugged way, it is the most majestic of trees. With age it becomes much too large for a small garden; but it grows slowly enough so that you may want to plant it anyway.

If surrounded by trees, the white oak grows tall and straight and is topped by a large but reasonably compact, rounded crown. But in the open, with nothing much around it, it usually has a short trunk from which the branches spread far, far to the sides. The latter trees look very much like live oaks; and as in the case of live oaks, the lower limbs often must be supported by guy wires from the upper limbs.

Plant in the sun in average, well-drained soil. Avoid damp spots. If you live in the east, spray the tree every spring to protect it against the gypsy moth and elm spanworm (all other oaks need the same protection, since oaks are the favorite targets of these vicious pests).

OAK, WILLOW. *Quercus phellos.* Zones 6–9. Deciduous. Moderate growth to 50 feet. Long, narrow, willowlike leaves turn yellow in the fall. Small hemispherical acorns.

Like the pin oak, the willow oak is erect, more-or-less round-topped, and narrow enough for planting in every garden. Its shape is refined and

*The king of the oaks is the great white oak. This is a beautifully shaped specimen but not by any means exceptionally large. It is just leafing out.*

*Valley oaks have massive trunks and limbs with distinctive bark.*

orderly; and when in leaf, its texture has a delicacy that is not found in other members of the genus.

Plant in sun in average but humusy soil. It does especially well in moist locations.

*The willow oak is more shapely and refined than most oaks. In warm weather it is covered with willowlike leaves.*

OLIVE. *Olea europaea.* Zones 8b–10. Broadleaf evergreen. Slow growing to 25 feet and equal width. Gnarled trunk with smooth gray bark. Beautiful gray-green, willowlike foliage. Black fruits edible only when pickled.

This important tropical fruit tree has long been rated as one of the most ornamental evergreens in California. Many home owners plant it only for its decorative qualities. They prevent fruiting by pruning out the branch growth made in the previous year (the fruit is borne only on such growth) or by spraying with a hormone spray.

Olives need sun and are actually more productive in average soil than in good soil. Plant where they will be safe from late spring and early fall frosts. If you want the fruit, water the trees deeply in the spring before they bloom and in the summer after the fruit is set. Fertilize annually with a nitrogen fertilizer and prune moderately to encourage growth of new fruiting wood.

Although olives are self-fruitful, you should not count on this, so it is advisable to plant two different varieties together. Favorites are Ascolano, Manzanillo, Mission and Sevillano. A variety named Fruitless is available for those who don't want fruit; but unfortunately, Fruitless doesn't always live up to its name.

ORANGE. *Citrus sinensis.* Zones 9b–10. Broadleaf evergreen. Moderate growth to 25 feet. Dwarf plants also available. Lustrous oblong leaves. Fragrant white flowers followed by familiar orange fruits.

Like other citrus trees, the orange develops into a compact, dense, very handsome plant that sweetens the air as well as the palate. Start with plants which have been grafted on roots that are known to thrive in your area. Plant in full sun in a frost-free location with well-drained loam to which you should add considerable humus. Prune only enough to keep out dead and broken branches and all suckers. Water regularly if you live in an arid climate. Fertilize and spray according to schedules developed by your state agricultural extension service.

Orange trees are self-fruitful, so you don't need to plant more than one to have a good supply of fruit after the tree has been in the ground about five years. Good varieties are Hamlin, Parson Brown, Pineapple, Valencia and Washington Navel.

*Citrus trees are superlative ornamentals, especially when they attain full size. This is a young orange tree. Visually it is very similar to a grapefruit tree.* (Photo by the Florida Agricultural Extension Service)

PALM, COCONUT. *Cocos nucifera.* Zones 9b–10. Broadleaf evergreen. Makes moderately fast growth to 100 feet. Clean, slender, leaning, single trunk. Large crown of fronds arranged feather fashion. Clusters of large green-to-brown nuts ripening one at a time almost the whole year round.

The beautiful coconut palm is most often associated with the seashore, where it grows well despite salt spray; but it also grows inland and is equally decorative there. The tree has two drawbacks, however. One, not so serious, is that falling nuts can damage humans, automobiles or terrace roofs on which they land. The second is the susceptibility of tall coconut palms in southernmost Florida (but apparently not in Hawaii) to a new disease called lethal yellowing. This causes nuts to fall prematurely; then the leaves yellow and the tree dies. At the moment there is no known control except prompt destruction of infected trees. Fortunately, dwarf varieties from Malaya are resistant or immune to the disease—and these are the ones to plant if you live in Florida.

You will have fun growing your own coconut palm from the nut, and the tree you produce will be every bit as good as one you might buy. The nut should be cut down from an existing tree when the husk turns brown and starts to dry. Plant it horizontally in partial shade without removing the husk. The longest side of the husk should be turned up and the eye end should be slightly higher than the opposite end. Fill in humusy soil around the bottom two-thirds and keep it moist. A single sprout will appear in about three months. When this is just under a foot tall, transplant the nut to its permanent position in the garden. For fastest growth, prepare a large planting hole and fill it with sandy loam which has been well enriched with humus. Cover the husk slightly. Water regularly for the next year. Cover the soil with a mulch to keep down weeds. Apply a balanced fertilizer every three months.

PALM, DATE. *Phoenix dactylifera.* Zone 10. Broadleaf evergreen. Fast growth to 60 feet. Large, straight trunk covered with the stubs of old fronds. Suckers form around the base. Large crown of gray-green, arching, 10- to 20-foot fronds arranged in feather fashion; leaflets with wicked spines. Large dense clusters of flowers in early spring followed by huge pendent bunches of fruits which ripen in the fall.

Although the date palm is not quite so ornamental as some of the other members of the *Phoenix* genus, it's a handsome tree; and if you want to raise dates at their best, it is definitely the one to plant. Both male and female trees are required for production of fruit.

Start with offshoots cut from existing trees. Plant these in sun in fertile, humusy, well-drained soil. Water regularly if you want good fruit (though the tree is actually very drought-resistant). If you let the trees fend pretty much for themselves, they will reward you with *some* fruit, but for maximum production, you must tend to them regularly. The process is too complicated to be discussed here. You can find the details in my book *Gardens Are for Eating*, or Bulletin A-22 published by the Arizona Agricultural Extension Service, or Agriculture Information Bulletin No. 207 published by the U.S. Department of Agriculture.

PALM, ROYAL. *Roystonea regia.* Zones 9b–10, but not in California. Broadleaf evergreen. Grows fast to 80 feet. Smooth, clean, gray trunk, fatter in the middle than at the top and bottom. Large crown of graceful fronds arranged feather-fashion.

This regal Florida palm is generally rated the most beautiful of all palms. In the unusually graceful crown, the 15-foot lower fronds are drooping; the upper central fronds are erect. When the wind blows, the tree sways and dances.

Grow in sun in average soil containing humus.

PALM, MEXICAN FAN. *Washingtonia robusta.* Zones 9b–10. Broadleaf evergreen. Very rapid growth to 90 feet. Slender, curving trunk, clean at the bottom, shaggy above. Compact crown of rather coarse fronds arranged fan-fashion.

The Mexican fan palm is much used in southern California, particularly along the streets. It's a handsome, undemanding tree if grown in good soil in a sunny location; but its appearance is somewhat marred by the thatch of dead leaves that hang down around the trunk below the crown.

PEACH. *Prunus persica.* Zones 5–9. Deciduous. Fast growth to 25 feet. Dwarf varieties much smaller. Long elliptical leaves that remain green and hang on the tree into late fall. Small deep-pink flowers in the spring before the leaves. Luscious fruits in late spring and summer.

*As the fruit swells, the weight drags down the glossy leaves and branches of this peach tree. Eventually the branches had to be supported on crotched sticks to keep them from breaking.*

The peach is a pleasantly attractive tree, especially when the ripe fruits weigh down the branches. It is not very particular about soil although it does best when grown in sandy loam containing ample humus. But it does need full sun and should not be placed in a frost pocket.* Apply fertilizer in the spring and keep well watered right up to harvest. Prune annually in very early spring. To control pests, follow a regular spray schedule recommended by your state agricultural extension service.

There are innumerable excellent varieties—most with yellow-fleshed fruits but some with white flesh. Good yellows include Elberta, Blake,

* A low or sheltered place in which frost collects.

*Beautiful royal palms—one large, one small. Note the interesting taper of the trunk of the larger tree.* (Photo by the Florida Agricultural Extension Service)

Golden Jubilee, Halehaven and Southland. Vedette is an especially hardy variety; Keystone and Redskin are recommended for Zone 9, where most varieties do poorly. George IV, Georgia Belle and Redrose are white-fleshed varieties. All of these are self-fruitful as are most, but not all, other varieties.

PEAR. *Pyrus communis.* Zones 3–9, but best in 5–8. Deciduous. Moderate growth to 40 feet; usually kept lower. Oval leaves. White flowers in spring as the leaves appear. Delicious fruits from late summer into late fall.

Pear trees are pruned like apples and have much the same informally attractive appearance in the garden. Their greatest problem is their susceptibility to fire blight, which kills branches (and sometimes trees) and often ruins a tree's lines. Unhappily there is no positive control for this disease, although you should not have trouble with it if you fertilize rather sparingly and do all pruning in the winter.

Plant in full sun in deep, loamy soil. Maintain an organic mulch around the tree to hold in moisture and supply nutrients to the soil. Spray on a regular schedule recommended by your state agricultural extension service.

Pears are usually self-unfruitful, so you should plant two different varieties. Bartlett is the top favorite. Other excellent varieties are Anjou, Beurre Bosc, Clapp's Favorite, Comice, Kieffer, Magness and Seckel.

PECAN. *Carya illinoiensis.* Zones 6–9. Deciduous. Grows fast to 150 feet. Large compound leaves with 9 to 17 slender elliptical leaflets turning yellow in the fall. Sweet, smooth-shelled nuts in dark-brown husks in the fall.

If left to develop naturally, the pecan is a massive, craggy tree; but if cultivated primarily for its delicious nuts, it is pruned to form a large vase which will ornament a sunny, open space in any good-sized garden.

A very deep-rooted tree, the pecan requires a very large planting hole filled with the best soil and humus you can find. Given this kind of start, plus annual feeding, ample moisture in dry spells, and careful pruning when young to develop a system of large, open, spreading

*A row of pear trees in a flower border laid out in diamonds and triangles.*

*Pecan trees left to their own devices have a craggy look, as here. When pruned for maximum nut production, they are vase-shaped.*

branches, the tree should yield a bountiful harvest every year for as long as you live.

There are three groups of pecans: eastern varieties growing in the southeast; western varieties growing from central Texas westward; and northern varieties growing in colder climates. Stuart, Schley and Mahan are good eastern varieties; Apache, Sioux and San Saba Improved are good western varieties; Major is the most common northern variety, but unhappily, like other northern varieties, you can't count on it to produce mature fruit. To be sure of getting nuts, you should plant two different varieties from the same group.

PERSIMMON, JAPANESE. *Diospyros kaki.* Zones 7b–10. Deciduous. Grows rapidly to 40 feet. Spreading limbs. Big, oval, leathery leaves turn from light green to dark green to orange or scarlet in the fall. Handsome, delectable but astringent, orange fruits in the fall hang on after the leaves drop.

The Japanese persimmon is a pretty tree to grow in the middle of the lawn or a sunny corner in a shrubbery border. It is a delight in all seasons, and is very easy to grow, since it requires almost no attention. Plant it in well-drained, very humusy soil and keep it staked for several years until the trunk can support the crown. Prune annually to let light into the crown.

Fuyu, Peiping, Tamopan and Tanenashi are good varieties which are usually self-fruitful. Hachiya is self-fruitful in California, where it is the top variety, but in other areas you should plant male and female specimens.

*Oriental persimmons stand out bright orange against the sky. They will hang on the tree for several weeks after all the leaves have fallen.* (Photo by Eugene Griffith)

PINE, AUSTRIAN. *Pinus nigra.* Zones 4–7. Needled evergreen. Fast growth to 90 feet. Long, dark-green, very stiff needles grow in pairs. Rough, dark-brown bark. Two- to 3-inch yellow-brown cones with short spines on the tips of the scales.

This is a very handsome, but stiff, pyramidal pine. Its dense, dark-green needles glisten in the sun. If grown in an open location where they get sun from all sides, fairly young plants are clothed with foliage to the ground and make superlative windbreaks. But as the trees grow taller and wider, the upper branches shade the lower branches and the latter eventually die. At this stage, an Austrian pine is excellent for shading a terrace.

Plant in average soil. Requires little attention and is not bothered by the pests which attack some other pines.

*The long, stiff needles of an Austrian pine (foreground) contrast with the feathery foliage of the hemlocks in the hedge. The columnar tree is an American arborvitae.*

A *beautiful specimen of one of the world's loveliest and most useful trees—*
*the eastern white pine.*

PINE, EASTERN WHITE. *Pinus strobus.* Zones 3–6. Needled evergreen.
Fast growth to 150 feet. Fine, slender, soft green needles to about 4
inches long; borne in bundles of five. Slender, rather open cones up to
8 inches long.

Historically, the white pine was the tree that built our country, because until the greedy loggers leveled the great forests of the north, it
was our most important timber tree. It was also—and still is—one of our
most beautiful trees. No gardener can go wrong in planting it as a
specimen in the lawn, for shade over the house or terrace, or as a background for smaller deciduous trees and shrubs. (Flowering dogwoods
in front of white pines are a sight to behold.)

When young, white pines form a round-topped pyramid, but as they
get older, they become more irregular and flat-topped. The effect is
exceedingly picturesque. Also promoting flat-topped, irregular growth is
the white pine weevil, which attacks and kills the leaders of young trees.
When this happens, the trees put up several leaders, which destroys

their value as timber trees and also frequently detracts from their beauty.

White pines that are allowed to develop naturally have fairly wide spaces between branches. This is especially noticeable in young trees, but to my mind is not a serious drawback. However, many nurserymen correct the problem by shearing the young trees. This promotes denser branching and also makes for more stiffly pyramidal trees. But unless the gardener who buys these trees continues shearing them (and that is not an easy job to do properly), the trees eventually lose their artificial symmetry; and like natural trees, they also lose their closely spaced lower limbs as they grow older and the upper limbs shade them out.

White pines must be grown in the sun, but they are not demanding about soil. They sprout and grow freely in New England's worn-out stony pastures; and I have also found that they make amazing growth in clay that is so dense and soggy that many other trees drown in it.

In addition to being attacked by weevils (for the control of which, see page 104, eastern white pines and also western white pines are sometimes attacked by the white pine blister rust. This causes the branch ends to leak an orange liquid. The following year white blisters appear on the bark and discharge orange spores. To control the disease, cut out infected branches and spray with Acti-Dione. If gooseberries or currants are growing within 900 feet of the trees, remove them because they are the alternate host for the disease.

PINE, LONGLEAF. *Pinus palustris.* Zones 8–9. Needled evergreen. Very slow growth for the first ten years; then slow to moderate growth to 120 feet. Very rough, orange-brown bark. Slender, flexible, bright-green needles sometimes as long as 18 inches; borne in bundles of three. Large red-brown cones up to almost a foot in length; each scale with a sharp, curved spine.

Even as a seedling, this important southern tree is a large tuft of beautiful needles; and as it grows and begins to fill out, it looks like an upright, slender cone of billowing green. But with age, it loses its lower branches and develops a crown of widely spaced, more or less horizontal limbs dripping with graceful needles.

The longleaf pine does not tolerate the slightest amount of shade; but it grows very well in dry, sandy soil.

*The Scotch pine has an open-branching structure, and with age it commonly loses its symmetry. Note how the trunk has begun to curve at the top.*

PINE, SCOTCH. *Pinus sylvestris.* Zones 2–8. Needled evergreen. Fast growth to 75 feet. Stiff, twisted, 3-inch blue-green needles in bundles of two. Mature cones rather shapeless, up to 2 inches long and almost as wide at the middle. Bark on trunks and older branches is distinctly red or orange.

The Scotch pine is pyramidal and open in its early years; but there is no telling what strange, picturesque shape it will be when old. I have yet to find an old tree that isn't twisted and irregular in a delightful way. Plant in sun in average soil.

PINE, WESTERN WHITE. *Pinus monticola.* Zones 6–8. Needled evergreen. Fast growth to 90 feet. Almost identical to the eastern white pine except that it is native to the far west, has longer cones and forms a narrower pyramid. A beautiful tree requiring sun and average soil—though it will do even better in moist, humusy soil.

PITTOSPORUM, QUEENSLAND. *Pittosporum rhombifolium.* Zone 10. Broadleaf evergreen. Slow growth to 30 feet. Glossy leaves 4 inches long and almost diamond-shaped. Small white flowers in spring. Orange-to-yellow ½-inch fruits in clusters in fall and winter.

Queensland pittosporum is a shapely, rounded tree in all seasons and very showy when the fruits are ripe. It can be used as a specimen or background plant, or for screening.

Grow in sun or partial shade. Average soil but must be moisture-retentive. Fertilize every spring.

PLANE-TREE, LONDON. *Platanus acerifolia.* Zones 6–10. Deciduous. Grows fast to 100 feet. Bark flakes off, exposing yellowish underbark. Large, three- to five-lobed leaves with coarse teeth. Brown fruit balls in clusters of two, or sometimes three, in the fall.

The London plane-tree becomes massive with age but is more refined in appearance than our native sycamore, to which it is closely related. It is an excellent tree for metropolitan-area gardens because it resists smog better than most. It is also a good shade tree over terraces because the crown develops high above the ground and the foliage lets some sunlight through.

Plant in sun in average soil. Grows best when given ample moisture but does not demand this.

PLUM. *Prunus* species. Zones 3–9. Deciduous. Fast growth to 25 feet. Dwarf and semidwarf varieties also available. Toothed, elliptical leaves. White flowers in spring followed by juicy blue, red or yellow fruits in the summer.

*The western white pine is slightly less beautiful than its eastern cousin, but it's a winner anyway.* (Photo by R. S. McFarland, USDA Forest Service)

*An outstanding tree for smoggy metropolitan areas—the London plane-tree.
This is really two trees.*

Like the other fruit trees to which they are related, plums are perfectly good ornamental trees but far from exceptional. If you are like most people, therefore, you will grow them mainly for fruit.

Plant them in a sunny, frost-free location in average soil containing humus. Prune in late winter. Fertilize annually. Follow a regular spray schedule recommended by your state agricultural extension service.

Three types of plum are grown: European varieties with blue fruits grow in Zones 5–7; Japanese varieties with mainly red fruits grow in Zones 5–9; native varieties with small red or yellow fruits grow in Zones 3–7. Some of the good varieties are French Damson, Green Gage and Oneida (European); Abundance, Elephant Ear and Santa Rosa (Japanese); Red Coat, South Dakota and Underwood (natives). Some plums, primarily European varieties, are self-fruitful; but it is generally advisable to plant two different varieties of the same basic type (that is, two European or two Japanese or two natives—but don't try to mix them).

POINCIANA, ROYAL. Also called Flamboyant. *Delonix regia.* Zone 10. Deciduous. Very fast growth to 40 feet. Broad, rounded crown. Compound, 2-foot leaves with innumerable small leaflets resemble fern

*The royal poinciana is very fast-growing and wide-spreading. It has beautiful foliage and striking flowers in spring and summer.* (Photo by the Florida Agricultural Extension Service)

fronds. Three-inch scarlet and yellow flowers in clusters in spring and summer.

The royal poinciana is southern Florida's gaudiest, most popular tree. The flowers are so numerous you can see them for miles; but even when not in bloom, the tree derives rare grace from the delicate foliage. Plant it just for its beauty, or also to shade your terrace, which it does well.

You might think that such a brilliant ornamental would require extraordinary attention, but such is not the case. The tree grows in sun in any average soil, it flowers at a tender age, and develops to full size in a matter of a few years.

RED CEDAR, EASTERN. *Juniperus virginiana.* Zones 2–8. Evergreen with tiny, sharp needles in fernlike sprays. Moderate growth to 60 feet. Shredding brown bark.

This is a shapely, well-mannered, good-looking plant for gardens large and small. Whether narrowly pyramidal or lance-shaped, it forms a striking accent at the back of the garden or silhouetted against a high wall. Occasionally old trees become windblown-looking and picturesquely gnarled.

Red cedars tolerate some shade but are much better in full sun. If you give them soil of average quality you will be spoiling them, because in the wild they are more accustomed to poor, dry soil.

RUSSIAN-OLIVE *Elaeagnus angustifolia.* Zones 2–9. Deciduous. Grows at moderate speed to about 10 feet but more slowly thereafter to 20 feet. Brown shredding bark. Branches sometimes spiny. Slender, gray-green leaves to about 3 inches long. Small fragrant yellow-and-silver flowers in late spring followed by yellow-and-silver berries in early fall.

The Russian-olive develops into a dense, wide, shrublike specimen which is of surprising interest in the winter; but it is best when fully leafed out. The leaves have a delightful grace as they dance in the breeze, and they are a splendid foil for the more usual green foliage of other trees and shrubs.

Plant in the sun in average soil. The tree is exceptionally undemanding and hardy; it is frequently used in windbreaks in the northern plains states.

*The gray-green leaves of the Russian-olive respond to the merest whisper of a breeze. The tree normally has branches close to the ground, but they were cut out here so that the owner could ride a mower underneath without being badly scratched by the thorns.*

SCHEFFLERA. Also called Queensland Umbrella tree. *Brassaia actino-phylla*. Zones 9b–10. Broadleaf evergreen. Fast growth to 25 feet. Giant, compound leaves have 7 to 16 oblong 1-foot leaflets with a high gloss. They spread outward and down like umbrella ribs. Small red summer flowers in long, narrow clusters arch above the tree like octopus arms. These are followed by little purple fruits.

This is a truly exotic and striking plant used in shrubbery borders as a foil for shrubs and trees with more delicate foliage. It can also be effectively silhouetted against a wall.

Plant in rich soil in the sun. Keep well watered and fertilize several times a year. In early spring, pinch back the top growth and cut leggy stems to the ground to keep the plant from getting gawky. Be alert for scale insects.

*The large glossy leaves of the schefflera make bold contrast with the smaller leaves of other plants.*

*Two trees that respond to the breeze: a large-leaved sea-grape (here growing in front of a gardenia) and a coconut palm.*

SEA-GRAPE. *Coccoloba uvifera.* Zones 9b–10. Broadleaf evergreen. Moderate growth to 20 feet. Angular, multitrunked tree with mottled bark. Leathery, almost round leaves to 8 inches across. Inconspicuous greenish-white flowers in clusters followed by bunches of purple grapelike fruits that can be made into jelly.

The sea-grape is a striking tree whether displayed against the sea, the sky or a wall. The crowns of large leaves above the bare trunks responds to the wind whipping off the tropical sea. The effect is bold, modern and handsome.

The sea-grape grows in full sun. The fact that it grows naturally on the sandy shore indicates that it does not need anything very special in the way of soil or attention. In fact, if you treat it too well, it is likely to curl up its toes.

*The white bellflowers of the Japanese snowbell hang in clusters below the branches. The leaves grow up from the branches.*

SNOWBELL, JAPANESE. *Styrax japonica*. Zones 6–10. Deciduous. Moderate growth to 30 feet. Flat-topped and wider than high. Elliptical 2- to 3-inch leaves grow upright on the branches. Small, white, fragrant, bell-shaped flowers hang below the branches in late spring.

The Japanese snowbell is an almost shrublike tree with slender trunk and horizontal branches. In leaf it has a fine-textured look; and in flower it is a pleasingly delicate composition of alternating green lines (the leaves) and white lines (the flowers). Seen from below in the spring, it is a blanket of flowers.

Grows in partial shade but prefers sun. The soil should be of average quality, well drained and humusy.

SORREL-TREE. Also called Sourwood. *Oxydendrum arboreum.* Zones 6–9. Deciduous. Grows slowly to 75 feet, but usually less. Furrowed gray bark tinged with red. Slender, lance-shaped, finely toothed leaves are lustrous dark green above, lighter beneath; turn scarlet in the fall. Tiny bell-shaped white flowers in delicate panicles in early summer. These develop into dry gray capsules that hang on the tree for a long time in the fall and winter.

In partial shade the sorrel-tree loses all but its upper branches, and while it puts on a gay show in the fall and is pretty in flower in the spring, it is nothing to get excited about. But in an open, sunny location, where it keeps all its branches, it is very decorative—a top choice for small gardens and large.

Plant in average, well-drained soil. Water in dry spells.

*The lily-of-the-valleylike flower panicles are half developed on this sorrel-tree.*

SOUR-GUM. Also called Tupelo, Black Gum and Pepperidge. *Nyssa sylvatica.* Zones 5–10. Deciduous. Grows slowly to 90 feet. Innumerable slender branches in irregular whorls around the straight trunk; sometimes definitely horizontal, sometimes slightly pendulous. Lustrous, oblong, 2- to 5-inch leaves with pointed tips turn rich red in the fall. Small blue berries on female plants in midsummer, but hidden among the leaves.

The sour-gum is more or less pyramidal but with a blunt top. It is good-looking in leaf, interesting and unusual when bare. Primarily it is a tree to be viewed from a little distance. As a shade tree for a terrace, it must have its lower branches removed, and even then it isn't outstanding, because it spreads over a rather small area.

Grow in the sun in average soil. In nature the tree is often found in swamps, which indicates that it does well in moist situations. But in my garden it grows in dry, gravelly soil. One drawback is that the tree puts up numerous suckers from the roots, and if you don't keep these cut out, you'll end up with a thicket of sour-gums.

SPRUCE, NORWAY. *Picea abies.* Zones 2–7. Needled evergreen. Fast growth to form a wide, 150-foot pyramid. Branches that curve upward are densely festooned with pendulous branchlets. Stiff, pointed, curving, dark-green needles grow from all sides of the branchlets and twigs. Slender cones to 7 inches long hang in clusters from the branch tips.

Once you know the characteristics of the Norway spruce, you can hardly fail to identify it at a distance; and you certainly cannot miss it, because it rises up so spectacularly among other trees. In its early years it does not take up very much ground space, but with time it gets much broader.

Plant in an open, sunny place in average soil. Avoid very exposed locations because vicious winds occasionally whip the branches about so violently that the area is blanketed with snapped-off twigs and branchlets. Spray in the spring with malathion or Sevin to control the aphids, which cause galls on new twigs.

Several attractive small, shrubby varieties of the Norway spruce are available in nurseries. They are used in rock gardens, shrubbery borders and foundation plantings.

*The sour-gum tree (center) has innumerable, closely spaced, outstretching branches. The eastern red cedar is spearhead-shaped.*

*A young Serbian spruce. With age it will grow tall and slender and have graceful hanging branchlets.*

SPRUCE, SERBIAN. *Picea omorika.* Zones 5–7. Needled evergreen. Moderate growth to 90 feet. Forms a very slender pyramid with upward-curving branches and hanging branchlets. Short, flattened needles dark green on top, whitish beneath. Two-and-a-half-inch cones.

The Serbian spruce is a beauty—infinitely graceful at all times but especially when the wind causes the branches to billow and show their light-colored undersides. It can easily fit into a small garden, but it needs some rather sizable trees around it to keep it from looking too much like a small green Eiffel Tower; so it is really a tree for large gardens only. One of the country's best-known landscape architects rates it just about at the top of his conifer list.

Needs sun and average soil.

*The Japanese stewartia is a small, shapely, upright tree with lovely camellia-like flowers and very attractive two-colored bark.*

STEWARTIA, JAPANESE. *Stewartia pseudo-camellia.* Zones 6–10. Deciduous. Grows slowly to 60 feet. Bright-green elliptical leaves pointed at both ends turn more-or-less purple in the fall. In early summer, 2½-inch, cup-shaped, fragrant white flowers with yellow and red centers appear. They resemble single camellias. Reddish-brown bark comes off in large flakes to reveal lighter-colored inner bark.

The Japanese stewartia is a tree for all seasons. I fell for it initially because of its striking bark and its distinctive, irregular branching habit. These features make for extraordinary winter interest and suggest that you should plant the tree close enough to the house so you can enjoy it through the windows. But the tree is even more beautiful when it is in flower, and again when the foliage colors up in the autumn.

Plant the Japanese stewartia in the sun or, even better, where it will get morning and afternoon sun but will be in light shade around noon. The soil should be of average quality, slightly acid and loaded with humus.

There are several other good stewartias. In fact, the Korean species is even better than the Japanese because of its bigger flowers; but you will have trouble finding it.


SWEET-GUM. *Liquidambar styraciflua.* Zones 6–10. Deciduous. Moderate growth to 120 feet. Corky wings on the branches. Leaves form perfect stars except that they are flattened at the stem end; lustrous green in summer, a scarlet conflagration in the fall. Pendent, round, brown, somewhat prickly fruits in the fall are favorites of flower arrangers.

The sweet-gum is an outstanding deciduous tree forming a tall, symmetrical pyramid above a rather long, clear (branchless) trunk. It is among the most brilliant of autumn trees. Plant it in sun in rich, moisture-retentive soil. It does especially well in damp locations.


TEA TREE, AUSTRALIAN. *Leptospermum laevigatum.* Zones 9b–10. Broadleaf evergreen. Moderate growth to 30 feet. Dull green, 1-inch-long, oval leaves. Covered with little white flowers in early spring.

This popular California tree is variable in its habit of growth. If you set plants close together, they form an excellent dense hedge. But ideally, the tree should be planted by itself in a sunny location. It then develops a sturdy, twisted trunk, or trunks, with twisted main branches surmounted by an umbrellalike canopy of delicate leaves and flowers. The effect is unusual, Oriental and delightful.

Plant in average soil which is well drained and a little acid.


*A nice mixture of textures and, in the fall, colors. The star-shaped leaves of the sweet-gum turn brilliant red. The small heart-shaped leaves of the gray birch turn yellow. The short needles of the low Japanese yew are dark green the year round.*

THORN, WASHINGTON. *Crataegus phaenopyrum.* Zones 5–10. Deciduous. Moderate growth to 30 feet. Dense, thorny branches in a round head. Lustrous, roughly triangular, 2½-inch leaves with three- to five-toothed lobes; leaves turn red in the fall. Clusters of small white flowers in late spring. Tree densely covered with bright red berries in the fall.

This hawthorn is a choice tree for small gardens and should be planted in a prominent open place where you can enjoy it in late fall and winter particularly. At that time it is like a small cloud of red, its berries are so thick. But it is a mannerly, attractive plant in other seasons as well.

Plant in average, well-drained soil on the alkaline side. Prune out dead wood and cankers every year after flowering.

TULIP TREE. Also called Yellow Poplar. *Liriodendron tulipifera.* Zones 5–10. Deciduous. Moderately fast growth to 175 feet. Unusual big leaves with four pointed lobes, the two lobes at the end separated by only a very shallow sinus; leaves turn yellow in the fall. In late spring, tree bears many solitary tulip-shaped, yellow-green flowers. Conspicuous brown, conelike pods up to 3 inches long from fall through winter.

The tulip tree has the distinction of being our tallest native deciduous tree. It is an impressive sight—huge trunk rising straight up and up and finally branching out at various angles in no set pattern. Unquestionably, when full-grown, it would be out of scale on small properties. But, unhappily, if you planted it today, I doubt that you would live to see the day when you thought it oppressive.

Needs sun and average soil. If leaves develop spots, spray with malathion to kill the aphids causing the trouble.

UMBRELLA PINE. *Sciadopitys verticillata.* Zones 6–10. Needled evergreen. Slow growth to form a 50-foot pyramid. Very dark green, up to 5-inch needles radiate out from the twigs like the ribs of a many-many-ribbed umbrella. Occasionally produces 3- to 5-inch cones.

This is one tree I'd give almost anything to have in my own garden, but I can't figure out a place to put it. It is simply stunning: dark green, very dense, very shapely, with branches all the way to the ground. And the arrangement of the needles is so interesting and unique that you want to study them at length.

With time this Washington thorn will become more rounded, but it will not grow much taller. It is a good tree for small properties.

*An unusually large umbrella pine seen through the white flowers of a weeping crab apple. The umbrella pine is 30 feet tall and almost 60 years old.*

Plant the tree in a sunny place in average soil that is well drained but moisture-retentive. Don't crowd it in so that it cannot develop its symmetrical form. A good place to use it might be as a screen between the terrace and a neighboring property. Or use it anywhere as a striking accent plant.

*A tulip tree about 25 years old. When it reaches maturity several generations hence, it may be 4 times taller.*

WILLOW, GOLDEN WEEPING. *Salix alba tristis.* Zones 3–10. Deciduous. Very fast growth to 75 feet. Slender, lance-shaped, hairy leaves turn yellow in the fall. Slender, pendulous branches—the young growths—yellow the year round.

It's a toss-up whether this or the Babylon weeping willow is the better. I prefer this because it is a much hardier tree and its yellow branch color in winter is a promise of spring to come. On the other hand, the Babylon weeping willow is smaller, therefore better suited to small gardens; and it has somewhat more pendulous, longer branches.

Be that as it may, the golden weeping willow is everything you can ask for in a weeping willow. It is exceedingly graceful, and because of its speedy growth, it permits you to get beauty and shade into a new garden in jig time. You can very easily propagate your own trees simply by making greenwood stem cuttings in the spring, or if you have a brook or pond, by sticking a long branch into one of the banks.

Plant in sun in average soil, preferably moist. But beware of placing it close to septic or drainage lines, because the invasive roots will soon clog the pipes.

Other faults of the tree—and of all willows—are: its very weak wood; its propensity for cluttering the garden with twigs and hard-to-rake-up leaves; its susceptibility to disease in some areas; and its inability to stand up to hurricanes. These are all matters you should consider carefully before planting a willow. But you'll probably decide in its favor anyway.

YELLOW-WOOD. *Cladrastis lutea.* Zones 3b–9. Deciduous. Moderate growth to 50 feet high and almost equal width. Rounded. Attractive smooth, light-gray bark. Dense compound leaves with 5 to 11 oval yellow-green leaflets turning orange to yellow in the fall. Hanging clusters of fragrant white flowers very similar to the wisteria in late spring.

One of my neighbors has a yellow-wood in the center of a terrace, and there are few more attractive sights or more pleasant places to sit on a hot day. The tree, like most of this genus, has a short trunk and large branches reaching up and out. It's just about as good-looking in winter as in other seasons.

Unfortunately the yellow-wood cannot be counted on to bloom every

*A delight in all seasons: a golden weeping willow.*

year; but you appreciate the unusual display just that much more when it does come along.

Plant in sun in average soil. Prune after flowering.

YEW, HICKS. *Taxus media hicksii.* Zones 3–10. Needled evergreen. Moderate growth to 20 feet, but can be held much lower by pruning. Flat, wide-pointed needles on all sides of the twigs are dark green above, lighter green beneath.

The Hicks yew forms a rather narrow column—if it is kept pruned—and is very useful as a dark accent plant standing by itself or in front of a wall, or mixed in with other plants. If not pruned, it grows almost as wide as it is high and loses some of its effectiveness, but it is useful for screening.

Plant in sun or partial shade in average soil. All parts of the tree are poisonous if eaten.

YEW, IRISH. *Taxus baccata stricta.* Zones 7–10. Needled evergreen. Slow growth to 25 feet. Wide, flat, pointed needles more than 1 inch long; dark green above, yellow-green below. Large red berries on female plants.

When well grown, this is a quietly sensational plant forming a substantial, stiffly upright column of green from the ground up. It is a marvelous accent plant, not too big for a fairly small garden; and when several are lined up in a well-spaced row in a large garden, the great formal English gardens instantly come to mind.

Plant in sun or light shade in soil of average quality; but tree will grow more vigorously if there is ample humus. If you wish to keep the tree neatly trimmed (yews take kindly to shearing), you'll need a very tall ladder.

Foliage and fruits are poisonous if eaten.

*Irish yews look more massive than they actually are, simply because they form such a solid mass from top to bottom.*

# ·10·

# THE NEXT BEST TREES

| Common name | Botanical name | Climate zones | Hgt. (ft.) | Type* | Sun or shade | Growth speed |
|---|---|---|---|---|---|---|
| Arborvitae, giant | Thuja plicata | 5–10 | 150 | E | S or Sh | Slow |
| Arborvitae, Oriental | Thuja orientalis | 6b–10 | 50 | E | S or Sh | Slow |
| Ash, blue | Fraxinus quadrangulata | 3b–7 | 70 | D | S | Fast |
| Ash, European | Fraxinus excelsior | 3b–10 | 120 | D | S | Fast |
| Ash, flowering | Fraxinus ornus | 6–10 | 60 | D | S | Fast |
| Ash, white | Fraxinus americana | 3b–10 | 120 | D | S | Fast |
| Avocado | Persea americana | 9b–10 | 25 | E | S | Fast |
| Bald cypress | Taxodium distichum | 5–10 | 150 | D | S | Slow |
| Brisbane-box | Tristania conferta | 10 | 60 | E | S | Moderate |
| Cajeput-tree | Melaleuca leucadendra | 10 | 40 | E | S | Very fast |
| Camphor-tree | Cinnamomum camphora | 9–10 | 40 | E | S | Slow |
| Carob | Ceratonia siliqua | 10 | 50 | E | S | Moderate |
| Carrot-wood | Cupaniopsis anacardioides | 10 | 30 | E | S | Slow |
| Cedar, Atlas | Cedrus atlantica | 6b–10 | 120 | E | S | Slow |
| Chinaberry | Melia azedarach | 7b–10 | 50 | D | S | Very fast |
| Chinese flame-tree | Koelreuteria formosana | 9b–10 | 30 | D | S | Fast |
| Chinese parasol-tree | Firmiana simplex | 9–10 | 40 | D | S | Fast |
| Clethra, Japanese | Clethra barbinervis | 6–9 | 30 | D | S | Moderate |
| Coral-tree | Erythrina caffra | 10 | 40 | D | S | Fast |
| Cryptomeria | Cryptomeria japonica | 6–10 | 150 | E | S | Moderate |
| Cucumber-tree | Magnolia acuminata | 5–10 | 90 | D | S | Very fast |
| Cypress, columnar Italian | Cupressus sempervirens stricta | 7b–10 | 50 | E | S | Fast |
| Dawn-redwood | Metasequoia glyptostroboides | 6–10 | 100 | D | S | Very fast |
| Desert-willow | Chilopsis linearis | 8–9 | 25 | D | S | Fast |

* D—deciduous; E—evergreen

| Common name | Botanical name | Climate zones | Hgt. (ft.) | Type* | Sun or shade | Growth speed |
|---|---|---|---|---|---|---|
| Dogwood, Pacific | *Cornus nuttallii* | 7b–10 | 60 | D | S or Sh | Moderate |
| Douglas fir | *Pseudotsuga menziesii* | 5–10 | 250 | E | S or Sh | Fast |
| Dovetree | *Davidia involucrata* | 6b–10 | 60 | D | S or Sh | Slow |
| Elm, American | *Ulmus americana* | 3–9 | 120 | D | S | Very fast |
| Empress-tree | *Paulownia tomentosa* | 6–10 | 45 | D | S | Very fast |
| False cypress, hinoki | *Chamaecyparis obtusa* | 5–7 | 120 | E | S | Slow |
| False cypress, Lawson | *Chamaecyparis lawsoniana* | 6–7 | 120 | E | S | Moderate |
| Fern pine | *Podocarpus gracilior* | 10 | 60 | E | S or Sh | Slow |
| Fig, fiddleleaf | *Ficus lyrata* | 10 | 20 | E | S or Sh | Fast |
| Fig, India-laurel | *Ficus retusa* | 10 | 30 | E | S | Moderate |
| Fig, India-laurel | *Ficus retusa nitida* | 10 | 30 | E | S | Moderate |
| Fig, rustyleaf | *Ficus rubiginosa* | 10 | 40 | E | S | Moderate |
| Filbert | *Corylus maxima* | 6–9 | 30 | D | S | Slow |
| Fir, Nikko | *Abies homolepis* | 5–8 | 90 | E | S | Moderate |
| Firewheel-tree | *Stenocarpus sinuatus* | 9b–10 | 25 | E | S | Slow |
| Frangipani | *Plumeria rubra* | 10 | 15 | D | S | Moderate |
| Golden-chain tree | *Laburnum watereri* | 6–10 | 30 | D | S | Slow |
| Golden shower tree | *Cassia fistula* | 10 | 25 | D | S | Slow |
| Gum, dwarf blue | *Eucalyptus globulus compacta* | 9–10 | 70 | E | S | Fast |
| Gum, red | *Eucalyptus camaldulensis* | 8–10 | 120 | E | S | Fast |
| Gum, red flowering | *Eucalyptus ficifolia* | 9b–10 | 40 | E | S | Fast |
| Hackberry, European | *Celtis australis* | 6b–10 | 75 | D | S | Fast |
| Hawthorn, English | *Crataegus oxyacantha* | 5–10 | 20 | D | S | Moderate |
| Hawthorn, Lavalle | *Crataegus lavallei* | 5–10 | 20 | D | S | Moderate |
| Hemlock, Carolina | *Tsuga caroliniana* | 5–8 | 75 | E | S or Sh | Moderate |
| Holly, long-stalk | *Ilex pedunculosa* | 6–10 | 30 | E | S | Slow |
| Hong Kong orchid-tree | *Bauhinia blakeana* | 10 | 20 | E | S | Moderate |
| Hop-hornbeam | *Ostrya virginiana* | 5–8 | 40 | D | S | Slow |
| Hornbeam, European | *Carpinus betulus* | 6–10 | 60 | D | S or Sh | Slow |
| Horse-chestnut, common | *Aesculus hippocastanum* | 3b–10 | 75 | D | S | Fast |
| Horse-chestnut, red | *Aesculus carnea* | 3b–10 | 75 | D | S | Fast |
| Incense-cedar | *Libocedrus decurrens* | 5–10 | 125 | E | S | Fast |
| Jerusalem-thorn | *Parkinsonia aculeata* | 9–10 | 30 | D | S | Fast |
| Joshua tree | *Yucca brevifolia* | 9–10 | 30 | E | S | Slow |
| Jujube | *Zizyphus jujuba* | 7b–10 | 30 | D | S | Slow |
| Juniper, Chinese | *Juniperus chinensis* | 5–10 | 60 | E | S | Moderate |
| Kaffir plum | *Harpephyllum caffrum* | 10 | 35 | E | S | Fast |
| Katsura-tree | *Cercidiphyllum japonicum* | 5–8 | 60 | D | S or Sh | Slow |
| Kentucky coffee-tree | *Gymnocladus dioicus* | 5–10 | 90 | D | S | Fast |
| Kumquat | *Fortunella* species | 9b–10 | 12 | E | S | Moderate |

* D—deciduous; E—evergreen

| Common name | Botanical name | Climate zones | Hgt. (ft.) | Type* | Sun or shade | Growth speed |
|---|---|---|---|---|---|---|
| Larch, eastern | *Larix laricina* | 2–7 | 60 | D | S | Fast |
| Larch, European | *Larix decidua* | 2–9 | 100 | D | S | Fast |
| Lilac, Japanese tree | *Syringa amurensis japonica* | 5–8 | 30 | D | S | Moderate |
| Lily-of-the-valley tree | *Clethra arborea* | 9–10 | 25 | E | S or Sh | Moderate |
| Linden, American | *Tilia americana* | 3–8a | 120 | D | S | Fast |
| Linden, Crimean | *Tilia euchlora* | 5–10 | 60 | D | S | Fast |
| Linden, pendent silver | *Tilia petiolaris* | 6–10 | 75 | D | S | Moderate |
| Locust, black | *Robinia pseudoacacia* | 3b–10 | 75 | D | S | Fast |
| Loquat | *Eriobotrya japonica* | 9b–10 | 20 | E | S | Fast |
| Magnolia, anise | *Magnolia salicifolia* | 6–10 | 30 | D | S | Slow |
| Magnolia, Yulan | *Magnolia denudata* | 6–10 | 60 | D | S | Moderate |
| Maple, columnar red | *Acer rubrum columnare* | 3b–10 | 75 | D | S | Fast |
| Maple, hedge | *Acer campestre* | 6–9 | 25 | D | S | Slow |
| Maple, trident | *Acer buergerianum* | 6b–10 | 20 | D | S | Moderate |
| Maple, vine | *Acer circinatum* | 6–10 | 25 | D | S or Sh | Moderate |
| Mayten-tree | *Maytenus boaria* | 9–10 | 40 | E | S | Slow |
| Moreton Bay chestnut | *Castanospermum australe* | 10 | 60 | E | S | Fast |
| Mountain-ash, Folgner | *Sorbus folgneri* | 6–10 | 25 | D | S | Moderate |
| Mountain-ash, Korean | *Sorbus alnifolia* | 5–10 | 60 | D | S | Moderate |
| Mulberry, white | *Morus alba* | 5–10 | 50 | D | S | Fast |
| Oak, California live | *Quercus agrifolia* | 9–10 | 90 | E | S | Fast |
| Oak, canyon live | *Quercus chrysolepis* | 7b–10 | 60 | E | S | Moderate |
| Oak, cork | *Quercus suber* | 7–10 | 60 | E | S | Moderate |
| Oak, English | *Quercus robur* | 7–10 | 100 | D | S | Moderate |
| Oak, holly | *Quercus ilex* | 9–10 | 70 | E | S | Moderate |
| Oak, red | *Quercus rubra* | 3–8 | 75 | D | S | Fast |
| Oak, sawtooth | *Quercus acutissima* | 6b–8 | 45 | D | S | Moderate |
| Oak, scarlet | *Quercus coccinea* | 5–10 | 75 | D | S | Moderate |
| Oak, shingle | *Quercus imbricaria* | 6–8 | 75 | D | S | Moderate |
| Oak, Shumard | *Quercus shumardii* | 6–8 | 120 | D | S | Moderate |
| Oak, swamp white | *Quercus bicolor* | 3b–8 | 60 | D | S | Slow |
| Osage-orange | *Maclura pomifera* | 6–10 | 60 | D | S | Fast |
| Palm, Canary Island date | *Phoenix canariensis* | 10 | 60 | E | S | Slow |
| Palm, Christmas | *Veitchia merrillii* | 10 | 20 | E | S | Fast |
| Palm, European fan | *Chamaerops humilis* | 8–10 | 20 | E | S or Sh | Slow |
| Palm, Florida thatch | *Thrinax parviflora* | 9b–10 | 25 | E | S | Slow |
| Palm, Guadalupe | *Erythea edulis* | 9–10 | 30 | E | S | Slow |
| Palm, Mexican blue | *Erythea armata* | 10 | 40 | E | S | Slow |
| Palm, Senegal date | *Phoenix reclinata* | 10 | 30 | E | S | Slow |
| Palm, windmill | *Trachycarpus fortunei* | 8–10 | 50 | E | S | Fast |
| Pear, Bradford | *Pyrus calleryana* Bradford | 5–10 | 50 | D | S | Moderate |
| Peppertree, California | *Schinus molle* | 9–10 | 40 | E | S | Fast |
| Pignut | *Carya glabra* | 5–8 | 120 | D | S | Slow |
| Pine, Aleppo | *Pinus halepensis* | 9–10 | 60 | E | S | Moderate |
| Pine, Canary Island | *Pinus canariensis* | 8–10 | 80 | E | S | Fast |
| Pine, Coulter | *Pinus coulteri* | 8–10 | 80 | E | S | Fast |

* D—deciduous; E—evergreen

| Common name | Botanical name | Climate zones | Hgt. (ft.) | Type* | Sun or shade | Growth speed |
|---|---|---|---|---|---|---|
| Pine, Italian stone | *Pinus pinea* | 9–10 | 80 | E | S | Moderate |
| Pine, Japanese black | *Pinus thunbergii* | 4–9 | 90 | E | S | Moderate |
| Pine, Japanese red | *Pinus densiflora* | 5–8 | 90 | E | S | Fast |
| Pine, Korean | *Pinus koraiensis* | 3–7 | 90 | E | S | Slow |
| Pine, limber | *Pinus flexilis* | 2–7 | 75 | E | S | Slow |
| Pine, Monterey | *Pinus radiata* | 8–10 | 100 | E | S | Very fast |
| Pine, ponderosa | *Pinus ponderosa* | 6–10 | 150 | E | S | Fast |
| Pine, red | *Pinus resinosa* | 2–6 | 75 | E | S | Fast |
| Pine, slash | *Pinus caribaea* | 8–10 | 100 | E | S | Very fast |
| Pine, Swiss stone | *Pinus cembra* | 2–7 | 75 | E | S | Slow |
| Pistache, Chinese | *Pistacia chinensis* | 9–10 | 50 | D | S | Moderate |
| Pittosporum, willow | *Pittosporum phillyraeoides* | 9–10 | 20 | E | S or Sh | Slow |
| Plane-tree, Oriental | *Platanus orientalis* | 7–10 | 90 | D | S | Fast |
| Privet, glossy | *Ligustrum lucidum* | 7b–10 | 30 | E | S or Sh | Fast |
| Redbud, eastern | *Cercis canadensis* | 5–10 | 35 | D | S or Sh | Moderate |
| Redbud, western | *Cercis occidentalis* | 6–10 | 18 | D | S or Sh | Moderate |
| Red cedar, western | *Juniperus scopulorum* | 6–10 | 35 | E | S | Moderate |
| Redwood | *Sequoia sempervirens* | 7b–10 | 350 | E | S or Sh | Very fast |
| Shadblow | *Amelanchier canadensis* | 5–7 | 60 | D | S | Fast |
| Silk oak | *Grevillea robusta* | 9b–10 | 100 | E | S | Very fast |
| Silverbell, Carolina | *Halesia carolina* | 6–10 | 30 | D | S | Moderate |
| Silverbell, mountain | *Halesia monticola* | 6–10 | 90 | D | S | Moderate |
| Spruce, Colorado blue | *Picea pungens* | 2–7 | 100 | E | S | Fast |
| Spruce, Engelmann | *Picea engelmannii* | 2–7 | 150 | E | S | Fast |
| Spruce, Sitka | *Picea sitchensis* | 6b–8 | 140 | E | S | Fast |
| Spruce, white | *Picea glauca* | 2–7 | 90 | E | S | Fast |
| Sweet bay | *Laurus nobilis* | 7–10 | 30 | E | S or Sh | Slow |
| Sweet bay | *Magnolia virginiana* | 6–10 | 60 | D or E | S | Slow |
| Sweet-gum, Chinese | *Liquidambar formosana* | 7b–10 | 60 | D | S | Moderate |
| Sycamore | *Platanus occidentalis* | 5–10 | 120 | D | S | Very fast |
| Sycamore, California | *Platanus racemosa* | 7b–10 | 120 | D | S | Fast |
| Tangerine | *Citrus reticulata* | 9b–10 | 20 | E | S | Moderate |
| Thorn, cockspur | *Crataegus crus-galli* | 5–10 | 35 | D | S | Moderate |
| Thorn, Jerusalem | *Parkinsonia aculeata* | 9b–10 | 25 | D | S | Moderate |
| Victorian-box | *Pittosporum undulatum* | 10 | 40 | E | S or Sh | Moderate |
| Walnut, Carpathian | *Juglans regia* Carpathian | 5–8 | 90 | D | S | Moderate |
| Walnut, Persian | *Juglans regia* | 8–10 | 90 | D | S | Moderate |
| Willow, Babylon weeping | *Salix babylonica* | 6b–10 | 30 | D | S | Very fast |
| Willow, corkscrew | *Salix matsudana tortuosa* | 5–9 | 30 | D | S | Fast |
| Willow, Niobe weeping | *Salix blanda* | 5–10 | 40 | D | S | Very fast |
| Willow, Thurlow weeping | *Salix elegantissima* | 4–10 | 40 | D | S | Very fast |
| Yaupon | *Ilex vomitoria* | 7b–10 | 25 | E | S | Slow |
| Zelkova, Japanese | *Zelkova serrata* | 6–10 | 90 | D | S | Moderate |

* D—deciduous; E—evergreen

# ·11·

## THE 100 BEST SHRUBS

ABELIA, GLOSSY. *Abelia grandiflora.* Zones 6–10. Evergreen in warm climates; deciduous elsewhere. 6 feet. Dense, glossy, oval leaves to 1½ inches long turn bronze in fall. Tubular, white to pink flowers in small clusters from early summer into fall.

Glossy abelia is a graceful hybrid shrub with slender arching branches. It is ideal for use in shrubbery borders and also makes a good, dense hedge. Grows best in sun but does well in partial shade. Average soil containing plenty of humus. Cut a few of the stems to the ground in the winter to make a more open, arching plant. In cold climates, if the shrub is killed back, it will make substantial new growth the following summer. Propagate by hardwood stem cuttings.

ANDROMEDA, JAPANESE. *Pieris japonica.* Zones 6–9. Broadleaf evergreen. 9 feet. Lustrous, dark-green, elliptical leaves to 3½ inches long; new leaves in spring reddish-bronze. Creamy-white lily-of-the-valleylike flowers in pendulous sprays in early spring. In winter the flower buds hang from red stems.

Very few shrubs, evergreen or deciduous, are as good as the slow-growing Japanese andromeda. It is beautiful in every season—a magnificent, rounded plant for shrubbery borders or specimen planting. Its foliage shows little reaction to subzero temperatures; even in the dead of

*Japanese andromeda is a sheet of white flowers in the spring. This large specimen was in bloom for 4 weeks.*

winter the red-stemmed panicles of tiny flower buds are attractive and promising. It is one of the first northern plants to bloom in the spring, and in good years it is an almost solid sheet of creamy white. The bronzy color of the young leaves that follow the flowers is pretty and unusual. And unlike the mountain laurel, which I consider its major rival in colder climates, it is clothed with foliage all the way to the ground.

Finally, it requires little attention. Plant in full sun if possible; but if you must plant it in partial shade, it will also do very well. The soil needs to be of only average quality but should be slightly acid and as humusy as you can make it. Prune after flowering—if pruning is necessary. Spray in the spring with malathion to control lace bugs. Propagate by layering.

ANDROMEDA, MOUNTAIN. *Pieris floribunda*. Zones 5–9. Broadleaf evergreen. 6 feet. This is very similar to the foregoing. The major difference is that the nodding little flowers grow in upright clusters and appear a bit later in the spring. The plant is also a little hardier and smaller. The leaves and stems are not reddish.

Mountain andromeda is not quite so ornamental as the Japanese species, but it is nevertheless a very good, easy-going shrub and should be more widely planted than it is. Grow in sun in average soil. Prune after flowering. Propagate by layering.

AUCUBA, JAPANESE. *Aucuba japonica*. Zones 7b–10. Broadleaf evergreen. 10 feet high and about as wide. Glossy, toothed, elliptical leaves up to 8 inches long. Tiny, dark-red flowers in spring. Clusters of conspicuous bright red berries on female plants in fall and winter.

The Japanese aucuba is a topnotch shrub for gardens in warm climates because it requires shade—does quite well even in deep shade—and can therefore be counted on to fill in those otherwise difficult dark spots in the garden. A number of varieties are available, some with all-green leaves, others with variegated leaves. The most popular is known as the gold-dust plant (*A. japonica variegata*) because its large leaves are so splattered with gold marks that they leap out at you in the shade. You must plant both male and female specimens of aucuba to have berries.

Plant aucuba in better-than-average soil which is well drained and fortified with humus. Needs plenty of water. Prune, if necessary, before flowering; however, the plant is usually so slow-growing and orderly that it needs little attention of this kind. Propagate by half-hardwood stem cuttings.

Azalea, Exbury hybrid. *Rhododendron* hybrids. Zones 6b–10. Deciduous. 10 feet. Mostly single flowers as large as 4 inches across, borne in rounded clusters of 10 to 30 flowers; white, pink, red, yellow and orange; sometimes fragrant. They appear in mid- to late spring.

The Exbury hybrid azaleas are well-shaped plants with incredibly lovely flowers. When you see them you will want to rush out and buy a dozen plants for your garden; but then you will discover that there are so many sensational named varieties that you cannot make up your mind about which you want. I'm not going to try to help you.

Like other azaleas and rhododendrons* that develop into large plants, the Exbury hybrids can be treated as specimen plants or placed in a border with other shrubs and trees. If you mass the plants, take care not to put clashing colors together. And if you set them in a foundation planting, make sure you don't place them under windows, because they will ultimately grow up and block the view—and you will not be able to make yourself cut them down to proper size.

The Exbury hybrids should be planted in partial shade in a spot protected from winter winds. An ideal location is where the plants get sun part of the day, but not at midday. The soil, which must be acid, should be deeply dug and mixed with considerable humus. Water plants in dry spells and maintain a mulch of oak leaves or pine needles to hold in moisture, keep down weeds and keep the soil cool in summer. Fertilize in the spring with cottonseed meal or Hollytone, but don't try to work this into the soil with a cultivator because the roots of these hybrids are shallow and should not be disturbed. Snap off spent flowers with your fingers before seed heads develop. Prune after flowering to remove dead wood. Pinch out leaf buds (but not the tiny buds at their base) to promote bushier growth. Propagate by layering.

Azaleas and to a lesser extent rhododendrons are often hit by a blight

---

* Azaleas are members of the rhododendron genus.

*Exbury hybrid azaleas have large flowers in amazing colors.*

that causes spots on the blossoms. Within a very short time the blossoms drop and turn slimy. The problem is most common in the south. It can be controlled by spraying every other day with zineb from the time the buds show color until they are open; then spray every fourth day. Lace bugs, mites and mealybugs are other fairly common pests.

Knapp Hill hybrid azaleas are similar to Exbury hybrids. De Rothschild hybrids are special selections of Exbury plants.

*The hardy flame azalea does well in sun and also in partial shade.*

AZALEA, FLAME. *Rhododendron calendulaceum*. Zones 6–10. Deciduous. 15 feet. Broad, elliptical leaves to 3 inches long; woolly underneath.
Yellow, orange or scarlet flowers about 2 inches across in large clusters
in mid-spring.

The flame azalea is the most striking of our native species. Because
of its hardiness, it is especially suited to northern gardens. Grows well
in full sun or light shade. Use and handle like the preceding.

*These enormous Ghent hybrid azaleas are more than 100 years old. A grove of tulip trees towers above them.*

AZALEA, GHENT HYBRID. *Rhododendron gandavense.* Zones 5–10. 10 feet. Deciduous. Single or occasionally double flowers in rounded clusters in mid-spring; white, pink, red, orange or yellow.

These are exceptionally hardy hybrid azaleas which thrive even in northern New England. Use and grow the upright plants like Exbury hybrid azaleas. You will find many excellent varieties to choose from.

AZALEA, INDIAN HYBRID. *Rhododendron* hybrids. Zones 8b–10. Broadleaf evergreen. 6 feet. Single or double flowers up to 3 inches across in large clusters in early spring; white, pink, red, violet.

These rather large-leaved azaleas are grown only in warm climates, where they need considerable protection from the sun. Plant in filtered sun or in a shaded place where they get only a few hours of direct sun a day. Follow directions for using and growing Exbury hybrid azaleas.

AZALEA, KURUME. *Rhododendron obtusum.* Zones 7–10. Broadleaf evergreen. 3 feet. Elliptical leaves about 1 inch long, glossy green above. Small white, pink or red, single or double flowers in great profusion in mid-spring.

The Kurume azaleas are low, spreading, dense plants with small leaves. When in bloom, the flowers completely blanket the plants and the foliage is almost invisible. They are favorite plants for foundation borders in warm climates, but, unhappily, too many people using them mix varieties with clashing colors.

Grow Kurume azaleas like the Exbury hybrids. Pruning (after flowering) is mainly a matter of clipping or even shearing the plants to the desired shape: new leaves soon cover the stubs of twigs and branches.

*Kurume azaleas: one in bloom, those on either side, finished blooming. The flowers are so dense that they hide the foliage.*

*Among the showiest of azaleas are the Mollis hybrids.*

AZALEA, MOLLIS HYBRID. *Rhododendron kosterianum.* Zones 6–10. Deciduous. 5 feet. Oblong leaves to 6 inches, gray-green underneath, turning yellow or orange in the fall. Flowers up to 4 inches across in clusters of up to a dozen; white, yellow, orange, pink or red. They appear in mid-spring.

This is another very showy group. Plants are erect, not too spreading. Because of their size, they can often be used in foundation plantings under windows. Grow in partial shade or sun like the Exbury hybrids.

AZALEA, ROYAL. *Rhododendron schlippenbachii.* Zones 5–10. Deciduous. 15 feet. More-or-less oval leaves wider toward the pointed end and up to 5 inches long; clustered in whorls at the ends of branches. They turn yellow, orange and red in the fall. Fragrant pink flowers 3 inches across in clusters of three to six appear in mid-spring.

This is a fine shrub with many branches. The flowers are an unusual pure pink—very showy in a restrained way. Use and grow like the Exbury hybrid azaleas.

AZALEA, SNOW. *Rhododendron mucronatum.* Zones 6b–10. Broadleaf evergreen. 6 feet. Elliptical gray-green leaves to 2½ inches long. Fragrant, snow-white 2-inch flowers in clusters of one to three appear in mid-spring.

The snow azalea is an excellent foil for the more colorful azaleas. Use it with these in a shrubbery border. Since it does not grow high, you might also be tempted to use it in a foundation planting if the foliage color were not so drab.

Grow the snow azalea like the Exbury hybrids.

AZALEA, TORCH. *Rhododendron obtusum kaempferi.* Zones 6–8. Evergreen in warmer climates, almost deciduous in cold. 10 feet high and about as wide. Elliptical, 1-inch-long leaves dark green above, hairy on the underside of the midrib. Fiery red flowers about 2½ inches across in clusters of two or three in mid-spring. Because there are many blossoms on each large plant, the effect is electric. Maybe it is too brilliant for a small property—I'm not sure.

Since it needs partial shade (and also does well in deep shade), plant it partly under trees, which will serve as a toning-down background. Grow like Exbury hybrid azaleas.

*This small torch azalea is still in a nursery bed but is already putting forth individual flowers.*

BAMBOO, YELLOW-GROOVE. *Phyllostachys aureosulcata.* Zones 6b–10. Broadleaf evergreen. 25 feet. Slender, upright, jointed green stems with vertical yellow grooves. Long slender leaves on side branches.

Most bamboos grow in warm climates; but yellow-groove also thrives fairly far north. It is a delightful sight because the bright green canes and leaves move constantly in the slightest breeze. Ideally you should display it in front of a wall, so that the canes are silhouetted; but it also makes a superb screen for blotting out neighboring lots or work or play areas on your own lot.

The main difficulty with yellow-groove is that it belongs to the so-called "running bamboos," meaning that it puts out roots in every direction and new canes spring up from these; thus a small clump eventually turns into a forest. The best way to prevent this is to confine the plant in a terrace plant pocket,* or to surround it with galvanized steel to a depth of 18 inches or more. The alternative is to keep cutting off the spreading roots with a sharp spade.

Grow in sun or partial shade in average soil. For fastest growth, fertilize and water as you do your lawn (bamboos belong to the grass family). Propagate by cutting off the rooted canes that grow up outside the clump. The very young, succulent shoots are edible.

BARBERRY, JAPANESE. *Berberis thunbergii.* Zones 5–9. Deciduous. 7 feet high and almost as wide. Very dense branches and twigs covered with spines. Small, egg-shaped leaves a little wider at the top than at the stem end turn fiery red in the fall. In mid-spring, small yellow flowers touched with red on the outside. Small, elliptical, bright-red berries from fall through winter.

The Japanese barberry is one of our most widely planted shrubs because it makes a hedge that is virtually impenetrable by man and beast. Once you plant the shrub in sun or partial shade in average soil, you can forget it except for pruning in early spring to keep it shapely and within bounds.

There are several varieties to choose from. One of the best is the box

* A small bed surrounded by walls or paving.

*A thicket of yellow-groove bamboo surrounds the base of a loblolly pine.*

*The Japanese barberry leafs out early in the spring. It grows in the sun or, as here, in partial shade.*

barberry (*B. thunbergii minor*). This is somewhat smaller in every way than the true Japanese box and grows to only 3½ feet. Another is Crimson Pygmy, only 2 feet tall, with red-to-reddish leaves if grown in full sun.

You can propagate this and other barberries by planting the berries outdoors in the fall or by making greenwood stem cuttings in the spring. But thanks to the birds, you will discover that little plants spring up naturally from seed all over the garden.

BARBERRY, WINTERGREEN. *Berberis julianae*. Zones 6–9. Broadleaf ever-green. 6 feet. Upright plant with thorny twigs. Narrow, elliptical leaves as long as 3 inches with spines along the edges, dark green above, lighter beneath. Clusters of small yellow flowers in mid-spring. Blue-black berries in the fall.

The wintergreen barberry is extremely thorny and makes another out-standing hedge plant. Single plants can also be used here and there for their decorative value. Plant in sun or light shade in average soil.

*Wintergreen barberry has long, leathery, spiny-edged leaves and small bright-yellow flowers in the spring.*

BEAUTYBUSH. *Kolkwitzia amabilis.* Zones 5–10. Deciduous. 12 feet. Upright, arching stems and branches covered with peeling brown bark. Oval leaves to 3 inches long, reddish in the fall. Shrub covered in late spring with profuse clusters of small, weigela-like pink flowers with yellow throats. Conspicuous dry, reddish-brown, bristly fruits in late summer.

This popular shrub is very showy when in bloom and quite showy in other seasons as well; but if you let it grow to full size in a small garden, it takes up more space than it's worth. Plant in sun or light shade in average soil. Thin out excess branches after flowering. Propagate by greenwood stem cuttings.

BLUEBEARD. *Caryopteris clandonensis.* Zones 6–10. Deciduous. 2 feet. More-or-less oval, toothed leaves to 3 inches long. Many clusters of bright-blue flowers with protruding stamens on upright stems appear in late summer and fall.

There are not many shrubs with bright-blue flowers, and almost none that bloom at the end of summer. That's good reason for using this erect little plant in a shrubbery border, in a border by itself, or in flower beds.

Needs full sun; average, well-drained soil. As it is often killed back by frost, it benefits by being cut almost to the ground in the spring; this promotes better growth and flowering. Propagate by stem cuttings in the summer.

BLUEBERRY, HIGHBUSH. *Vaccinium corymbosum.* Zones 5–7. Deciduous. 12 feet. Upright. Dense branches and twigs that are reddish in winter. Elliptical 2- to 3-inch leaves turn scarlet in the fall. Clusters of tiny bell-shaped white or pinkish flowers in mid-spring. Delicious blue or blue-black berries in summer.

As an ornamental plant the highbush blueberry must be given high marks because it contributes to the beauty of the garden in all seasons. But, understandably, most people consider its fruit to be its main attraction. The only argument I have against this is, if you want berries

*A beautybush needs lots of space (unless you prune it hard) but it rewards you with lots and lots of bloom.*

the size of those sold in the supermarket, you must prune the plant very hard in early spring—and this detracts from its beauty. I recommend, therefore, that you go a little easy with your pruning shears and settle for somewhat smaller but still delicious berries.

Blueberries require full sun. Plant in average, well-drained soil into which you must mix a large quantity of rotted oak leaves, pine needles, peat moss or sawdust to make it acid (4.0 to 5.2 pH). Water in dry spells. Fertilize twice in the spring. Prune out weak stems and branches and some of the young shoots on which the big, round, plump fruit buds have formed.

To have fruit, you must plant two different varieties. Among the best to choose from are Bluecrop, Concord, Coville, Darrow, Earliblue, Herbert, Jersey and Pemberton.

*A highbush blueberry in bloom in early spring gives promise of a bountiful crop of fruit in midsummer.*

Box, COMMON. Also called Boxwood. *Buxus sempervirens.* Zones 6b–9. Broadleaf evergreen. 20 feet. Very dense foliage. Lustrous, dark-green oval leaves to 1¼ inches.

This is the most widely planted species of box—the kind associated with the gardens of old Virginia homes. It is such a dense dark-green plant that it stands out prominently wherever it is used. It somehow seems to represent solidity and formality. Allowed to grow naturally (at its natural slow pace), it develops into a large, rounded mound (although there are varieties which are pyramidal, treelike, and even weeping). But it responds well to shearing and is often used for neatly shaped hedges and in topiary work.*

Plant box in the sun or partial shade. The soil should be of average or better quality, well drained and humusy. Water regularly and very heavily in the fall before the ground freezes. Prune in late summer. Spray in late spring with malathion to control boxwood psyllids (small green flies). Leaf miners may also attack plants.

During heavy snowfalls, get out every hour with a pole to shake off the snow. In cold, windy areas, plants must be shielded with burlap to keep them from being winter-killed. Plants exposed to the southern sun in such areas must also be screened. (However, since there is nothing pretty about burlap-shielded plants of any description, I recommend not using box in such areas.)

Of the numerous varieties of common box, the best are *suffruticosa* —edging box or dwarf box—which grows very slowly to 3 or 4 feet, but is commonly held much lower; flat-topped Vardar Valley, which is hardy in Zone 5 and stays green in winter even in that zone; and Inglis, also green and hardy in Zone 5 but forming a pyramid.

BRIDAL WREATH. *Spiraea vanhouttei.* Zones 5–9. Deciduous. 6 feet. Pointed, oval leaves to 1¾ inches occasionally turn orange in the fall. White flowers in clusters in late spring. Of the many species and varieties of spirea, this hybrid rates as the best. It has lovely arching branches. The flowers are profuse and brilliant. Growth is vigorous and fast.

Grow in either sun or light shade, but preferably the former. Average soil which is well drained but retains moisture. Cut some of the oldest

* The practice of shearing and training plants into ornamental (and sometimes grotesque) shapes.

stems to the ground after flowering to promote stronger new growth. Propagate by layering the tips of young branches.

BROOM, WARMINSTER. *Cytisus praecox*. Zones 6–10. Deciduous. 6 feet. Forms a mounded, spreading mass of slender, upright twigs that are bright green the year round. Leaves tiny and inconspicuous. Covered with pealike yellow flowers in mid-spring.

Like other brooms, the Warminster broom is an odd-looking shrub with a swirling, often fountainlike form which is bound to fascinate you. It is literally a solid mass of yellow when in bloom; and in winter a solid mass of bright green that stands out beautifully against the bleak landscape. It is good in a shrubbery border or rock garden.

Plant in sun in average, well-drained soil. Also does well in extremely sandy soil. Prune after flowering to keep the plant orderly but informal.

*Warminster broom—a mass of tiny yellow flowers in the spring. In the winter it is a swirling mound of bright-green twigs.*

BUTTERFLY-BUSH. *Buddleia davidii.* Zones 6–10. Deciduous. 8 feet. Thin, oval, toothed leaves to 9 inches long, green above, whitish beneath. Large upright spikes of fragrant blue, purple, white, pink or red flowers from midsummer till fall.

Butterfly-bush is widely planted for its very colorful late-season flowers. Although the foliage is somewhat coarse, the upright plant with slender, arching branches is quite graceful and fits well into a sunny shrubbery border.

Plant in well-drained, average soil with plenty of humus. Prune in early spring. The shrub is very slow to leaf out. In cold climates it is often killed to the ground in the winter but makes a rapid comeback and blooms on normal schedule. In any climate, it often pays to pinch out the stem ends to encourage bushier growth. Propagate by greenwood stem cuttings in summer.

*The butterfly bush in the foreground has not bloomed; the closely related fountain buddleia behind it has.*

CAMELLIA, SASANQUA. *Camellia sasanqua*. Zones 7b–10. Broadleaf evergreen. 20 feet. Oval, glossy, dark-green leaves. Flowers to 3 inches across, usually single or semidouble, white or pink; occasionally faintly fragrant. These are heavily produced in fall and early winter.

The sasanqua camellia is smaller and somewhat less showy than the common camellia; but if you like camellias, it is a valuable shrub because it blooms many weeks before the common species. Consequently, by planting both species, you get a much longer season of bloom.

The shrubs are generally rather open and informal—some upright, some rounded, some spreading and even vinelike. Use them wherever you would use common camellias. They are also good for espaliering. Grow like the common camellia (page 125).

CAROLINA ALLSPICE. Also called Sweetshrub. *Calycanthus floridus*. Zones 5–10. Deciduous. 9 feet. Aromatic, glossy, elliptical leaves to 5 inches long turn yellow in the fall. Dark red-brown flowers, 2 inches across and very fragrant, appear in mid-spring.

Carolina allspice is a native shrub widely planted for its fragrance; but it has a nice, dense, rounded habit that enhances almost any shrubbery border. Plant it in sun or partial shade in average soil. It is well suited to moist locations. Prune after flowering. Propagate by layering or seeds.

CEANOTHUS, POINT REYES. *Ceanothus gloriosus*. Zones 7–10. Broadleaf evergreen. 2 feet; spreads to 5 feet. Leathery, toothed, dark-green, more-or-less round leaves to 1½ inches long. Rounded clusters of lavender-blue flowers in early and mid-spring.

The ceanothus genus is native to California and grows there better than anywhere else. Even so, many species and varieties do poorly in home gardens because they cannot tolerate as much moisture as other plants require. Point Reyes ceanothus, however, is one of several that does well under frequent watering—provided the soil is very well drained. Plant in sun. Prune, if necessary, after flowering. Propagate by layering.

*Buds and flowers of the Carolina allspice are a strange but pleasing dark red-brown.*

CHERRY, NANKING. *Prunus tomentosa.* Zones 2–10. Deciduous. 9 feet. Broad oval leaves to 3½ inches long with toothed edges. Small white or pinkish flowers in small clusters in early spring followed in early summer by edible scarlet cherries about ½ inch in diameter.

When the Nanking cherry is in flower, the clusters of blossoms appear up and down each stem; and since there are a great many stems growing at all angles in the spreading, rounded plant, the effect is rather like that of a shrub lightly encrusted with snow. It is charming. Then, a few months later, the entire plant sparkles with red fruits that can be eaten fresh or made into jam.

Plant the shrub as a specimen, incorporate it in a shrubbery border, or buy a number of plants and use them as an informal flowering hedge. In any case, the shrub requires sun and average soil, but does best in a fairly rich, moist soil. Prune after harvesting fruit or in late winter.

*The Nanking cherry is a small rounded plant with outstretched fruit-laden branches.*

*When fall comes, the innumerable berries of the red chokeberry will turn crimson and hang on the shrub for months.*

CHOKEBERRY, RED. *Aronia arbutifolia.* Zones 3–9. Deciduous. 9 feet. Elliptical, toothed leaves to 5 inches long, hairy and gray underneath, turn bright red in the fall. White and faintly pink little flowers in dense clusters in mid-spring. Brilliant red berries in fall may last well into winter.

This informal eastern native is fairly slender and irregular in habit; usually placed toward the rear of shrubbery borders. But you won't be able to overlook it even so, because it makes a good display throughout the growing season.

Plant in sun or partial shade in average soil containing humus. If you have a moist spot in the garden, put the shrub there. Prune after flowering; little pruning is needed, however. Propagate by suckers or greenwood stem cuttings.

*This row of shrubby cinquefoils is studded with gay little yellow flowers throughout the summer. This is Katherine Dykes, an especially good variety.*

CINQUEFOIL, SHRUBBY. *Potentilla fruticosa.* Zones 3–10. Deciduous. 4 feet. Small, feather-shaped compound leaves with 3 to 7 slender 1-inch leaflets covered with silky hair. Innumerable small yellow flowers from mid-spring to the end of summer.

There are many varieties of shrubby cinquefoil and you'll be hard put to pick out the ones you like best. All are delightful plants, usually not more than 2 feet high and about as wide. When in bloom they are covered with pretty flowers of varying shades of yellow. Use them as informal hedges or edgings; in the front of shrubbery borders or foundation plantings; or as specimens, say at the end of your front walk.

Plant in sun in average soil. Needs virtually no attention. Propagate by half-hardwood stem cuttings in the fall.

*A row of rockspray cotoneasters overhanging the wall flank a Pfitzer juniper at the corner. Flowering dogwoods in the background are dazzling white.*

Cotoneaster, rockspray. *Cotoneaster horizontalis.* Zones 5–10. Deciduous. 3 feet. Somewhat rounded, tiny, glossy leaves turn red and orange in the fall. Small, faintly pink flowers in late spring followed in fall by countless little bright-red fruits.

Rockspray cotoneaster can spread over an area 12 to 15 feet wide and is therefore excellent for planting in rock gardens, on banks and as fillers in shrubbery borders. It can also be trained into an attractive espalier.

Grow in sun in average soil. Prune in late winter to remove awkward branches. If you want to keep the plant from spreading too far, cut back the lengthening branches inside the plant so you can't see the stubs. Propagate by layering. Like most cotoneasters, this one may be attacked by scale insects and fire blight.

COTONEASTER, SPREADING. *Cotoneaster divaricata.* Zones 6–10. Deciduous. 6 feet. Rather stiff branches arching from the center of the shrub. Oval leaves to ¾ inch turn red in fall. Profuse, small pink flowers in mid-spring. Innumerable small egg-shaped red berries in fall.

This tall spreading cotoneaster is ideal for the shrubbery border or as a hedge or screen. It is among the very best of the large cotoneasters. Grow in sun and average soil. Prune in late winter to accent the graceful branches.

COTONEASTER, WILLOWLEAF. *Cotoneaster salicifolia.* Zones 6b–10. Evergreen in warm climates; deciduous or semi-evergreen in cold. 15 feet. Long, arching branches with slender, willowlike leaves to 3½ inches long. Small white flowers in clusters in late spring, followed by somewhat rounded bright-red fruits in fall.

The foliage of this vigorous cotoneaster is distinctive; the plant itself, very graceful. It is a good background shrub anywhere and also a fine screen. Plant in sun and average soil. Prune in late winter to accent the arching branches. Variety *floccosa* is somewhat hardier than the true willowleaf species and the leaves are very hairy on the undersides.

*The spreading cotoneaster has larger leaves than many members of this useful family.*

*The slender deutzia is bright with little white flowers in mid-spring.*

DEUTZIA, SLENDER. *Deutzia gracilis.* Zones 5–9. Deciduous. 3 feet. Toothed, elliptical leaves about 2½ inches long. Profuse, white, ¾-inch flowers in upright clusters in mid-spring.

This is the best of the many deutzias; even so, it doesn't rank among the many outstanding shrubs. I include it here mainly because it is so well known, and I must admit that, when in bloom, it is a very pretty sight—a small fountain of brilliant white. At other times it is simply a pleasant green, dense plant with branches arching nicely from the ground.

Grow it either in sun or partial shade in average soil. Because it is often damaged by winter cold, prune in early spring if you live in the north; elsewhere, after flowering. Propagate by greenwood stem cuttings.

A *row of autumn elaeagnus. The open shrubs have beautiful silvery foliage.*

ELAEAGNUS, AUTUMN. *Elaeagnus umbellata.* Zones 3b–8. Deciduous. 12 feet. Oval leaves to 3½ inches long are silver-colored underneath. Small, fragrant, yellow-white flowers in mid-spring. Little berries in the fall are silver-colored mixed with brown, which later turns to red.

The autumn elaeagnus is an informal, open, spreading shrub which is planted alone or in shrubbery borders for its beautiful silvery foliage and berries. It is also used in windbreaks. Plant in sun in average soil. Prune in late winter. Propagate by layering.

ELAEAGNUS, THORNY. *Elaeagnus pungens.* Zones 7b–10. Broadleaf evergreen. 12 feet. Spiny branches. Oblong, wavy-margined leaves to 4 inches are olive-green above, silvery underneath. Small, silvery-white, fragrant, pendulous flowers in autumn. Small brown-to-red berries in spring.

Allowed to grow naturally, the thorny elaeagnus has a somewhat sprawling, very informal look; but it is effective at the back of a shrubbery border, and when the wind blows it is a knockout—it glistens like silver. With pruning, the shrub can be made much more orderly and compact. You can even use it as a 4-foot hedge.

Thorny elaeagnus is a very fast-growing shrub tolerant of wind, salt spray, reflected heat and other difficult conditions. Plant in sun or partial shade in average soil. Prune at any time. Propagate by layering.

Several varieties with variegated leaves are on the market. Fruitland is a favorite in the deep south.

*Fragrant little flowers and silvery leaves grace the thorny elaeagnus.* (Photo by the County of Los Angeles Arboreta and Botanic Gardens)

ENKIANTHUS, REDVEIN. *Enkianthus campanulatus.* Zones 5–10. Deciduous. 20 feet. Oval leaves 1 to 3 inches long turn scarlet in the fall. Yellowish to pale orange lily-of-the-valleylike flowers in clusters are veined with red; appear in mid-spring. They are followed in the fall by small seed capsules.

Redvein enkianthus is a superb shrub that is not so well known as it should be. If kept under control with pruning shears, it forms a wide column with many upright stems from which smaller branches spread slightly to the side and sometimes droop. The effect is informal but pretty in all seasons—especially in the spring and fall. Use the shrub in shrubbery borders as a vertical contrast to more rounded plants. I have also seen it used to excellent advantage at the front corners of one-story houses.

Redvein enkianthus prefers sun but grows in light shade. It requires somewhat acid soil that is well drained and humusy. Prune after flowering. Propagate by layering.

EUONYMUS, EVERGREEN. *Euonymus japonicus.* Zones 8–9. Broadleaf evergreen. 15 feet. Narrow, elliptical, glossy leaves with blunt-toothed edges, to 3 inches long. Unimportant greenish-white flowers in spring. Small pink and orange fruits in the fall.

The evergreen euonymus is a useful, attractive, fast-growing plant widely used in shrubbery borders and hedges because of its lustrous foliage. Grow in sun or shade in average soil. It is a reliable plant but troubled sometimes by mildew and scale insects. Prune whenever you feel like it. Propagate by half-hardwood stem cuttings.

Varieties with variegated foliage are numerous and particularly popular; but frequently parts of these plants revert to solid green. This detracts from their appearance to some extent.

EUONYMUS, WINGED. *Euonymus alatus.* Zones 3b–8. Deciduous. 10 feet. Dense, irregular branches with corky, longitudinal wings. Elliptical leaves 1½ to 3 inches long turn brilliant red in the fall. Unimportant yellowish flowers in the spring are followed by equally unimportant purplish fruits.

If the redvein enkianthus is a superb shrub, the winged euonymus must be called a superlative shrub. This may seem strange, since nei-

*The winged euonymus in early spring: a thicket of slender, outreaching branches with prominent corklike wings and little bright-green leaves.*

ther its flowers nor its fruits are anything to brag about. Yet after living with it for untold numbers of years, I find myself liking it more every day. It is a beautiful, rounded plant which is clothed with dense, fine foliage throughout the warm months. The fall coloring is unbelievably rich (more about this later). In winter the interesting light-brown branches twist and cross every which way. Because of the way the wings are arranged, the smaller branches look, from a distance, like a line of penciled dashes; and after a snowfall they become long-lasting lines of white. And to complete the story, birds find the shrub a marvelous place to build nests.

Use the plants as specimens or in shrubbery borders. The compact variety also makes a good hedge which can be clipped or allowed to grow informally. The cultural requirements are of the easiest. Sun or partial shade (but the fall color is not so good in shade); average soil. Prune at any time.

The one trouble with the winged euonymus is that in recent years the nurseries seem to have "discovered" it, and the plants they now generally offer simply are not to be compared with the true species. The leaves are longer, coarser, and a fiery red that doesn't look like a product of nature (interestingly, most nurseries have renamed the plants Burning Bush). And on many plants the wings are small and often nonexistent. Happily, you don't have to be saddled with these inferior varieties if you know someone who has any of the original shrubs (and many people do). This is because the winged euonymus self-seeds like mad, and it is no trick at all to dig up and transplant some of the countless seedlings to be found. Or you can simply collect some of the ripe fruits and sow them in your garden in the fall.

FATSHEDERA. *Fatshedera lizei.* Zones 7b–10. Broadleaf evergreen. 7 feet. Glossy leaves up to 8 inches across and about as long, usually with five pointed lobes, bear a close resemblance to large ivy or sweet-gum leaves.

Fatshedera is a cross between fatsia and English ivy (*Hedera helix*). It has the leaves of the former; its vinelike tendency comes from the latter. A handsome plant, it is best grown as an upright shrub. By occasionally pinching off the tips of the twisting stems that rise from the roots, you can force it to make side growth and gain width and density.

*Fatshedera has handsome glossy foliage. It usually needs staking, as here, to hold it upright.*

Plant in a relatively wind-free, frost-free spot near your terrace or front door. The shrub requires partial to deep shade. Average soil with a good supply of humus. Frequent watering, but don't let the soil get waterlogged. Fertilize once or twice during the growing season.

FATSIA. *Fatsia japonica.* Zones 7b–10. Broadleaf evergreen. 8 feet. Glossy, dark-green leaves as much as 15 inches across with five to nine lobes. Clusters of small whitish flowers in fall and winter followed by black berries.

Fatsia is an extremely handsome foliage plant sometimes used to give bold, contrasting texture to shrubbery borders, but best displayed by itself against a wall. It looks tropical, and, unfortunately for northerners, it actually does grow outdoors only in warm climates.

Plant in the shade; it doesn't need any sun at all. Improve average soil with humus. Water regularly and fertilize several times during the growing season. Prune in early spring to open the plant somewhat; it is most attractive when you can see some of the branches. Remove suckers that come up from the roots and use them to propagate new plants. If you cut off the flower clusters after they bloom, the plant will put all its energy into producing even larger than normal leaves.

FIRETHORN, LALAND'S SCARLET. *Pyracantha coccinea lalandei.* Zones 6b–10. Evergreen in warm climates; frequently deciduous in cold. 10 feet. Very thorny branches. Toothed, oval, 1-inch leaves turn purplish in cold weather if they do not drop. Clusters of small whitish flowers in late spring followed in the fall by very showy clusters of brilliant scarlet berries. If the birds leave these alone, they last well into winter.

There are other fine species of firethorn, and in warmer climates, these are often planted—but Laland's scarlet firethorn might be called the standard variety, because it is the most widely used throughout the country. Not only is it the hardiest, but it also has the most brilliant berries in greatest profusion.

Firethorn is a favorite for planting in front of walls, where it can be allowed to develop more-or-less naturally but is usually espaliered. It is also a splendid candidate for shrubbery borders and foundation plantings, and it makes a handsome, formidable hedge.

Grow in sun or partial shade. Average soil preferably reinforced with humus. Prune in late winter. Propagate by layering. I've never had any insect or disease problems with firethorn, but lace bugs and the fire blight may attack the plants.

*An espaliered firethorn being trained to wires.*

*In a color photograph this border forsythia would be almost blindingly golden against the green backdrop of an eastern white pine.*

FORSYTHIA, BORDER. *Forsythia intermedia.* Zones 6–8. Deciduous. 9 feet. Toothed, elliptical leaves. Yellow flowers as large as 2 inches across in early spring.

This fast-growing hybrid is the most spectacular forsythia and the one most commonly planted today. The flower color differs somewhat between varieties; but in the best—Beatrix Farrand, Lynwood Gold, Spectabilis and Spring Glory—it is a brilliant, deep yellow. And the flowers are borne so profusely on the upright to slightly arching branches that from a distance they look like long, solid spikes. Few plants make such a dazzling show.

Forsythia is one of the easiest shrubs to grow. It does best in sun but is tolerant of light shade. The soil need be of only average quality, although the plant responds to an occasional light dose of fertilizer and/or an organic mulch. Prune after flowering. The proper procedure is to cut out entire stems at the ground to keep the plant reasonably open and free of dead wood. Don't bob the ends of the branches, and, if you value the beauty of the plant, never shear it into a rigid shape. Propagate by layering the tips of the branches.

FOTHERGILLA, ALABAMA. *Fothergilla monticola.* Zones 6–9. Deciduous. 6 feet. Rounded, oval, toothed leaves turn yellow, orange and red in the fall. White flowers in mid-spring are suggestive of large, elongated clover blossoms.

Alabama fothergilla is a first-class shrub of rather spreading habit for use in shrubbery borders and foundation plantings. It is especially effective when planted in front of evergreens, because the dark backdrop accentuates the whiteness of the spring flowers and brilliant fall foliage.

Plant in partial shade in average, humusy soil which holds moisture. Prune after flowering. Propagate by suckers.

*The fothergillas have small white, thimble-shaped flowers and large leaves that turn brilliant yellow-orange-red in the fall.*

*Fuchsias have heart-shaped leaves with toothed edges and beautiful pendulous flowers which show up poorly in a black-and-white photo but are visible here in the foreground and upper right of the plant.*

FUCHSIA. *Fuchsia* species. Zones 7b–10. Deciduous or evergreen. 3 to 12 feet, depending on variety and habit of growth. Leaves more-or-less heart-shaped. Very beautiful, complex, tubular flowers with protruding stamens, pendulous and usually growing in clusters, which bloom throughout the summer. Each flower is multicolored in white and soft pastels of red, blue or purple.

In California, where the hybrid fuchsias grow best, they are indispensable shrubs, and no wonder—the flowers are indescribably lovely. You have undoubtedly seen fuchsias in florist shops, but until you have seen a large plant in a California garden you haven't seen anything.

Fuchsias are exceedingly variable in the way they grow. Some are trailers that are grown in containers; others are upright shrubs that are planted in shrubbery borders or used as specimens around the terrace. These are often espaliered.

Plant in filtered sun in a spot protected from wind. The soil should be light, humusy, well drained and slightly acid. Keep it slightly damp at all times, and spray the plants themselves with water every few days. Fertilize lightly once a fortnight. In the spring, remove weak branches and cut back strong ones. Propagate by greenwood stem cuttings.

HAWTHORN, YEDDO. *Raphiolepis umbellata.* Zones 7b–10. Broadleaf evergreen. 10 feet. Broadly oval leaves to 3 inches long are thick, leathery, lustrous, almost black-green. Fragrant white flowers in dense, upright clusters in late spring. Blue-black berries in fall and winter.

This ornamental shrub is excellent for providing texture and color contrast in shrubbery borders. It can also be used to create an informal hedge because it makes moderately slow growth and can be kept as low as 4 feet by pruning after the flowers fade.

Although the shrub grows in light shade, it is then not so dense as it is in full sun. Average soil. Propagate by half-hardwood stem cuttings.

HEAVENLY BAMBOO. *Nandina domestica.* Zones 8–10. Broadleaf evergreen. 8 feet. Compound leaves with 1- to 2-inch pointed, oval leaflets; these are pinkish when young but turn light green in summer and then red in fall and winter. White flowers in big, loose, upright clusters in early summer followed by informal clusters of bright-red berries in fall and winter.

Only one negative can be applied to heavenly bamboo: it is not a true bamboo. But it looks like bamboo, and it most certainly is heavenly. I wish it grew in the north, because if it did, I'd have it planted everywhere.

It is a neat, very delicate shrub with a cluster of slender, upright canes topped by lacy foliage that moves in the slightest breeze. There is no reason why you cannot use it to advantage in a shrubbery border; but it should really be planted in front of a wall so you can enjoy its exquisite silhouette. Or you might plant a row on a hillside where the shrubs would stand out against the sky.

Heavenly bamboo tolerates partial shade and needs some in the southwest; but it grows better and colors more brilliantly in the sun. The soil should be rich, full of humus, and well drained. Water regularly. Prune in early spring, but not too much. Never cut back the top; remove old canes at the ground instead. If a single plant does not produce many berries, put in a second plant.

HIBISCUS, CHINESE. *Hibiscus rosa-sinensis.* Zones 9–10. Broadleaf evergreen. 15 feet. Large shiny leaves, oval and with toothed edges. Single, semidouble and double flowers to 8 inches across in summer, in count-less shades of white, pink, red, yellow and orange.

The Chinese hibiscus is one of the most spectacular flowering plants that grow in warm climates. As a rule, each flower lasts only one day; but there are many of them over a long period. In habit the plants range from dense to open, rounded to upright. Use them as specimen shrubs, in shrubbery borders, or in hedges. In the latter case, use a single variety for the entire hedge; otherwise the growth and appearance of the hedge will be uneven.

Hibiscus will take a little shade (and needs it in the southwest), but much prefers full sun. The soil can be average in quality but definitely should be well drained and slightly acid. In southern Florida, where the plants never really stop growing, fertilize them lightly every month during the most active growth periods. See that plants are deeply watered by hose or rain once a week. Prune in the spring after all danger of frost is past. Spray with malathion to control scale insects and thrips. Propagate by half-hardwood stem cuttings in summer.

The excellent varieties of Chinese hibiscus are too numerous to list. Buy whichever appeals to you.

HOLLY, CHINESE. *Ilex cornuta.* Zones 7b–10. Broadleaf evergreen. 10 feet. Dark-green leaves up to 5 inches long, so shiny they appear to be waxed, usually with two spines at the base and three at the top. Large, brilliant red berries in fall and winter.

Chinese holly is one of the most beautiful hollies and has unusually big berries. Furthermore, unlike most hollies, you don't have to plant more than one specimen to have berries. These are good reasons for using this species.

Burford holly (*I. cornuta burfordii*) is an outstanding variety. It is a more rounded plant than the species; and the leaves have only one spine.

Plant in a protected, sunny spot (though some shade will do no harm). Average soil must be well drained and very slightly acid. Prune in early spring.

HOLLY, JAPANESE. *Ilex crenata.* Zones 6–10. Broadleaf evergreen. 20 feet. Oval, dark-green leaves resembling those of boxwood range from ½ to 1½ inches long. Small black berries in the fall on female plants.

*Burford variety of the Chinese holly at left; mountain andromeda at right.
Two excellent evergreen shrubs.*

The Japanese holly doesn't look like the plant we think of as holly. In fact, it is easily confused with boxwood. But in many respects it is the most versatile and useful of the hollies, since you can plant it as a specimen, in shrubbery borders, in foundation plantings, in edgings and for hedges.

In shape and size the shrub is variable. Some varieties grow upright and tall; most are low and wide. *Convexa* is one of the best and largest in the latter category. Heller's holly is one of the best and smallest.

Grow in sun or partial shade in average, well-drained, slightly acid soil. Prune in early spring to remove any long branches that may shoot out. The plants can also be sheared into formal shapes. If you want berries, you must plant both male and female specimens, but the berries do not contribute materially to the beauty or usefulness of the shrub.

HONEYSUCKLE, TATARIAN. *Lonicera tatarica.* Zones 3b–10. Deciduous. 9 feet. Oval, dark- or bluish-green leaves 2 inches long. White, pink or almost red flowers in late spring followed by red berries in summer.

The tatarian honeysuckle is a hardy, fast-growing, upright, dense shrub that makes a grand display of flowers and berries during warm weather. Dependable and trouble-free, it can be used to advantage in mass plantings anywhere in the garden. Grow in average soil in sun or partial shade. Prune in early spring. Propagate by layering or greenwood stem cuttings.

*After the flowers fade, the tatarian honeysuckle is covered with shiny red berries.*

*Japanese hollies take kindly to shearing but are equally attractive when allowed to develop naturally like the boxwood at the end of the wall. The small tree is a flowering dogwood.*

HONEYSUCKLE, WINTER. *Lonicera fragrantissima.* Zones 6–10. Deciduous in cold climates, evergreen in warm. 6 feet. Stiff, oval leaves to 3 inches long are blue-green underneath, dull green above. Very fragrant white flowers in early spring, or in winter in warmest areas. Red berries in late spring.

The winter honeysuckle develops into a spreading, rounded mass with excellent foliage. But the fragrant flowers so very early in the year are its chief asset. Use in shrubbery borders or hedges.

Plant in sun in average soil. Prune after flowering. Propagate by hardwood cuttings.

HYDRANGEA, GARDEN. *Hydrangea macrophylla.* Zones 6–10. Deciduous. 12 feet but usually less. Broad, oval, pointed, toothed leaves to 6 inches long, lighter green underneath than above. Big balls of blue or pink flowers in midsummer.

I am undoubtedly in the minority, but I must confess that this is not

*A garden hydrangea of the Lacecap variety just starting to bloom.*

one of my favorite shrubs. The foliage is coarse; the flower clusters, lurid. I have never seen a garden that was enhanced by the plant. But it certainly is widely used, particularly in warm climates, where it thrives. In colder areas it is often killed to the ground in winter; it then takes a long time to come back the following summer and may not bloom.

The garden hydrangea is interesting because the color of the flowers depends on the condition of the soil. If the soil is acid, the flowers are blue; if it is alkaline or neutral, the flowers are pink. To change the flowers from pink to blue, all you have to do is give each plant a gallon of water containing 3 ounces of dissolved aluminum sulfate. Make the first application as soon as the ground is free of frost and follow with 4 to 6 additional applications at 10-day intervals. To turn the flowers from blue to pink, work a cupful of superphosphate into the soil in early spring, and water it in well.

Garden hydrangeas grow in sun or partial shade in the north, but should be in partial shade in warm climates. The soil should contain a lot of humus. Water regularly. Prune after flowering. Propagate by half-hardwood stem cuttings.

There are numerous varieties. The so-called Lacecaps are among the prettiest. Their flowers are in more-or-less flat clusters with the largest flowers forming a ring around small inner flowers.

HYDRANGEA, OAKLEAF. *Hydrangea quercifolia.* Zones 6–10. Deciduous. 6 feet. Leaves 8 inches long have sharp-pointed lobes like the red and black oaks; they turn bronzy-red in the fall. Small white flowers in upright clusters in early summer.

This wide, rounded hydrangea is much less showy than the garden hydrangea, but it is a finer shrub that is easier to accommodate in the garden and it makes more of a contribution to over-all garden beauty.

Plant in sun or partial shade. In our hottest climates, always plant in shade. Soil of average quality should be humusy and well drained. Prune in early spring. In cold areas, plants may be killed to the ground by freezing weather but will come back strongly the following summer. They probably won't have flowers, however.

Propagate hydrangeas by half-hardwood stem cuttings or by layering.

*The oakleaf hydrangea has handsome leaves and large clusters of white flowers.*

HYPERICUM, HIDCOTE. *Hypericum patulum* Hidcote. Zones 6b–10. Evergreen in warm climates; deciduous in cold. 3 feet. Oval leaves to 2½ inches long. Fragrant, bright-yellow, cuplike flowers up to 3 inches across from late spring to mid-autumn.

The common name for hypericum is St. Johnswort, but this variety is rarely identified in this way. Be that as it may, this is a rounded shrub, almost as wide as it is high, which is grown for its all-summer display of many flowers. Use it by itself where you want a low, neat, colorful plant, at turns in walks, for instance, or at the corners of steps; or in the foreground of shrubbery borders and foundation plantings. It also makes a delightful untrimmed hedge.

Plant in sun in average soil. Prune in early spring. In cold climates it may be killed to the ground, but it recovers rapidly the following summer.

JUNIPER, MEYER. *Juniperus squamata meyeri.* Zones 5–10. Needled evergreen. 12 feet, but can be held lower. Short, pointed needles in groups of three are bluish-green.

Meyer juniper is an upright shrub with stiff branches growing at unusual angles. Its bluish color is distinctive. Plant in sun in average soil. Prune in late winter to maintain orderly compact growth.

JUNIPER, PFITZER. *Juniperus chinensis pfitzeriana.* Zones 5–10. Needled evergreen. 10 feet. Very prickly little leaves encircling twigs which are arranged in flat sprays. Small bright-blue berries borne in profusion in fall and winter on female plants.

The Pfitzer juniper is a large, spreading, flat-topped plant which is much used in foundation plantings and shrubbery borders. It has a feathery appearance but should be planted far enough away from walks and paths so that its sharp needles don't scratch the passerby.

The shrub is hardy, tolerant of difficult conditions (including polluted air) and fast-growing. It needs to be pruned almost every winter to keep it within the space allotted to it. Plant in sun in average soil.

*Nurserymen often represent the Meyer juniper as a good medium-size plant for the foundation border—as indeed it is if you keep it pruned. But if you neglect pruning, you will wind up with something like this massive 12-foot specimen.*

*A large mountain laurel just after coming into bloom. The beautifully shaped flowers in big clusters are normally very pale pink, but in the newest varieties are much rosier.*

LAUREL, MOUNTAIN. *Kalmia latifolia.* Zones 5–8. Broadleaf evergreen. 30 feet. Elliptical leaves to 5 inches long. Large clusters of small, beautifully shaped flowers in late spring.

I can't find enough superlatives for the mountain laurel. It is just a perfect plant—more-or-less rounded, dense, unfazed by zero weather; and when it is in bloom, it is blanketed with exquisite flowers. Usually these are white or very pale pink, but plants with deep pink, sometimes almost red, flowers, pop up, and eastern nurserymen are now working hard to propagate these in quantity.

I like to use mountain laurel by itself as a specimen plant, but it fits into shrubbery borders and wooded areas beautifully. It is not, however, particularly desirable in foundation plantings (where it is often used), because it eventually grows up to cover the windows. (You could, of course, keep it low by pruning; but that is sacrificing the full beauty of the plant.) Furthermore, as the plant ages, it usually loses its lowest branches, which means you must place smaller plants in front of it to cover up the bare space.

Mountain laurel grows and blooms well in either sun or partial shade. It also grows in deep shade but doesn't bloom. It requires acid soil but is otherwise undemanding. Just mix plenty of humus into any reasonably well-drained soil and let it go at that. Growth is slow and pruning is rarely necessary except to remove dead wood. Do whatever cutting seems indicated after flowering.

LAVENDER. *Lavandula officinalis.* Zones 6–10. Broadleaf evergreen. 3 feet. Slender, lance-shaped, aromatic, gray leaves to 2 inches long. Spikes of fragrant lavender flowers on upright stems in early summer.

This old, old favorite is grown primarily for its fragrance. On warm days it perfumes the air throughout the garden. During the rest of the year you can enjoy the aroma by drying the flowers and storing them in plastic bags or sprinkling them through bureau drawers and closets.

When not in bloom, the plant is conspicuous only for its gray foliage; but it is so small that it must be planted in the foreground of the shrubbery border, rock garden or even the flower bed to be seen at all.

Grow in sun in average, well-drained soil. Prune lightly in late winter to promote neat, compact growth. Propagate by greenwood stem cuttings in the spring.

*Old-fashioned yet always new-fashioned favorite—lavender.*

LEUCOTHOE, DROOPING. *Leucothoe fontanesiana.* Zones 5–9. Broadleaf evergreen. 6 feet. Slender, lance-shaped leaves to 6 inches long turn bronze-color in the fall. Small, white, bell-shaped flowers in short clusters from the arching branches in late spring.

If you have a shrubbery border or foundation planting in partial shade, the drooping leucothoe is ideal for inclusion in it. The plant is wide and low (though capable of reaching 6 feet in height, it usually is only 3 feet). The foliage is attractive in color and texture. And the flowers, though much like those of several other plants, are delightful.

Plant in average soil that contains a good amount of humus and is rather acid. Pick off flower heads after they die and do whatever pruning is necessary at the same time. It's a good idea to cut a few of the old stems close to the ground every once in a while to encourage new, more vigorous growth. Propagate by dividing the roots.

LILAC, COMMON. *Syringa vulgaris.* Zones 3b–8. Deciduous. 20 feet. Oval or heart-shaped leaves 2 to 4 inches long. Deliciously fragrant flowers in gorgeous upright clusters of purple, lilac, blue, white, pink or red appear in mid-spring.

Common lilacs have been planted in American dooryards and gardens since pioneer days. Our ancestors were so attached to them that whenever they moved to a new part of the country they carried lilacs with them. You can do this, too, but it isn't really necessary. Numerous beautiful varieties of the common lilac (many are called French lilacs) are sold in local nurseries; and even more varieties are available from the leading mail-order nurseries.

The common lilac is an erect plant that normally puts up many stems. The crown is more-or-less rounded and informal. The plant lends itself to many uses in the garden. I like it particularly when planted by itself at the corners of the house, by gates or on both sides of the garage doors. But it can also be used in shrubbery borders; and it makes a good screen.

Plant lilacs in full sun (except in hottest climates) in well-drained, average soil with a pH of about 7. The depth of planting depends on the way the plants were propagated. If they are grafted plants, set them 4 inches deeper than they grew in the nursery. On the other hand, if they are "own-root" plants propagated from suckers or cuttings, they

*A common lilac at the corner of the house grows almost as tall as the wisteria vine.*

*It's a time-consuming job, but if you want maximum flower production from lilacs you should remove the twiggy remains of the flower clusters soon after the flowers die. This is the littleleaf species.*

should be set at the depth at which they previously grew.

Once established, lilacs do not require any more watering or feeding than other shrubs. But watch out for scale insects and borers. Mildew on leaves is not serious but is unsightly. It can be controlled by spraying with zineb.

Prune out deadwood and most of the suckers every year after flowering. Cut a few of the old stems to the ground every two or three years and let a few of the suckers grow to take their place. Cutting off dead flowers before seeds are set forces plants to put maximum energy into the development of bigger flowers the next year.

You can propagate your own lilacs by rooted suckers that are dug up in early spring, or by greenwood stem cuttings in late spring.

LILAC, LITTLELEAF. Also called Daphne Lilac. *Syringa microphylla superba*. Zones 6–8. Deciduous. 6 feet. Oval leaves about 1 inch long. Reddish buds open to display deep-pink trusses of fragrant flowers in mid-spring and sometimes again in fall (but not heavily).

This is a unique lilac because it develops into a rounded mound almost twice as wide as high. When it blooms in the spring, the entire shrub is covered with flowers with a two-tone effect. The largest clusters are at the branch ends and smaller clusters are borne further down the branches. Use the plant as a specimen or in a shrubbery border where it has ample space to spread.

Plant in sun in average, well-drained, neutral soil; however, light shade is best in hottest climates. Prune after flowering—just enough to control the shape of the shrub. Propagate by greenwood stem cuttings.

LILAC, PERSIAN. *Syringa persica.* Zones 6–8. Deciduous. 6 feet. Lance-shaped, sometimes lobed leaves to 2½ inches long. Fragrant, pale-lilac flowers in small clusters frequently covering the branches appear a little after those of the common lilac.

The Persian lilac is the smallest lilac species. It is a compact, upright shrub with arching, slender branches. Grow like the common lilac.

MAHONIA, LEATHERLEAF. *Mahonia bealei.* Zones 7–10. Broadleaf ever-green. 10 feet. Large compound leaves with 7 to 15 spiny-toothed, oval leaflets which are gray-green and leathery. Fragrant lemon-yellow flow-ers in upright clusters in early spring followed by blue grapelike berries in summer.

The leatherleaf mahonia is a striking plant which is ideal for planting in front of a wall. The stems are rather stiffly erect, the big leaves stiffly horizontal. If you grew the plant only for its form and foliage you would be happy with it. But the bonus of splendid flowers and fruits will make you even happier.

Plant in partial shade. The soil should be a rich mixture of loam and humus. Give plenty of water. Prune after fruiting. Propagate by layering.

*A leatherleaf mahonia and snow azalea in the foreground of a thickly planted shrub and tree border.*

MANZANITA, STANFORD. *Arctostaphylos stanfordiana.* Zones 7b–10. Broadleaf evergreen. 6 feet. Crooked branches covered with smooth, red-brown bark. Glossy, oval, dark-green leaves about 1½ inches long. Clusters of pink flowers in late winter and early spring are followed by reddish-brown berries in the fall.

The Stanford manzanita is a good-looking, informal, spreading plant for shrubbery borders in California gardens. In bloom, it is sometimes so covered with flowers that you can hardly see the leaves.

Plant in sun in average soil, which must be very well drained. Even with excellent drainage, the shrub should not be overwatered. Pinch off new growths here and there during spring and summer to shape the plant and promote bushiness. Propagate by greenwood stem cuttings.

MOCK-ORANGE, LEMOINE. *Philadelphus lemoinei.* Zones 6–9. Deciduous. 8 feet. Small elliptical leaves, hairy underneath. Small clusters of very fragrant, white single or double flowers up to 2 inches across appear in late spring.

Mock-oranges are overrated plants, because they are undistinguished except for the brief period that they are in bloom—but they are too popular for me to exclude them from this list.

The Lemoine mock-oranges are hybrids, as showy and fragrant as any. Depending on the variety, the shrubs range from 4 to 8 feet in height; they are upright, mounded or arching. Plant them in sun or light shade in average soil. Prune after flowering. Propagate by layering or hardwood stem cuttings.

MYRTLE, TRUE. *Myrtus communis.* Zones 8–10. Broadleaf evergreen. 15 feet. Lustrous, green, pointed, oval leaves to 2 inches long give off an aromatic fragrance when crushed. Small, fuzzy white flowers in summer. Bluish-black berries in fall.

Not to be confused with the groundcover sometimes called myrtle, the true myrtle is a fine dense, rounded shrub about as wide as it is high. It is used in the shrubbery border or foundation planting, and it makes an excellent clipped hedge. Grow it in sun or partial shade in average soil, which must be well drained and should be reinforced with humus. Prune in late winter. Propagate by half-hardwood stem cuttings.

*Pale pink flowers of the Stanford manzanita are followed by reddish-brown berries. (Photo by the County of Los Angeles Arboreta and Botanic Gardens)*

*An all-around shrub for our warmest climates—the evergreen natal plum. The white, star-shaped, fragrant flowers appear in small numbers almost throughout the year.* (Photo by the Florida Agricultural Extension Service)

NATAL PLUM. *Carissa grandiflora.* Zones 9–10. Broadleaf evergreen. 15 feet. Spines on branches and at ends of twigs. Leathery, glossy, oval leaves to 3 inches long. Star-shaped, 2-inch white flowers smell like jasmine; they appear more or less throughout the year but especially in winter and spring. Edible red fruits 1 inch long and tasting like cranberries are produced in summer. These are used in making jelly and sauces.

The natal plum grows rapidly into a rounded, somewhat open shrub that deserves to be displayed as a specimen because it is so attractive. But it will enhance a shrubbery border, and it makes an outstanding clipped or informal impenetrable hedge. However you use it, plant it close enough to the house or terrace so you can enjoy its fragrance.

This is a tough plant that withstands salt spray and other difficult conditions. Grow it in sun or partial shade in average soil. Water deeply in dry weather. Prune annually to control the shape and stimulate production of the new growth on which fruit is borne. Propagate by layering.

NINEBARK, EASTERN. *Physocarpus opulifolius.* Zones 2–8. Deciduous. 9 feet. Shredding bark. Leaves to 3½ inches long with three rounded lobes and rounded teeth around the edges. Tiny white flowers in dense, umbrellalike clusters in late spring. Dry red or brown seed capsules in clusters of five appear in the fall and persist through the winter.

Eastern ninebark resembles spirea but is coarser-looking. Showy only when in bloom, it is important mainly because it is so hardy. Use it only in a northern garden where other more ornamental shrubs will not survive. Even there, it should be planted in the back of shrubbery borders. A dwarf variety, *nanus,* can be used in hedges.

Plant in sun in average soil. Prune after flowering. Propagate by greenwood stem cuttings.

*A low hedge of eastern ninebark separates lawn from shrubbery borders. Two American elms have so far escaped the Dutch elm disease, which is killing so many of these gorgeous trees.*

OLEANDER. *Nerium oleander*. Zones 8–10. Broadleaf evergreen. 20 feet. Narrow, oblong, leathery leaves to 12 inches are dark green above, lighter underneath. Single or double flowers as large as 3 inches across in clusters at the ends of branches and twigs, borne from mid-spring to mid-autumn. White, pink, red and yellow; sometimes fragrant.

An indispensable shrub in warm climates, the oleander is used for screening, for bordering driveways, in the background of shrubbery borders, even as a specimen. Left to its own devices, the plant grows big, wide and rather untidy. As a rule, therefore, it should be pruned yearly after flowering to eliminate suckers and cut back the branches. By really hard pruning, it is possible to develop the shrub into an olive-like tree with single or multiple trunks.

Oleanders require sun, but do well in average soil. They are quite resistant to drought, but may be attacked by scale insects, aphids and caterpillars. All parts of the plant are poisonous if eaten. The smoke of the burning wood may cause skin irritations.

*Oleander is a mainstay in warm-climate gardens.* (Photo by the Florida Agricultural Extension Service)

*An Oregon grape photographed in winter when the leaves are a glistening, brilliant purple.*

OREGON GRAPE. *Mahonia aquifolium.* Zones 6–10. Broadleaf evergreen. 6 feet. Compound leaves with stiff, leathery, spiny-edged leaflets turn from dark green in summer to bronze or rich purple in the fall and winter. Bright-yellow flowers in small, erect, pyramidal clusters in early spring followed by blue-black grapelike fruits that are made into jelly in summer.

Oregon grape has just about everything you can ask for in a plant: rich and varied color in all seasons, edible fruit and an upright, spreading habit. Small, rather sparse plants are effective when displayed against a wall. Larger plants are gorgeous in a shrubby border, though I feel that they should be planted along with evergreens as well as deciduous plants because the former help to tone down the almost unreal coloring of the winter foliage.

Oregon grape is a favorite for planting in partial shade but does well in full sun. Grow in average soil that is well drained and contains humus. Prune after flowering. Cut out stems that stick out of the mass; or, to keep the plant low, cut back stem ends. If you don't want the plant to spread to form a tall mat, cut back the roots occasionally with a sharp spade or cut off new stems arising around the outer margins of the plant. Propagate by layering.

*Holly osmanthus is almost a dead ringer for the true hollies.*

OSMANTHUS, HOLLY. *Osmanthus heterophyllus.* Zones 6b–10. Broad-leaf evergreen. 18 feet. Hollylike, shiny, dark-green oblong leaves to 2½ inches with spines on the edges. Fragrant, yellowish, but not showy flowers in early summer. Blue-black berries in the fall.

This so closely resembles a large, wide, rounded holly that you will probably think it is holly the first time you see it. It's a very handsome evergreen which should be used as a specimen if you have the space. You can also plant it in with other shrubs and trees—but close enough to the house or terrace for you to be able to smell the flowers. Or use it in a hedge and keep it clipped.

Plant in sun or partial shade in average soil. Prune lightly after flowering. Propagate by half-hardwood stem cuttings.

*A tree peony with 17 large, exquisite flowers and still more to come.*

PEONY, TREE. *Paeonia suffruticosa.* Zones 6–10. Deciduous. 5 feet. Compound leaves with lobed leaflets. Spectacular single, semidouble or double white, pink, red, yellow or purple flowers as much as 1 foot across in mid-spring.

The flowers of the well-known perennial peonies are lovely, but these are unbelievably so. Inexperienced gardeners might well think, "I could never grow anything like that." But they can and without a great deal of effort.

Tree peonies, like our most popular roses, are usually planted in beds devoted to nothing else. But there is no reason why you must follow this practice. However, the picturesque plants do show off to best advantage when not forced to compete with close neighbors.

Plant the shrubs in partial shade, preferably in a location where they get protection from afternoon sun. Also protect them from wind. The soil should be deep, rich, well drained and with a pH of about 7. Set the plants with the thick graft joint 4 to 6 inches below ground level. Water regularly. Fertilize in early spring. Spray about three times in the spring with Ferbam to prevent botrytis blight. Remove dead flowers; cut out dead wood in the spring. Propagate by cutting the roots into sections, each with several buds.

Excellent varieties are too numerous to list. Note that Japanese varieties tend to hold their flowers above the foliage; European varieties have somewhat drooping flowers that may be lost in the foliage.


PINE, MUGO. *Pinus mugo mughus.* Zones 2–9. Needled evergreen. 8 feet, but often much lower. Dark-green needles 1½ to 3 inches long, borne in pairs. Small cones.

Mugo pines are excellent plants for foundation plantings, for the foreground of shrubbery borders and for rock gardens. They are also planted in rows to serve as divider or barrier plants. They are especially effective placed at the top of low walls and steps.

The plants spread slowly to form large mounds of varying height and contour, depending on the specimen and also on the variety. Some plants are almost prostrate; others are fairly tall and upright. Some are quite symmetrical; others, irregular.

Grow in sun in average soil. To slow upward growth and make the plant bushier, prune the new candles (whitish end growths) in the spring before their needles open. Cut the candles to half length if you want the branches to continue growing slowly. Remove them entirely to stop branch growth and force out side branches.


PITTOSPORUM, JAPANESE. *Pittosporum tobira.* Zones 8–10. Broadleaf evergreen. 15 feet. Leathery leaves to 4 inches long, oval but with blunt tips, arranged in rosettes. Small, creamy-white flowers in clusters in early spring smell like orange blossoms. Green to brown fruits in fall split to reveal orange-colored seeds.

You can use the Japanese pittosporum as a big specimen plant or a smallish hedge plant. It also makes a dense screen. It is handsome, whichever way you use it.

*This spreading mugo pine grows considerably lower than many specimens. But all members of this species are splendid evergreens with many uses.*

Plant in sun or partial shade in average soil. Water regularly and feed in the spring to encourage best growth; even so, it makes progress slowly. Prune after flowering. Propagate by half-hardwood stem cuttings. Aphids and scale insects can cause trouble.

PRIVET, CALIFORNIA. *Ligustrum ovalifolium.* Zones 6–10. Evergreen in warmest climates, half-evergreen to deciduous elsewhere. 15 feet. Dark-green, oval, 2½-inch leaves. Small clusters of fragrant, creamy-white flowers in early summer followed by black berries.

This is the most widely used hedge plant in the United States. Despite its name, it is planted less in California than in other areas.

Grow in sun or partial shade. Average soil is satisfactory; but for fastest growth, mix in humus, loam and a little fertilizer. Buy two- or three-year-old plants and set them about 2 inches deeper than they formerly grew. Space them 9 to 12 inches apart in the row. After planting, cut back the branches by one third.

During the first summer, trim the shrubs about three times. Let them grow 1 foot, then cut them back 6 inches. This forces them to bush out. In succeeding years, clip as often as you like to maintain height and shape, but make sure that the hedge is narrower at the top than at the bottom.

You can propagate your own privet by greenwood stem cuttings in the spring. Thrips—tiny winged insects that feed on young privet leaves —can be controlled by spraying in midsummer with Sevin.

*When a neighbor bought this property, the hedge of California privet was 4 feet high and about as wide. He cut it to the ground and now keeps it like this. About 8 inches high and just a shade wider, it is so dense that you cannot see the thick old stems.*

*Bright-yellow leaves of the Vicary golden privet are impossible to miss in a green world.*

PRIVET, JAPANESE. *Ligustrum japonicum.* Zones 7b–10. Broadleaf evergreen. 12 feet. Rounded oval leaves to 4 inches long, darker above than below, with a thick, spongy texture. Small clusters of fragrant white flowers in early summer followed by black berries in fall.

This is a first-class hedge plant, which can also be trained as an upright shrub or small tree. It is excellent for topiary work. Grows in sun or partial shade in average soil to which humus has been added. Prune in early spring. If grown in a hedge, space plants 3 feet apart and avoid the hard clipping given to California privet. Spray with malathion if you find webworms feeding on the foliage. Propagate by greenwood stem cuttings.

PRIVET, VICARY GOLDEN. *Ligustrum vicaryi.* Zones 5–10. Deciduous. 12 feet. Small elliptical leaves are bright yellow from spring through fall. Clusters of small white flowers in early summer followed by blue-black berries in the fall.

Plants with colored foliage are not always easy to accommodate in a garden, but this golden privet fits in well. It's like having a forsythia in bloom throughout the growing season.

A dense, rounded, spreading plant, this can be used as a specimen or planted in with ordinary green plants in a shrubbery border. Or you can use it as a hedge or even a low edging, because it can be trimmed to a height of only 12 inches.

Requires full sun for maximum color. Average, well-drained soil with humus added. Prune in early spring; however, it is a slow grower, usually neat, and requires little pruning. Propagate by greenwood stem cuttings in the spring.

QUINCE, FLOWERING. *Chaenomeles speciosa.* Zones 5–10. Deciduous. 8 feet. Dense branches, usually well covered with thorns. Oval leaves to 3 inches long. Countless showy white, pink or red flowers in mid-spring. Small green fruits like apples or true quinces in late summer can be used for jelly-making, but usually are not.

Your forebears knew this shrub by various botanical names. *Chaenomeles speciosa* is the currently accepted appellation; but everyone will know what plant you're talking about if you say "flowering quince." It is a popular and useful shrub, usually spreading to cover quite a lot of ground and therefore making a stunning display when in bloom. Birds and rabbits find large specimens excellent places to set up

*Flowering quince normally blooms before the leaves are quite as big as these. The mound in the background is a huge specimen of this plant.*

*A Carolina rhododendron well covered with pale rosy-purple flower clusters.*

housekeeping. And unfortunately, leaves blowing across the landscape in autumn also find the plants good resting places.

Flowering quince is a tough, undemanding shrub. Plant it in sun in average soil. Prune after flowering to remove dead wood and to control shape. Propagate by layering.

RHODODENDRON, CAROLINA. *Rhododendron carolinianum.* Zones 6–8. Broadleaf evergreen. 6 feet. Narrowly elliptical leaves to 3 inches long; brown underneath. Pale rosy-purple flowers about 1½ inches across, in mid-spring in clusters of five to ten.

The Carolina rhododendron is a compact, rounded plant that can be used as a specimen, planted in masses or combined with other shrubs and trees in a shrubby border. It is low enough also to fit under some windows if used in a foundation planting; but, since the leaves start to roll up and the whole plant looks sad as soon as the temperature falls ten degrees below freezing, such a prominent spot is not recommended for it except in warm climates.

Grow this lovely plant in partial shade in soil enriched with humus. Culture is the same as for the Exbury hybrid azaleas. Plants that become leggy can be rejuvenated by cutting stems to within a few inches of the ground and applying fertilizer. They will start making new growth in a month or two.

*A gorgeous example of the Catawba hybrid rhododendron.*

RHODODENDRON, CATAWBA HYBRID. *Rhododendron catawbiense.* Zones 5–8. Broadleaf evergreen. 15 feet. Oblong leaves to 5 inches long, glossy green on top, paler beneath. Flowers up to 3 inches across, appearing in large clusters in late spring, are white, pink, red, violet or purple.

These are among the handsomest of all rhododendrons, and there are many varieties from which to choose. Mass them, use them as specimens or combine with other shrubs and trees. Whatever you do, you can't go wrong. Grow like Exbury hybrid azaleas.

RHODODENDRON, KOREAN. *Rhododendron mucronulatum.* Zones 5–10. Deciduous. 6 feet. Narrow, lance-shaped leaves to 3 inches long turn yellow to bronze in the fall. Rosy-purple flowers 1½ inches wide in early spring before the leaves open.

This upright-branching, open rhododendron is one of the first shrubs to bloom in the spring. It usually coincides with forsythia, and the two together make a splendid show.

If you live in an area where you often have a late frost, plant the Korean rhododendron in partial shade on the north side of the house, along a high wall, a high hedge or slope, so the southern sun will not encourage the flowers to open too early. Otherwise, grow like Exbury hybrid azaleas.

Korean rhododendron is often called Korean azalea.

*Two early bloomers: A small rosy-purple Korean rhododendron and a young pink Higan weeping cherry.*

*A yellow shrub rose. The newest varieties stay in bloom from spring to fall.*

Rose, shrub. *Rosa* species. Zones 4–10. Deciduous. 8 feet. Dense, thorny stems. Toothed, oval leaves. Lovely single, semidouble or double flowers in white, pink, red, purple or yellow; often fragrant. Time of bloom varies. Small red fruits, called hips, in summer and fall.

All roses, including the familiar hybrid teas, floribundas, climbers, etc., are shrubs; and by rights I should cover all of them here. But I bypass them because (1) most people think of them as flowers, like zinnias and chrysanthemums, and (2) they are usually not located and grown in the garden like rhododendrons, spirea and other plants known as shrubs.

Shrub roses are another matter. They are called shrubs; they look like shrubs; and they are used like shrubs. Specifically, they are large, dense, rather spreading plants which can be planted as specimens, mixed into shrubbery borders, or massed to make informal hedges. There are many species and varieties. The older varieties usually bloom only in the spring, though some bloom a second time in the fall. Many of the

*Rose of Sharon has late-summer flowers in a variety of colors. In this instance they are pale pink with rose-red centers.*

newest varieties, on the other hand, bloom from spring until frost. These are not necessarily more beautiful than the older varieties, but since they do give continuous bloom, they are the first you might consider. They include Frau Dagmar Hartopp, Mabelle Stearns, Poulsen's Park Rose, Sarah Van Fleet, Elmshorn and Gruss an Aachen.

Plant shrub roses in full sun. The soil should be a well-drained nourishing mixture of loam, humus and sand. Water regularly. Fertilize in the spring when growth starts and again in early summer. Prune in early spring to remove dead wood and excess branches, and to cut the plants back to manageable size if necessary. Since shrub roses have few pests, they need little spraying. No winter protection is called for. Propagate by greenwood stem cuttings.

ROSE OF SHARON. Also called Althea. *Hibiscus syriacus.* Zones 6–10. Deciduous. 15 feet. Leaves shaped something like arrowheads with rounded teeth and sometimes three lobes. Single or double flowers (white, pink, red, blue or purple), as large as 4 inches across in late summer.

Rose of Sharon is usually an upright, reasonably compact shrub, but old plants often develop quite a spreading crown. To my mind, plants look best when trained to a single trunk. Plant them in an open shrubbery border where they are not too tightly hemmed in and where the fallen flowers do not make too much mess.

Plant in sun in average soil that is well drained but contains enough humus to retain moisture. If you prune early every spring to remove dead wood, excess branches and branches that crisscross, flowering will be better and the shrub will look a great deal neater. There are many varieties to choose from.

SARCOCOCCA, DWARF. *Sarcococca hookeriana humilis.* Zones 7–10. Broadleaf evergreen. 3 feet. Glossy, lance-shaped leaves, pointed at the end, to 3 inches long. Inconspicuous, fragrant white flowers in early spring followed by black berries.

Dwarf sarcococca is a tidy, slow-growing plant which spreads as much as 8 feet and is therefore often used as a tall groundcover. But it can also be very useful in the foreground of shrubbery borders and foundation plantings. And it is good for filling in narrow strips between the house wall and a walk.

Grows in partial to fairly deep shade. Average soil, with lots of humus added. Prune in early spring. Propagate by greenwood stem cuttings.

SKIMMIA, REEVES. *Skimmia reevesiana.* Zones 7b–9. Broadleaf evergreen. 2 feet. Dark-green, elliptical leaves to 4 inches long, aromatic when crushed. Clusters of small fragrant white flowers in mid-spring. Dull-red berries in fall.

Every garden has a few places for small shrubs. These are usually in the foreground of shrubbery borders and foundation plantings; but they may also be under floor-to-ceiling windows, in rock gardens, in low-growing hedges and dividers, etc.

Reeves skimmia is an outstanding plant for such locations. It is slow-growing and orderly, forms a dense mound and blends well with other plants, but it is attractive enough to be grown alone.

Plant only in partial shade. Average soil. Do whatever pruning is called for after flowering.

*Several varieties of smokebush in a mass planting. Some have yellowish plumes; some, pink; some, purple.*

SMOKEBUSH. *Cotinus coggygria.* Zones 6–10. Deciduous. 15 feet. Oval leaves, very narrow at the base, to 3 inches long, turn yellow to orange in the fall. Inconspicuous yellowish flowers in late spring develop into large, feathery pink or purplish plumes that cover the plant for weeks during the summer and into the fall.

If you like the unusual, this is one plant you should not miss buying. Since it grows about as wide as high, plant it in an open space in a prominent location, then sit back and wait for your neighbors' exclamations. You won't be disappointed. When the smokebush is covered with its large, colorful plumes, it looks like a dense cloud of smoke; and, though the plumes gradually lose their color, the leaves continue to make a vibrant show well into the fall.

Plant in sun in average soil. A location sheltered from cold winter winds is needed in the north. Prune in early spring.

The name of the purple variety of smokebush is *purpureus*. The true smokebush has pink plumes.

STEPHANANDRA, CUTLEAF. *Stephanandra incisa*. Zones 6–8. Deciduous. 7 feet. Roughly triangular leaves 2½ inches long with sharp-pointed lobes turn red or reddish-purple in the fall. Small, greenish-white flowers in clusters in late June.

Cutleaf stephanandra should be used in shrubbery borders for its graceful arching habit and lovely chiseled leaves. Attractive alone, it is a good foil for plants with coarse foliage. And it is easy to grow in partial shade and average soil. Prune in early spring or any time thereafter. Propagate by layering.

Variety *crispa* is only 3 feet tall; recommended for use in hedges and holding banks.

SUMMERSWEET. Also called Sweet Pepperbush. *Clethra alnifolia*. Zones 4–7. Deciduous. 8 feet. Broad, oval, toothed leaves to 5 inches long turn yellow to orange in the fall. Small, white, unusually fragrant flowers in erect spikes in early summer.

Summersweet puts up slender, vertical stems from its spreading roots and eventually forms a wide clump that helps to fill in the shrubbery border. Be sure to plant it where you can enjoy its fragrance; but actually this is so powerful that a prevailing summer breeze will carry it to you over a considerable distance.

Plant in sun or partial shade in average soil that does not dry out rapidly. Prune in early spring. You can control the spreading growth by cutting back the roots with a sharp spade or removing the suckers that develop around the edges of the clump. Propagate by the suckers.

*Cutleaf stephanandra is planted because of its small, finely chiseled leaves.*

*Summersweet has good foliage but is prized mainly for its very fragrant white flowers.*

TALLHEDGE. *Rhamnus frangula columnaris.* Zones 2–8. Deciduous. 15 feet. Oval leaves to 2½ inches long are glossy, dark green, hairy underneath; turn yellow in autumn. Unimportant little greenish flowers followed in late summer by red berries that gradually turn black.

This is a new hedge plant which is already being proclaimed one of the best among the tall growers. It is good-looking, neat, hardy, free of pests and grows upward at a rapid pace. But it does not spread much more than 4 feet.

Plant in sun in average soil. Prune or shear in early spring or whenever trimming is required.

*Tallhedge has lustrous foliage, and berries which turn from green to red to purple.*

*The leaves of the tamarisk are so small they almost seem nonexistent, but they give the plant an airy texture that contrasts well with surrounding large-leafed shrubs.*

TAMARISK, KASHGAR. *Tamarix hispida.* Zones 6–9. Deciduous. 6 feet. Minute silvery leaves hugging the twigs. Masses of rose-pink flower clusters cover plant through much of the summer.

This shrub has an almost ethereal look. The branches are very slender and upright. The tiny leaves cover the plant like a veil. In addition the shrub is blanketed from top to bottom with delicate fluffy flowers. At that stage the plant looks like a large version of the feathery plumes women used to wear in their hats. Plant it as a specimen. It can also be used in the shrubbery border, but don't hem it in tightly and don't set it next to shrubs with large leaves because the contrast is too great.

Despite its delicacy, the Kashgar tamarisk is a very tough customer that came originally from the Asian deserts. Plant it in the sun or partial shade in average soil or poorer. Cut the long branches back severely in early spring. Propagate by greenwood stem cuttings.

*A Burkwood viburnum perfumes the air around a doorway.*

VIBURNUM, BURKWOOD. *Viburnum burkwoodii*. Zones 6–10. Deciduous. 6 feet. Oval leaves, blunt at the base, dark green and glossy above, and whitish and hairy underneath turn wine-red in the fall. Very fragrant flowers in 4-inch clusters turning from pale pink to white appear in mid-spring. Black berries in the fall.

As a group, the viburnums are noted for their very large, often fragrant flower clusters in spring, spectacular red berries in the fall, and fine foliage. Admittedly, not all the species within the genus have all these characteristics. But it is not hard to pick out a goodly number that are sufficiently notable for widespread use in American gardens.

The hybrid Burkwood viburnum rates highly because of its flowers and good fall color. The plant is dense, upright and vigorous; generally free of problems. Use it as a specimen or in shrubbery plantings. Or try it as an espalier.

Grow in sun or partial shade in average, well-drained soil. Prune after flowering. Propagate by greenwood stem cuttings.

VIBURNUM, DOUBLEFILE. *Viburnum plicatum tomentosum*. Zones 5–10. Deciduous. 9 feet. Oval leaves to 6 inches long with pronounced veins turn purple-red in the fall. Flowers in flat clusters borne in rows along the horizontal branches. The flowers in the outer ring are fully open and white; inner flowers are tiny and yellowish. Blooms appear in mid-spring. Fruits in fall are in flat, dense clusters, bright red at first, gradually turning black.

*Each branch of the doublefile viburnum becomes a flat line of white when the flowers bloom in mid-spring.*

This is an excellent shrub, spreading as wide as it is high and densely clothed with outreaching branches all the way to the ground. The flower clusters look something like delicate lace doilies. The berry clusters are brilliant.

Use as a specimen or in the shrubbery border. Grow in sun or partial shade. Average well-drained soil. Prune after flowering.

Marie's doublefile viburnum is another excellent variety, but not quite so widely available.

VIBURNUM, KOREAN SPICE. *Viburnum carlesii.* Zones 5–10. Deciduous. 5 feet. Toothed, oval leaves to 3 inches long turn reddish in the fall. In mid-spring, pink buds open to very fragrant white flowers in small clusters. Blue-black berries in summer.

This viburnum is not so shapely as others and should therefore not be featured so prominently. But do by all means plant it close to the house because you will be delighted by its perfume. Grow in sun or partial shade in average soil. Prune after flowering. There is a compact variety that grows to only 3 feet.

VIBURNUM, SIEBOLD. *Viburnum sieboldii.* Zones 5–9. Deciduous. 10 feet. Oblong, 6-inch leaves, dark green above, paler below, turn red in the fall. Creamy-white flowers in flat clusters about 4 inches wide in late spring. Large clusters of small oval berries are light red when they develop in midsummer, gradually turn dark red and finally black. They are borne on red stalks that hold their color for weeks after the black berries fall.

*The compact variety of the fragrant Korean spice viburnum tucks in easily under larger shrubs, provided they do not cast very deep shade.*

*The Siebold viburnum grows much larger than others in this genus, but this adds to rather than detracts from its usefulness.*

This is a superb shrub for planting in the lawn as a specimen. It is wide-spreading and irregular in a most attractive way; has flower- and fruit-laden branches all the way to the ground.

Plant in sun for maximum color; but it also grows in partial shade. Average soil, well drained and enriched with humus. Prune after flowering.

VIBURNUM, TEA. *Viburnum setigerum.* Zones 6–10. Deciduous. 12 feet. Oval leaves to 5 inches long are dark green, with silky hairs on the veins underneath. White flowers in flat clusters in early summer. Unusually large, shining, red berries in hanging clusters in the fall.

The tea viburnum has the most spectacular fruit of any viburnum; it is hard to think of any other genus of shrubs that can beat it in this department. Its only rival is its own variety, *aurantiacum,* which has brilliant orange berries.

Use and grow like other viburnums.

*By fall the small berry clusters of this tea viburnum will have developed into gorgeous plump, red fruits.*

*A 3-foot Wright viburnum blooming happily a year after planting. The common lilacs behind it are also in bloom.*

VIBURNUM, WRIGHT. *Viburnum wrightii*. Zones 6–9. Deciduous. 9 feet. Bright-green oval leaves with strong veins, to 5 inches long, turn red in the fall. White flowers in 4-inch-wide, flat clusters in late spring. Glistening, brilliant red fruits in large clusters from late summer into fall.

This is yet another outstanding viburnum of particular value for its beautiful, long-lasting fruit. Use and grow it like the preceding species.

WINTERBERRY. Also called Black Alder. *Ilex verticillata*. Zones 3b–8. Deciduous. 12 feet. Oval, toothed leaves, dull green above, hairy beneath, to 4 inches long, turn yellow in the fall. Bright-red holly berries in fall and winter.

This doesn't look like a holly most of the time because it is bare in winter and it throws up a cluster of slender stems. But when the berries appear in mid-autumn, before the leaves have fallen, you begin to suspect the truth: it's a holly all right—and even after the leaves fall, it makes a sterling show. In some years the berries are so thick that the plant looks like an upright, slenderly rounded cloud of color. They hang on the shrub through much of the winter if the birds leave them alone.

Use the winterberry as a specimen plant, especially in a location where it stands out against the sky or snow—or in a shrubbery border among evergreens. Grow in sun in average soil that is a little acid. Although the plant frequently grows wild in swamps, it does equally well in well-drained soil. Prune in late winter.

If you live in an area where winterberry is a common wild shrub, you can probably depend on these plants to pollinate the one you put into your garden. You therefore need to plant only a female specimen. But if winterberry does not abound in the wild, plant both male and female specimens to assure fruiting.

*Photographed in early March, this winterberry is still thickly covered with bright-red berries.*

YEW, JAPANESE. *Taxus cuspidata.* Zones 5–10. Needled evergreen. 25 feet. Flat, wide, pointed, dark-green needles about 1 inch long. Bright-red berries in the fall on female plants.

The Japanese yews are the hardiest, most widely used of all the yews. Wide-spreading, with more-or-less horizontal branch ends, they are in-dispensable for foundation plantings, hedges, rock gardens and specimen plantings. They vary greatly in size, and to a lesser extent in habit. The true Japanese yew forms a somewhat rounded pyramid about 25 feet high and almost as wide. Variety *nana* is more rounded, about 15 feet high and 20 feet wide at the maximum. *Expansa* is about 5 feet high, 8 feet wide and has a concave-to-flat top. Variety *densa* is about 4 feet wide and 8 feet high and is roughly rectangular in shape.

Plant in sun or light shade in average soil. If you are making a hedge, work a good amount of humus into the soil to nourish the com-peting root systems. Prune or shear in the spring.

The foliage and fruit are poisonous to human beings, but they do no harm to deer. This is unfortunate, because if you live in deer coun-try, you may find that they eat your yews (Japanese and all other species as well) to the ground in winter.

YEW, SPREADING ENGLISH. *Taxus baccata repandens.* Zones 6b–10. Needled evergreen. 3 feet. Wide, flat, pointed needles over 1 inch long; dark green above, yellow-green below. Red berries on female plants.

The spreading English yew is the hardiest variety of this species and one of the most attractive and useful shrub forms. Low and spreading, it has pendulous branchlets. If kept pruned it will remain reasonably upright; but left to itself, the branches are likely to dip down and creep across the ground.

Use the shrub in the foreground of foundation plantings and shrub-bery borders, and by themselves in rock gardens, next to steps, etc. Grow in sun or partial shade in average soil. Prune in spring. Shearing destroys the graceful lines of the plant. Protect from deer and warn your children not to eat the foliage or berries.

*Shrubby yew pines in a planter on either side of a picture window. They are slow-growing, upright, orderly.*

YEW PINE, SHRUBBY. *Podocarpus macrophyllus maki.* Zones 8–10. Evergreen. 10 feet. Narrow, upright plant with needlelike leaves resembling those of the yews, but much larger—up to 4 inches long.

The shrubby yew pine is a very beautiful, slow-growing evergreen that is used as an accent plant in the foundation or shrubbery borders. It can also be used for screening and espaliering. And it makes a superlative hedge that can be sheared or left more-or-less natural.

Plant in sun or partial shade in average soil. Prune whenever you like. Propagate by greenwood stem cuttings.

*Spreading English yews are excellent for covering hillsides and banks. Use them also in the foreground of foundation plantings and shrubbery borders.*

# ·12·

## THE NEXT BEST SHRUBS

| Common name | Botanical name | Climate zones | Hgt. (ft.) | Type* | Sun or shade | Soil† |
|---|---|---|---|---|---|---|
| Azalea, Glen Dale hybrid | *Rhododendron* species | 7–10 | 8 | E | Sh | Av, acid |
| Azalea, pinkshell | *Rhododendron vaseyi* | 5–8 | 10 | D | Sh | Av, acid |
| Azara, boxleaf | *Azara microphylla* | 8–10 | 18 | E | Sh | Av |
| Bamboo, dwarf whitestripe | *Arundinaria variegata* | 6b–10 | 3 | E | S | Av |
| Bamboo, palmate | *Sasa palmata* | 6–10 | 10 | E | S | Av |
| Barberry, Chenault | *Berberis chenaultii* | 6–9 | 4 | E | S | Av |
| Barberry, dwarf Magellan | *Berberis buxifolia nana* | 6–9 | 1½ | E | S | Av |
| Barberry, Korean | *Berberis koreana* | 6–9 | 6 | D | S | Av |
| Barberry, Mentor | *Berberis mentorensis* | 6–9 | 7 | D or E | S | Av |
| Barberry, three-spine | *Berberis triacanthophora* | 6–9 | 4 | E | S | Av |
| Barberry, warty | *Berberis verruculosa* | 6–9 | 4 | E | S | Av |
| Bayberry | *Myrica pensylvanica* | 2–7 | 9 | D or E | S | Av |
| Bottlebrush, lemon | *Callistemon lanceolatus* | 9–10 | 20 | E | S | Av |
| Box, Korean | *Buxus microphylla koreana* | 5–8 | 4 | E | S or Sh | Av |
| Breath of heaven | *Coleonema album* | 8–10 | 5 | E | S | Av, wd |
| Broom, Scotch | *Cytisus scoparius* | 5–10 | 6 | D | S | Av, wd |
| Broom, spike | *Cytisus nigricans* | 6–9 | 3 | D | S | Av, wd |
| Brunfelsia | *Brunfelsia calycina* | 9b–10 | 5 | E | S or Sh | Av |
| Buckeye, bottlebrush | *Aesculus parviflora* | 5–9 | 12 | D | S | Av |
| Buddleia, fountain | *Buddleia alternifolia* | 6–10 | 12 | D | S | Av |
| Buttonbush | *Cephalanthus occidentalis* | 5–10 | 15 | D | S | Av, damp |
| Ceanothus, Mountain Haze | *Ceanothus impressus* Mountain Haze | 7–10 | 4 | E | S | Av, wd |
| Ceanothus, Santa Ana | *Ceanothus griseus* Santa Ana | 8–10 | 8 | E | S | Av, wd |
| Chaste-tree | *Vitex agnus-castus* | 6b–10 | 9 | D | S | Av |
| Cherry-laurel | *Prunus laurocerasus* | 6b–9 | 18 | E | S | Av |
| Cleyera | *Cleyera japonica* | 9–10 | 10 | E | S or Sh | Av, acid |

\* D—deciduous; E—evergreen
† av—average; wd—very well drained

| Common name | Botanical name | Climate zones | Hgt. (ft.) | Type* | Sun or shade | Soil† |
|---|---|---|---|---|---|---|
| Coralberry | Symphoricarpos orbiculatus | 2b–10 | 6 | D | S or Sh | Av |
| Coralberry, Chenault | Symphoricarpos chenaultii | 5–10 | 3 | D | S or Sh | Av |
| Cotoneaster, bearberry | Cotoneaster dammeri | 6–10 | 1 | E | S | Av |
| Cotoneaster, cranberry | Cotoneaster apiculata | 5–10 | 3 | D | S | Av |
| Cotoneaster, creeping | Cotoneaster adpressa | 5–10 | 1 | D | S | Av |
| Cotoneaster, Diel's | Cotoneaster dielsiana | 6–10 | 6 | D | S | Av |
| Cotoneaster, Franchet | Cotoneaster franchetii | 6–9 | 10 | D or E | S | Av |
| Cotoneaster, Pyrenees | Cotoneaster congesta | 6b–10 | 3 | E | S | Av |
| Cotoneaster, redbox | Cotoneaster rotundifolia | 6b–10 | 10 | D or E | S | Av |
| Cotoneaster, wintergreen | Cotoneaster conspicua | 6b–10 | 4 | E | S | Av |
| Cranberry-bush, American | Viburnum trilobum | 2–9 | 12 | D | S or Sh | Av |
| Cranberry-bush, European | Viburnum opulus | 3b–9 | 12 | D | S or Sh | Av |
| Croton | Codiaeum variegatum | 10 | 5 | E | S or Sh | Av |
| Currant, alpine | Ribes alpinum | 2–8 | 7 | D | Sh | Av |
| Currant, winter | Ribes sanguineum | 6–10 | 12 | D | S | Av |
| Daphne, Burkwood | Daphne burkwoodii | 6–9 | 5 | D or E | S or Sh | Av, wd |
| Daphne, February | Daphne mezereum | 5–9 | 3 | D | S or Sh | Av, wd |
| Daphne, lilac | Daphne genkwa | 6–9 | 3 | D | S or Sh | Av, wd |
| Daphne, rose | Daphne cneorum | 5–9 | ½ | E | S or Sh | Av, wd |
| Daphne, winter | Daphne odora | 7b–9 | 6 | E | S or Sh | Av, wd |
| Dogwood, gray | Cornus racemosa | 5–8 | 15 | D | S | Av |
| Dogwood, Siberian | Cornus alba sibirica | 2–10 | 7 | D | S | Av |
| Elaeagnus, cherry | Elaeagnus multiflorus | 5–8 | 9 | D | S | Av |
| Euonymus, spreading | Euonymus kiautschovicus | 6b–8 | 9 | E | S or Sh | Av |
| Firethorn, Formosa | Pyracantha koidzumii | 8–10 | 10 | E | S or Sh | Av |
| Flamepea, heartleaf | Chorizema cordatum | 9–10 | 5 | E | Sh | Av |
| Forsythia, weeping | Forsythia suspensa | 6–8 | 10 | D | S or Sh | Av |
| Forsythia, white | Abeliophyllum distichum | 6–8 | 5 | D | S or Sh | Av |
| Fothergilla, dwarf | Fothergilla gardenii | 6–9 | 3 | D | Sh | Av |
| Fothergilla, large | Fothergilla major | 6–9 | 9 | D | Sh | Av |
| Fuchsia, Magellan | Fuchsia magellanica | 6–10 | 3 | D | S | Av |
| Gardenia | Gardenia jasminoides | 8–10 | 6 | E | Sh | Av |
| Germander | Teucrium chamaedrys | 6–10 | 1 | E | S | Av, wd |
| Harry Lauder's walking stick | Corylus avellana contorta | 4–10 | 7 | D | S | Av |
| Hawthorn, India | Raphiolepis indica | 7b–10 | 5 | E | S | Av |
| Heath, Cornish | Erica vagans | 6–9 | 1 | E | S | Av, wd, acid |
| Heath, cross-leaf | Erica tetralix | 3b–9 | 1½ | E | S | Av, wd, acid |
| Heath, Spanish | Erica lusitanica | 7–10 | 6 | E | S | Av, wd, acid |

* D—deciduous; E—evergreen
† av—average; wd—very well drained

| Common name | Botanical name | Climate zones | Hgt. (ft.) | Type* | Sun or shade | Soil† |
|---|---|---|---|---|---|---|
| Heath, spring | *Erica carnea* | 6–10 | 1 | E | S | Av, wd, acid |
| Heather | *Calluna vulgaris* | 5–8 | 1½ | E | S | Av, wd, acid |
| Holly, Perny | *Ilex pernyi* | 6b–10 | 30 | E | S or Sh | Av |
| Holly, Yunnan | *Ilex yunnanensis* | 6b–8 | 12 | E | S or Sh | Av |
| Honeysuckle, Amur | *Lonicera maackii* | 2–8 | 15 | D | S | Av |
| Honeysuckle, Morrow | *Lonicera morrowii* | 5–8 | 6 | D | S | Av |
| Huckleberry, box | *Gaylussacia brachycera* | 6–8 | 1½ | E | S | Av, acid |
| Hydrangea, peegee | *Hydrangea paniculata grandiflora* | 5–10 | 25 | D | S or Sh | Av |
| Hydrangea, smooth | *Hydrangea arborescens* | 5–10 | 10 | D | S or Sh | Av |
| Hypericum, Sungold | *Hypericum patulum Sungold* | 6b–10 | 2 | D | S | Av |
| Inkberry | *Ilex glabra* | 3b–8 | 9 | E | S or Sh | Av |
| Jasmine, primrose | *Jasminum mesnyi* | 7b–10 | 10 | E | S or Sh | Av |
| Jasmine, winter | *Jasminum nudiflorum* | 7–10 | 15 | D | S or Sh | Av |
| Juniper, Hetz | *Juniperus chinensis hetzii* | 5–10 | 15 | E | S | Av |
| Juniper, Irish | *Juniperus communis stricta* | 2–10 | 20 | E | S | Av |
| Juniper, tamarix | *Juniperus sabina tamariscifolia* | 5–10 | 2 | E | S | Av |
| Kerria | *Kerria japonica* | 5–10 | 6 | D | S or Sh | Av |
| Lantana | *Lantana* hybrids | 9–10 | 3 | E | S | Av |
| Laurel, sheep | *Kalmia angustifolia* | 2–8 | 3 | E | S or Sh | Av, acid, damp |
| Lilac, Korean | *Syringa palibiniana* | 5–8 | 3 | D | S | Av |
| Lilac, late | *Syringa villosa* | 3–8 | 9 | D | S | Av |
| Lilac, swegiflexa | *Syringa swegiflexa* | 6–8 | 9 | D | S | Av |
| Mexican orange | *Choisya ternata* | 7b–9 | 8 | E | S | Av, wd |
| Mock-orange, sweet | *Philadelphus coronarius* | 5–9 | 9 | D | S or Sh | Av |
| Mock-orange, virginalis | *Philadelphus virginalis* | 6–9 | 9 | D | S or Sh | Av |
| Palmetto, dwarf | *Sabal minor* | 8b–10 | 9 | E | S or Sh | Av, damp |
| Pearlbush, common | *Exochorda racemosa* | 6–8 | 15 | D | S | Av |
| Pernettya | *Pernettya mucronata* | 6b–9 | 2 | E | S or Sh | Av, acid |
| Photinia, Chinese | *Photinia serrulata* | 7b–10 | 35 | E | S | Av |
| Photinia, Fraser | *Photinia fraseri* | 7b–10 | 10 | E | S | Av |
| Photinia, oriental | *Photinia villosa* | 5–7 | 15 | D | S | Av |
| Pineapple guava | *Feijoa sellowiana* | 8–10 | 20 | E | S | Av |
| Pomegranate | *Punica granatum* | 7b–10 | 15 | D | S | Av |
| Privet, Amur | *Ligustrum amurense* | 3b–8 | 15 | D | S | Av |
| Privet, common | *Ligustrum vulgare* | 5–10 | 15 | D | S | Av |

\* D—deciduous; E—evergreen
† av—average; wd—very well drained

| Common name | Botanical name | Climate zones | Hgt. (ft.) | Type* | Sun or shade | Soil† |
|---|---|---|---|---|---|---|
| Privet, Regel | Ligustrum obtusifolium regelianum | 3b–8 | 5 | D | S | Av |
| Pussy willow, common | Salix discolor | 5–10 | 20 | D | S | Av, damp |
| Pussy willow, French | Salix caprea | 5–10 | 25 | D | S | Av, damp |
| Quince, Japanese | Chaenomeles japonica | 5–10 | 3 | D | S | Av |
| Rhododendron, Dexter hybrid | Rhododendron fortunei | 6b–10 | 10 | E | Sh | Av, acid |
| Rhododendron, Smirnow | Rhododendron smirnowii | 5–8 | 18 | E | Sh | Av, acid |
| Rock-rose, spotted | Cistus cyprius | 7b–10 | 6 | E | S | Av, wd |
| Rosemary | Rosemarinus officinalis | 6b–10 | 6 | E | S | Av, wd |
| St. Johnswort, Henry | Hypericum patulum henryi | 6b–10 | 3 | D or E | S | Av |
| St. Johnswort, Kalm | Hypericum kalmianum | 5–10 | 3 | D | S | Av |
| St. Johnswort, shrubby | Hypericum prolificum | 5–10 | 3 | D | S | Av |
| Sand cherry, purple-leaved | Prunus cistena | 2–8 | 7 | D | S | Av |
| Salal | Gaultheria shallon | 6–10 | 5 | E | S or Sh | Av |
| Sarcococca, fragrant | Sarcococca ruscifolia | 7b–10 | 6 | E | Sh | Av |
| Sea-buckthorn | Hippophae rhamnoides | 3b–8 | 30 | D | S | Sandy |
| Skimmia, Japanese | Skimmia japonica | 7b–9 | 4 | E | Sh | Av |
| Snowberry | Symphoricarpos albus | 3b–10 | 6 | D | S or Sh | Av |
| Spicebush | Lindera benzoin | 5–8 | 15 | D | Sh | Av |
| Spirea, Anthony Waterer | Spiraea bumalda Anthony Waterer | 6–9 | 2 | D | S or Sh | Av |
| Spirea, Thunberg | Spiraea thunbergii | 6–9 | 5 | D | S or Sh | Av |
| Stranvaesia | Stranvaesia davidiana | 7b–9 | 20 | E | S | Av |
| Sweet olive | Osmanthus fragrans | 8–10 | 10 | E | S or Sh | Av |
| Viburnum, Chinese snowball | Viburnum macrocephalum | 6b–10 | 12 | D or E | S or Sh | Av |
| Viburnum, fragrant | Viburnum carlcephalum | 6–10 | 9 | D | S or Sh | Av |
| Viburnum, Judd | Viburnum juddii | 6–10 | 8 | D | S or Sh | Av |
| Viburnum, leatherleaf | Viburnum rhytidophyllum | 6b–10 | 9 | E | S or Sh | Av |
| Viburnum, linden | Viburnum dilatatum | 6–9 | 9 | D | S or Sh | Av |
| Viburnum, sandankwa | Viburnum suspensum | 9–10 | 6 | E | S or Sh | Av |
| Viburnum, sweet | Viburnum odoratissimum | 8–10 | 10 | E | S or Sh | Av |
| Wax-myrtle | Myrica cerifera | 6b–9 | 35 | E | S | Av |
| Wax-myrtle, California | Myrica californica | 7b–10 | 30 | E | S | Av |
| Weigela | Weigela hybrids | 6–9 | 12 | D | S | Av |
| Willow, dwarf Arctic | Salix purpurea nana | 2–8 | 5 | D | S | Av, damp |
| Wintersweet | Chimonanthus praecox | 5–9 | 10 | D | Sh | Av |
| Witch-hazel, Chinese | Hamamelis mollis | 6–9 | 30 | D | S or Sh | Av |
| Witch-hazel, vernal | Hamamelis vernalis | 5–8 | 10 | D | S or Sh | Av |

\* D—deciduous; E—evergreen
† av—average; wd—very well drained

# APPENDIX

STATE AGRICULTURAL EXTENSION SERVICES

| | |
|---|---|
| ALABAMA | Auburn University, Auburn  36830 |
| ALASKA | University of Alaska, College  99701 |
| ARIZONA | University of Arizona, Tucson  85721 |
| ARKANSAS | Division of Agriculture, University of Arkansas, Fayetteville  72701 |
| CALIFORNIA | College of Agriculture, University of California, Berkeley  94720 |
| COLORADO | Colorado State University, Fort Collins  80521 |
| CONNECTICUT | College of Agriculture, University of Connecticut, Storrs  06268 |
| | Connecticut Agricultural Experiment Station, New Haven  06504 |
| DELAWARE | School of Agriculture, University of Delaware, Newark  19711 |
| FLORIDA | University of Florida, Gainesville  32601 |
| GEORGIA | College of Agriculture, University of Georgia, Athens  30601 |
| HAWAII | University of Hawaii, Honolulu  96822 |
| IDAHO | College of Agriculture, University of Idaho, Boise  83701 |
| ILLINOIS | College of Agriculture, University of Illinois, Urbana  61801 |
| INDIANA | Purdue University, Lafayette  47907 |
| IOWA | Iowa State University of Science and Technology, Ames  50010 |
| KANSAS | College of Agriculture, Kansas State University, Manhattan  66502 |
| KENTUCKY | College of Agriculture, University of Kentucky, Lexington  40506 |
| LOUISIANA | Agricultural College, Louisiana State University, Baton Rouge  70800 |
| MAINE | College of Agriculture, University of Maine, Orono  04473 |
| MARYLAND | University of Maryland, College Park  20740 |
| MASSACHUSETTS | College of Agriculture, University of Massachusetts, Amherst  01002 |
| MICHIGAN | College of Agriculture, Michigan State University, East Lansing 48823 |
| MINNESOTA | College of Agriculture, University of Minnesota, St. Paul  55101 |
| MISSISSIPPI | Mississippi State University, State College  39762 |
| MISSOURI | College of Agriculture, University of Missouri, Columbia  65201 |
| MONTANA | Montana State University, Bozeman  59715 |
| NEBRASKA | College of Agriculture, University of Nebraska, Lincoln  68503 |
| NEVADA | College of Agriculture, University of Nevada, Reno  89507 |

310 The Gardener's Basic Book of Trees and Shrubs

| | |
|---|---|
| NEW HAMPSHIRE | University of New Hampshire, Durham   03824 |
| NEW JERSEY | Rutgers—The State University, New Brunswick   08903 |
| NEW MEXICO | College of Agriculture, New Mexico State University, University Park   88070 |
| NEW YORK | College of Agriculture, Cornell University, Ithaca   14850 |
| NORTH CAROLINA | College of Agriculture, North Carolina State University at Raleigh, Raleigh   27600 |
| NORTH DAKOTA | North Dakota State University of Agriculture and Applied Science, Fargo   58102 |
| OHIO | College of Agriculture, Ohio State University, Columbus   43210 |
| OKLAHOMA | Oklahoma State University, Stillwater   74074 |
| OREGON | Oregon State University, Corvallis   97331 |
| PENNSYLVANIA | Pennsylvania State University, University Park   16802 |
| PUERTO RICO | University of Puerto Rico, Box 607, Rio Piedras   00928 |
| RHODE ISLAND | University of Rhode Island, Kingston   02881 |
| SOUTH CAROLINA | Clemson University, Clemson   29631 |
| SOUTH DAKOTA | South Dakota State University, Brookings   57006 |
| TENNESSEE | College of Agriculture, University of Tennessee, Knoxville   37900 |
| TEXAS | Texas A. & M. University, College Station   77843 |
| UTAH | College of Agriculture, Utah State University, Logan   84321 |
| VERMONT | State Agricultural College, University of Vermont, Burlington   05401 |
| VIRGINIA | Virginia Polytechnic Institute, Blacksburg   24061 |
| WASHINGTON | Washington State University, Pullman   99163 |
| WEST VIRGINIA | West Virginia University, Morgantown   26506 |
| WISCONSIN | College of Agriculture, University of Wisconsin, Madison   53706 |
| WYOMING | College of Agriculture, University of Wyoming, Laramie   82070 |

# INDEX